UNAPOLOGETIC THEOLOGY

Other books by William C. Placher

Readings in the History of Christian Theology,
Volume 1:
From Its Beginnings to the Eve of the Reformation

Readings in the History of Christian Theology,
Volume 2:
From the Reformation to the Present

A History of Christian Theology: An Introduction

UNAPOLOGETIC THEOLOGY

A Christian Voice
in a Pluralistic Conversation

William C. Placher

Westminster/John Knox Press
Louisville, Kentucky

Book design by Gene Harris

First edition

Published by Westminster/John Knox Press
Louisville, Kentucky

PRINTED IN THE UNITED STATES OF AMERICA

9   8   7   6   5   4   3   2   1

Library of Congress Cataloging-in-Publication Data

Placher, William C. (William Carl), 1948–
  Unapologetic theology: a Christian voice in a pluralistic
conversation / William C. Placher. — 1st ed.
     p.   cm.
  Includes index.
  ISBN 0-664-25064-5 (pbk.)

   1. Apologetics—20th century. 2. Theology—Methodology.
3. Philosophy, Modern—20th century. I. Title.
BT1102.P56 1989
230′.01′8—dc19
                       88-27706
                       CIP

To two admired teachers

Hans W. Frei

and

William A. Christian, Sr.

At one time nearly forty years ago he had been in Chicago as a visiting professor. I asked him what he thought of it. He said, with an air of surprise and puzzlement, "Those people don't know the Enlightenment is over."

—William A. Christian, Sr.
Remarks in memory of Robert L. Calhoun

Postmodern theology: Also called "postliberal theology"; the quest, initiated in recent years by the most interesting American followers of Karl Barth, to get beyond all forms of modernism in theology; either a *cul de sac* or the harbinger of a new theological age (too soon to tell).

—Jeffrey Stout
"Lexicon," in *Ethics After Babel*

CONTENTS

PREFACE

A good many people—myself included—have urged contemporary theologians to abandon their preoccupation with methodology and get on with the business of really doing theology. I therefore confess embarrassment at being the author of a sort of extended preface to contemporary discussions about theological method. Prologomena to prologomena! Worse and worse!

The explanation, and perhaps the excuse, is partly autobiographical. Several years ago I came round to sympathy with a broadly defined theological approach emerging in the work of a number of my friends and former teachers which George Lindbeck had just named "postliberal theology." This style of theology was in some ways uncongenial to my own religious upbringing and sensibilities. I have come to find it compelling for a number of reasons, but its initial attraction lay in the fact that it offered the best account of how to do theology, given the philosophical views I found most persuasive.

I have therefore found it unnerving to read critics of postliberal theology denouncing it for its indifference to philosophy and indeed to modern culture generally. I wondered if we were reading the same theological texts. I wondered, frankly, what philosophy they had been reading. Among other things, this book presents some of the philosophy I have been reading, as one context for thinking about a new way—or maybe it is a very old way—of doing theology. I think this book sorts out some important problems, but I am aware that it leaves an agenda of questions yet to be addressed. I find myself wanting to note that I just turned forty and seem to be in good health. I hope to have more to say.

I began thinking about this project during a semester as a visiting professor at Haverford. Ron Thiemann and Bill Werpehowski and I got together regularly to talk about matters only indirectly related to this project, but some ideas from those conversations have been percolating in my mind ever since, and I retain many fond memories of the living room of 7 College Lane.

Work on two volumes of readings in the history of Christian theology then diverted my attention, and I returned to this project only during a year as a member of the Center of Theological Inquiry at Princeton. I am grateful to James I. McCord and the staff of the Center for a wonderful year. The resident members helpfully discussed an earlier draft of my first chapter, and my colleague there, Russell Stannard, saved me from some mistakes in physics. Being in Princeton gave me rewarding opportunities for other conversations, especially with Jeffrey Stout and Mark Kline Taylor. I regret that the illness and death of Paul Ramsey, who welcomed me to the Center with such kindness and discussed this project with me in its early stages, prevented me from getting to know that remarkable man better than I did.

Cynthia Thompson has offered her characteristic helpfulness and good advice as editor. George Lindbeck was kind enough to read the manuscript and recommend its publication. Steve Webb not only taught my courses for me while I was gone but was the first person to read a full draft and managed the difficult task of making constructive comments on a text he thinks at many points quite misguided. My Wabash colleague Glen Helman read the manuscript with a philosopher's keen eye and made detailed and helpful comments. As I was completing this manuscript, my friend and colleague Eric Dean had a serious illness diagnosed. This will be, I think, the first thing I have ever written for publication that he did not read in manuscript. I know it would have been much better had it benefited from his insights.

The Yale-Washington Theology Group discussed my manuscript at its 1988 meeting, and I learned a lot from that discussion. Much more than that, though, the ongoing conversation and friendship of that group has made this book possible. I thought about dedicating it to them; I know they will be pleased at what I have done instead. This book tries to think clearly about how to do theology. It seemed fitting to dedicate it to two teachers. One taught me, and many others, the most about what it really means to be a Christian theologian; the other taught me, and many others, the most about how to think clearly. Neither will agree with everything I have said, but I hope it is not a book they will be ashamed of.

On September 13, 1988, two weeks after I had sent the manuscript of this book, including its dedication, off to the publisher, Hans Frei died tragically and unexpectedly. More than ever, I hope this is a book

of which he would not have been ashamed. At his memorial service the
congregation sang John Bunyan's hymn:

> "He who would valiant be 'gainst all disaster,
> Let him in constancy follow the Master.
> There's no discouragement shall make him once relent
> His first avowed intent to be a pilgrim."

1

INTRODUCTION

Contemporary pluralism
and three problems for theology

This volume bears the title *Unapologetic Theology*. I hope it was not a mistake to begin with a bad pun. "Apologetics" traditionally constitutes the part of Christian theology devoted to defending Christian faith to a non-Christian audience. It can be an honorable enterprise, but it always risks becoming "apologetic" in a bad sense: defensive, halfhearted. Christian apologists can adopt the language and assumptions of their audience so thoroughly that they no longer speak with a distinctively Christian voice. As a result, they not only cease to give a faithful account of the Christian tradition, they cease to be interesting to their non-Christian listeners because they do not seem to have anything new or different to say.

Contemporary Christian theology often seems to adopt such an "apologetic" tone.[1] Perhaps one reason is that ever since the Enlightenment in the seventeenth century, many forces in our culture have taught that "being rational" meant questioning all inherited assumptions and then accepting only those beliefs which could be proven according to universally acceptable criteria. "Tradition" and "authority" were bad words. If Christians wanted to join the general conversation, it seemed that these were the rules by which they would have to play. If that meant there were some things they could not say, or some ways they could not say them, then they would have to adjust accordingly—or else find themselves in increasing intellectual isolation. Those Enlightenment ideals remain strong today, whether in politically liberal suspicions of any traditional authority—especially if it is religious in origin—or in neoconservative polemics like those of William Bennett and Allan Bloom, which set forth a somewhat secularized version of "the Western tradition" as the only viable standard of intellectual respectability.

In the last several decades, however, the search for universal starting points and standards for rationality so characteristic of the Enlightenment and its heirs has come under attack from many sides—from philosophers, philosophers of science, literary critics, and anthropologists among others—and there seem to be new possibilities for a richer kind of intellectual pluralism, a pluralism that would also welcome voices unwilling to accept the Enlightenment's assumptions. Critical thinking would not have to begin by questioning all our previous beliefs at once; indeed, that seems impossible. Dialogue would not have to await *universally* acceptable starting points before it could begin; particular conversations could start with whatever their participants happened to share and go from there. We could admit that of course we all stand within traditions and can never achieve an "objective" point of view; we could try to learn from one another's traditions rather than casting them all aside.

Such a wider intellectual pluralism is particularly welcome just now because of the mess our society is in. Even the wealthiest young people often seek escape from reality through drugs, homeless people wander our cities, and ecological catastrophe and nuclear devastation threaten us all. It seems plausible that we need some *major* changes in our values and ways of thinking. Some would argue that we have only failed to press forward far enough with the projects of modernity. Perhaps so. But we should look for answers wherever we can find them. Maybe some non-Western cultures can suggest some alternatives to our competitiveness and materialism; maybe some societies we once would have dismissed as "primitive" can give us lessons in how to live more in harmony with nature. Many people are exploring such possibilities these days.

The Christian gospel too can offer a kind of countercultural critique of the values and beliefs of our times, but these days, at least in the world of universities and "high culture," those dissatisfied with secular modernity most often turn to the East or to the distant mythic past. One reason seems to be that Christianity cannot criticize our culture very effectively if it has already accepted many of the assumptions of that culture as the price of intellectual respectability. Perhaps the time has come for a more "unapologetic" theology.

My claim is that a new pluralistic model of conversation now being discussed in many quarters could encourage such theology. Two challenges, one from either side, would undercut such pluralism. One side would claim that the Enlightenment was right, and we really do have to find universally acceptable common ground for rational conversation. The other side would insist that we cannot find such common ground, and as a result people from different traditions cannot talk to one another at all.[2] Either way, genuinely pluralistic conversation would become impossible. I want to argue for some kind of middle position between those extremes of universalism and radical relativism and see what it implies for Christian theology.

Chapters 2, 3, and 4 will trace some of the philosophical developments I have mentioned—the end of an Enlightenment dream of universal rationality. Chapter 3 will look at the case of science in particular and at questions about its claims to a special authority and objectivity. By the end of chapter 4, I will have introduced my own point of view. I have described it as a middle position, and the best way to clarify it seemed to be by contrasting it with the extremes between which it lies. The next two chapters will undertake that task: chapter 5 looking at two strong defenders of Enlightenment ideals, and chapter 6 at two prominent relativists. Chapter 7 will then develop further the idea of pluralistic conversation, and chapter 8 will discuss what Christians might mean by claiming that their beliefs are "true" in a pluralistic context. Chapters 9 and 10 will then turn to three specific issues— religion and science, interreligious dialogue, and theological method—in the light of the intervening discussion in order to show some concrete implications of my proposals. In addition to arguing my own thesis, I hope to introduce interested readers to a good bit of recent philosophy along the way—to help students, teachers, and pastors find out something about what is going on in philosophy these days.

The argument of this book may seem paradoxical. I will be maintaining that Christians ought to speak in their own voice and not worry about finding philosophical "foundations" for their claims. Yet a good bit of my evidence will be drawn from the work of philosophers. Am I contradicting myself? Obviously, I do not think so, and that for two reasons. First, philosophers and theologians may sometimes wrestle with analogous problems, and when that happens, they can on occasion learn from one another without thereby presupposing any general theory about the relation of philosophy and theology. If something a philosopher has said happens to give me as a theologian a good idea, nothing necessarily follows about the priority of philosophy to theology.

Second, the claims I want to make for how Christian theology ought to go about its work need not ultimately depend on my philosophical evidence. Christians must remain faithful to their own vision of things for reasons internal to Christian faith, and if, in some contexts, that means intellectual isolation, so be it. In the contemporary intellectual context, I want to argue, it need not lead to such isolation. If one *can* make wider connections while still speaking faithfully in one's own voice, then that has some important implications for how to get on with the job at hand.

As examples of such implications, three issues will be considered— the relation between religion and science, dialogue among different religions, and theological method. As already noted, the last two chapters will examine these in detail, but it may be helpful to introduce them now as reminders of how the more abstract questions I will be discussing arise in practical contexts.

1. *Religion and science.* Since the beginning of the Enlightenment, the natural sciences have provided many in our culture with *the* model of good, clear thinking. Scientists, after all, seem to base their beliefs on evidence and argument: they don't believe what they can't prove. Religion, on the other hand, seems to rest on "faith." It is hard to imagine "proving" a religious claim, and therefore religion seems false, meaningless, or at least very peculiar. Quite apart from any other problems about "dialogue between science and religion," given this account, it is hard to think why a scientist would want to bother talking to a theologian.

The philosopher A. J. Ayer speaks for many when he proclaims, "I believe in science. That is, I believe that a theory about the way the world works is not acceptable unless it is confirmed by the facts, and I believe that the only way to discover what the facts are is by empirical observation."[3] Many of us grow up learning an account of modern intellectual history as the story of the steady triumph of science over superstition and ignorance.

Theology fares badly in such a story; indeed, one classic account of these matters is frankly entitled *A History of the Warfare of Science with Theology in Christendom,*[4] and its author consistently and vividly paints scientists as the war's heroes and theologians as its obscurantist villains. As one of the few scholars well trained in both fields describes "the popular stereotype": "The scientist makes precise observations and then employs logical reasoning; if such a procedure is to be adopted in all fields of enquiry, should not religion be dismissed as prescientific superstition?"[5] Little surprise, then, that a good number of the leading scientists and social scientists of our time should have signed a Humanist Manifesto declaring, "We believe . . . that traditional dogmatic or authoritarian religions that place revelation, God, ritual, or creed above human needs and experience do a disservice to the human species. Any account of nature should pass the tests of scientific evidence; in our judgment, the dogmas and myths of traditional religions do not do so."[6]

When one talks to philosophers of science or sophisticated working scientists these days, however, one discovers that many such contrasts between science and religion assume far too simple a picture of scientific method. Science itself turns out to be a surprisingly pluralistic affair, and some of those who talk about its methods even use terms like "faith" and "conversion." It does not follow that science is "just like" religion, but at least science too begins with assumptions and operates within a tradition or traditions. No one can escape the problems of pluralism and discover "universality" and "objectivity" simply by appealing to scientific method.

2. *The "other religions."* Increasingly in Western societies, we get to know people with a wide range of religious beliefs or none at all: not just Christians and Jews, but Muslims, Hindus, Buddhists, atheists, and others. At least some from each group seem intelligent, thoughtful folk. In such circumstances, members of any religious community often start wondering: How can we be sure that we're right and they're wrong? Do we even want to make that sort of claim?

The problem is not as new as we sometimes think it is. Even in seventeenth-century England, John Bunyan confessed that "the tempter" assaulted him with such questions as:

> How can you tell but that the Turks had as good Scriptures to prove their *Mahomet* the Saviour, as we have to prove our *Jesus* is; and could I think that so many ten thousands in so many Countreys and Kingdoms, should be without the knowledge of the right way to Heaven . . . and that we onely, who live but in a corner of the Earth, should alone be blessed therewith? Every one doth think his own Religion rightest, both *Jews* and *Moors* and *Pagans;* and how if all our Faith, and Christ, and Scriptures, should be but a thinks-so too?[7]

Still, Bunyan in all likelihood never met any "Turks," and the religious views known to him—Christianity, Judaism, Islam, and Deism—all shared belief in a single personal God and roughly similar moral codes. It was easier for him to still the tempter's voice.

The sociologists of knowledge tell us that we tend to share the beliefs of those around us, particularly those we like and respect. Conversely, if our friends and neighbors disagree with us, we often begin to have doubts about our own beliefs—or we rather desperately seek out a community of like-minded folk in order to shore up what we believe.[8] For example, college students away from home for the first time and thrust into association with friends who have very different ethical standards and political and religious beliefs often begin to question their own. Pope Leo XIII may have been bucking the modern world in many respects, but he was thoroughly up to date in sociological theory when, concerned about preserving strong Catholic faith, he advised, "Unless forced by necessity to do otherwise, Catholics ought to prefer to associate with Catholics."[9]

But in many societies that advice grows ever harder to follow. Not only do Catholics get to know, like, and respect Protestants, and vice versa, but Christians get to know, like, and respect Jews, Muslims, atheists, Buddhists, Hindus—both as the subjects of television documentaries and as neighbors down the street. It seems to grow harder to be sure that "we" are simply right and "they" are simply wrong.

Several years ago a commission of the United Church of Canada declared, "Without the particular knowledge of God in Jesus Christ, men do not really know God at all." Wilfred Cantwell Smith, a member of that church who has taught about Islam and other religions at Harvard for many years, reacted angrily:

> Let us leave aside for the moment any question of whether or not this is true. . . . My point here is simply that, in any case, it is arrogant. . . . It is morally not possible actually to go out into the world and say to devout, intelligent, fellow human beings: "We are saved and you are damned," or "We believe that we know God, and we are right; you believe that you know God, and you are totally wrong."[10]

However one feels about the statement to which he was responding, Smith's remark nicely exhibits several common features of many contemporary discussions of these matters. First, he seems to equate the question of whether non-Christians have real knowledge of God with the question of whether they are "saved or damned." But these are two quite separate issues. Few theologians, for instance, have denied more forcefully than Karl Barth that non-Christians can truly know God. Yet Barth at least strongly leaned toward belief in universal salvation. *All* are saved in Christ, but Christians are the only ones who know the good news.[11] Whether or not Barth is right about either claim, there seems at least nothing contradictory in his position. Therefore, while it makes a fine rhetorical flourish to denounce one's opponents for consigning most of humanity to hell, it is not necessarily a fair charge against those who deny the truth of faiths other than their own. Yet exactly such accusations appear over and over again in the literature on this topic.

Smith also says it is "morally not possible" to say to "devout, intelligent, fellow human beings" that in religious matters "we are right . . . and you are totally wrong." Why not? I know sincere, intelligent people who believe in supply-side economics or think that the United States "should have really tried to win" the Vietnam War. I think they are totally wrong, and I feel no moral impossibility in telling them so. We have no compunction, in fact, in saying such things about questions in physics or politics or history. There may be reasons why religion is a different case, but those reasons need to be set out and argued.

They rarely are. The assumption that it is intellectually and morally unacceptable to say that the central tenets of another religion are false grows so strong that scholars like Smith, John Hick, and Paul Knitter make it a kind of moral imperative to see "the great religious traditions as different ways of conceiving and experiencing the one ultimate divine reality."[12] Hick at least hopes for the day when "what we now call different religions will constitute the past history of different em-

phases and variations within something that it need not be too misleading to call a single world religion."[13] After all, otherwise we might have
to admit that religious traditions differ—and that choosing one means
rejecting many of the teachings of the others.

As Christian theologians, those who share such hopes for religious
unity need to minimize the elements that set Christianity apart, especially those which claim a unique status—much of traditional Chris-
tology, for instance, disappears. As historians of religion, they need to
claim that, if all religions are not exactly "saying the same thing," at
least they are aiming toward the same goal. Such a view risks becoming
what David Tracy calls "a kind of Will Rogers pluralism: one where
theologians have never met a position they didn't like."[14]

On the face of it, the great world religions seem to have quite
different views on whether there is a personal God (or more than one),
how and where that God has been revealed, what awaits us after death,
how we ought to live our lives, and so on. As two of Hick's critics
frankly say about the claim that different religions are only different
ways of conceiving the same reality:

> It may seem surprising, given the overwhelming weight of evidence
> against such a view, that anyone who thinks more than twice about reli-
> gion and religions could actually hold it. But the fact remains that it is a
> very widely held view, that eminent scholars such as Professor Hick seem
> to hold it, and that, except for a few isolated voices, it remains largely
> unchallenged in the scholarly world.[15]

Part of the explanation for this odd state of affairs lies in a nervousness
about pluralism we have inherited from the Enlightenment. We keep
thinking that any truly rational field has a clear method of inquiry and
common conclusions. Anyone who wants to preserve the intellectual
respectability of religion, therefore, seems to need a way of thinking
about all the world's religions as aspects of a common quest, moving
toward a single goal—however implausible that picture may be.

But maybe pluralism *is* intellectually respectable, maybe there is
something wrong with that Enlightenment model of rationality. If so,
we might be able to encourage a quite interesting kind of dialogue
among religious traditions—one in which they admit that they disagree, explore their differences, consider each other individually, and
do not try to see each other as alternative manifestations of a single
phenomenon called "religion."

3. *Revisionist and postliberal theology.* Christian theologians try to set
out the logic of what Christians believe, but they disagree about how
to undertake that task. In the United States in recent years, most have
adopted what David Tracy calls the "revisionist" model: they think it
particularly important to correlate Christian beliefs with concerns and

experiences that all people share and to stand ready to defend Christian convictions according to "publicly acceptable" criteria of truth.[16] But in the last few years a growing number of theologians—George Lindbeck has labeled them "postliberals"—have insisted that Christian theology should focus primarily on describing the *internal* logic of Christian faith—how Christian beliefs relate to each other and function within the life of a Christian community.[17] On this model, Christians may seek common ground with particular non-Christians for particular purposes, but they do not assume that theology needs to defend its case according to criteria acceptable to all rational persons. Indeed, they rather doubt that there *are* such criteria.

David Tracy introduced the term "revisionist theologians" to describe those, like himself, who continue to pursue, in modified and more sophisticated ways, many of the goals of nineteenth-century liberal theology.[18] Back at the beginning of the nineteenth century, Friedrich Schleiermacher worried that history might be moving to a point where "Christianity becomes identified with barbarism, and science with unbelief."[19] He wanted to make sure that one could be an intelligent, modern person and still be a Christian.

Tracy and many others share that concern. A cover story on Tracy in the *New York Times Magazine* quotes Archbishop Weakland of Milwaukee as saying that Tracy "has taken theology into the current academic world of the United States and made it again intellectually respectable as an intellectual discipline."[20] For Tracy, the key to such an accomplishment is that theology must offer *publicly* available explanations and arguments for its conclusions; it must "speak in a manner that can be disclosive and transformative for any intelligent, reasonable, responsible human being."[21] Gordon Kaufman of Harvard, another prominent revisionist, makes the same point. The right kind of theology, he says, "has public, not private or parochial foundations. It is not restricted . . . to the language and traditions of a particular esoteric community (the church)."[22] Theologians should not just address Christians. They should speak in a way that anyone can understand and offer arguments that seek to persuade everyone. Otherwise, they are retreating into a kind of ghetto.

A number of theologians, many connected with Yale, have recently been exploring a different way of thinking about how to do theology. George Lindbeck's 1984 book *The Nature of Doctrine* gave this approach a name: "postliberal theology."[23] Lindbeck rejected any notion that "different religions are diverse expressions or objectifications of a common core experience . . . present in all human beings" by reference to which "their adequacy or lack of adequacy is to be judged."[24] Instead, Lindbeck proposes a "cultural-linguistic model" of religion. A religion defines a language and a practice, shared by a community, and that language makes new kinds of experience possible. The primary task of Christian theology, as Lindbeck's colleague Hans Frei has put it, is therefore "Christian self-description," not correlation with universal "human, cultural quests for ultimate meaning."[25] Christian theology lays out how the world looks from a Christian perspective, with whatever persuasive force that account musters and whatever connections it may happen to make with other perspectives, but it does not systematically ground or defend or explicate that picture in terms of universal criteria of meaningfulness or truth.

Stanley Hauerwas has drawn some implications for ethics: "The church's social task is first of all its willingness to be a community formed by a language the world does not share. . . . The church's social ethic is not first of all to be found in the statements by which it tries to influence the ethos of those in power, but rather . . . in its ability to sustain a people who are not at home in the liberal presumptions of our civilization and society."[26] Confronted by our culture's standards of what makes sense and what doesn't, postliberal theology invites Christians to say, "We don't look at things that way," and to nurture communities that offer an alternative vision.

In terms of issues already mentioned in this chapter, the postliberals would make two charges against their revisionist opponents: (1) Appeals to explanations and arguments accessible to "any intelligent, reasonable, responsible human being" presuppose the kind of universal standard of rationality that the Enlightenment championed, the kind of argument that often lies behind claims that scientific method represents *the* legitimate way of inquiry. But pluralistic trends in contemporary thought raise doubts as to whether there is such a universal standard. (2) When they concern religious matters, such "public" arguments seem to appeal, explicitly or covertly, to a "common core of religion," so that the argument will not begin with specifically Christian premises. But the serious study of the world's religions suggests that there is no such common core.[27]

The revisionists would reply that we have to remember that we live in a pluralistic society. If Christianity is to be taken seriously, if it is to influence the direction of our society, it has to find a way to join the general conversation—and the postliberals sometimes sound as if they were beating a retreat to a theological ghetto where they need to explain and defend their ideas only to fellow Christians.

Discussions of revisionist and postliberal theologies have generated considerable passion. From the revisionist side, James Gustafson has denounced Lindbeck's position as a "pernicious . . . sectarian temptation" which "legitimates a withdrawal of Christianity from its larger cultural environs" and thereby leads it toward a "perilous fate."[28] A sympathetic summary of postliberal theology in *The Christian Century*

drew a virulent round of letters comparing its adherents to Jerry Fal-
well, Pontius Pilate, and the Athenians who killed Socrates.[29] From the
postliberal side, Lindbeck criticizes his opponents as "experiential-
expressivists" who claim that different religions simply express some
universal religious experience in different ways. He despairs of a situation in which

> religions are seen as multiple suppliers of different forms of a single
> commodity needed for transcendent self-expression and self-realization.
> Theologians, ministers, and perhaps above all teachers of religion in
> colleges and universities whose job is to meet the demand are under great
> pressure in these circumstances to emphasize the experiential-expressive
> aspects of religion. It is thus that they can most easily market it.[30]

Systematically beginning with "public criteria," Lindbeck is arguing,
means shaping one's faith to the needs, desires, and concerns of contemporary culture—and that inevitably distorts the faith.

In chapter 10, I will return to this debate and argue that the most
thoughtful writers on both sides are trying to say the right things. They
know that philosophy cannot provide us with a universal standard of
rationality but that Christians really do need to talk to non-Christians
and therefore need to find common ground from which those conversations can begin. But theologians have often lacked very clear ways
of talking about genuine pluralistic conversation. Partly as a result,
revisionists can sometimes *sound as if* they mean to let contemporary
culture set the theological agenda, and postliberals can *appear to be* in
full retreat from the intellectual debates of the modern world. I hope
I can provide some categories that let both parties say what they mean
in their best moments.

While I thus hope to find a kind of middle ground, candor compels
the confession that my sympathies lie more on the postliberal side. In
the world of American academic theology right now, helping Christian
theology speak forcefully in its own voice seems to me the most pressing task, and I think the postliberals therefore put the emphasis in the
right place. More of all that in chapter 10.

First, however, we need to turn to some philosophy. A good many
recent theological debates, as well as a good many assumptions about
the relation of religion and science and dialogue among different
religions, have stood in the shadow of the Enlightenment dream of a
universal standard of rationality, a single method for determining
what's true and what's false. Some theologians seem to accept that
view of the world; others want to break free of it—and therefore have
sometimes thought they had to turn a deaf ear to contemporary philosophy. But, as I have mentioned, these days most philosophers themselves no longer dream that dream. Chapters 2 and 3 will try to
describe why it fell apart, but first we need to see how it began, and

that means going back to the beginning of the Enlightenment in the seventeenth century.

NOTES

1. I write this book as someone concerned about Christian theology. Many of the same issues arise for other religious traditions too—and, for that matter, in some contexts outside religion—but they sometimes take quite different forms. One of my themes will be the danger of quick generalizations, and I am nervously aware that Christians have too often presumed to speak on behalf of others who are fully capable of speaking for themselves. So I will concentrate on the Christian case.

2. This is what Richard Bernstein diagnoses as "the Cartesian anxiety," the sense that "*either* there is some support for our being, a fixed foundation for our knowledge, *or* we cannot escape the forces of darkness that envelop us with madness, with intellectual and moral chaos" (Richard J. Bernstein, *Beyond Objectivism and Relativism*, p. 18; Philadelphia: University of Pennsylvania Press, 1983).

3. A. J. Ayer, "What I Believe," in George Unwin, ed., *What I Believe* (London: George Allen & Unwin, 1966), p. 13.

4. Andrew Dickson White, *A History of the Warfare of Science with Theology in Christendom*, 2 vols. (New York: D. Appleton & Co., 1896).

5. Ian G. Barbour, *Myths, Models, and Paradigms* (New York: Harper & Row, 1974), pp. 2–3.

6. *Humanist Manifestos I and II* (Buffalo, N.Y.: Prometheus Books, 1973), pp. 15–16. Among the admittedly varied but nonetheless impressive list of signatories are Isaac Asimov, Sir Alfred Ayer, Francis Crick, Arthur Danto, Antony Flew, Betty Friedan, Sidney Hook, Sir Julian Huxley, Jacques Monod, Gunnar Myrdal, Lord Ritchie-Calder, Andrei Sakharov, and B. F. Skinner.

7. John Bunyan, *Grace Abounding to the Chief of Sinners*, ed. Robert Sharrock (Oxford: Clarendon Press, 1962), p. 31.

8. See Peter L. Berger, *The Sacred Canopy: Elements of a Sociological Theory of Religion* (Garden City, N.Y.: Doubleday & Co., Anchor Books, 1969), pp. 29–51. For a fascinating case study, see Leon Festinger, Henry W. Reicken, and Stanley Schachter, *When Prophecy Fails* (Minneapolis: University of Minnesota Press, 1956).

9. Leo XIII, *Longinqua* (January 6, 1895), in Claudia Carlen Ihm, *The Papal Encyclicals 1878–1903* (New York: McGrath Publications, 1981), p. 368.

10. Wilfred Cantwell Smith, *Religious Diversity* (New York: Crossroad Publishing Co., 1982), p. 13.

11. See, e.g., Karl Barth, *Church Dogmatics*, IV/1, trans. G. W. Bromiley (Edinburgh: T. & T. Clark, 1956), p. 312.

12. John Hick, *Problems of Religious Pluralism* (New York: St. Martin's Press, 1985), p. 102. Hick makes the same rhetorical move that Smith did: his immediate argument in favor of this assertion is that "it is not a morally or religiously acceptable view that salvation depends upon being a member of the Christian minority within the human race." But who gets saved is simply a

different question from who knows the truth. For Knitter, see Paul F. Knitter, *No Other Name? A Critical Survey of Christian Attitudes Toward the World Religions* (Maryknoll, N.Y.: Orbis Books, 1985).

13. John Hick, "The Outcome: Dialogue Into Truth," in John Hick, ed., *Truth and Dialogue in World Religions: Conflicting Truth-Claims* (Philadelphia: Westminster Press, 1974), p. 151.

14. David Tracy, "Defending the Public Character of Theology," *The Christian Century* 98 (1981), p. 355.

15. Paul Griffiths and Delmas Lewis, "On Grading Religions, Seeking Truth, and Being Nice to People—A Reply to Professor Hick," *Religious Studies* 19 (1983), pp. 76–77.

16. See David Tracy, *Blessed Rage for Order: The New Pluralism in Theology* (New York: Seabury Press, 1975), pp. 32ff.

17. George A. Lindbeck, *The Nature of Doctrine: Religion and Theology in a Postliberal Age* (Philadelphia: Westminster Press, 1984), pp. 112ff.

18. Tracy mentions as examples Leslie Dewart, Gregory Baum, Michael Novak, Langdon Gilkey, Van Harvey, and Gordon Kaufman. Francis Fiorenza lists Paul Tillich, Karl Rahner, Peter Hodgson, Schubert Ogden, Edward Schillebeeckx, Hans Küng, Gilkey, and Tracy (Francis Schüssler Fiorenza, *Foundational Theology: Jesus and the Church*, pp. 276–277; New York: Crossroad Publishing Co., 1984).

19. Friedrich Schleiermacher, *On the Glaubenslehre: Two Letters to Dr. Lücke*, trans. James Duke and Francis Fiorenza (Missoula, Mont.: Scholars Press, 1981), p. 61.

20. Eugene Kennedy, "A Dissenting Voice," *New York Times Magazine*, Nov. 9, 1986, p. 23.

21. Tracy, "Defending the Public Character of Theology," pp. 351–352. See also James M. Gustafson, *Ethics from a Theocentric Perspective*, vol. 1 (Chicago: University of Chicago Press, 1981), p. 29; and Schubert M. Ogden, *On Theology* (San Francisco: Harper & Row, 1986), pp. 10–11.

22. Gordon D. Kaufman, *An Essay on Theological Method* (Missoula, Mont.: Scholars Press, 1975), p. 8.

23. Frankly, I wish Lindbeck had called his approach something else. "Post-anything" terminology always defines a position negatively, in contrast with some predecessor, rather than emphasizing its own character. Moreover, in the 1960s, when Lindbeck was developing the ideas that turned into his book, "postliberal" might have meant "radical," but by the time he published the book in the 1980s it carried unfortunate overtones of political conservatism.

24. Lindbeck, *The Nature of Doctrine*, p. 31. In addition to Lindbeck, a list of "postliberal theologians" might include Hans Frei, Stanley Hauerwas, Ronald Thiemann, William Werpehowski, and Charles Wood.

25. Hans W. Frei, "Eberhard Busch's Biography of Karl Barth," in H.-Martin Rumscheidt, ed., *Karl Barth in Re-View* (Pittsburgh: Pickwick Press, 1981), p. 103.

26. Stanley Hauerwas, *Against the Nations* (Minneapolis: Winston Press, 1985), pp. 11–12.

27. I should note David Tracy's recent remark: "There are family resemblances among the religions. But as far as I can see, there is no single essence, no one content of enlightenment or revelation, no one way of emancipation

or liberation, to be found in all that plurality" (David Tracy, *Plurality and Ambiguity,* p. 90; San Francisco: Harper & Row, 1987). My remarks here have oversimplified the issues. When I return to these matters in chapter 10, I will suggest how hard sorting out the real differences between revisionists and postliberals can get.

28. James M. Gustafson, "The Sectarian Temptation: Reflections on Theology, the Church, and the University," *Proceedings of the Catholic Theological Society* 40 (1985), pp. 93–94.

29. "A Challenge to Willimon's Postliberalism," *The Christian Century* 104 (1987), pp. 306–310.

30. Lindbeck, *The Nature of Doctrine,* p. 22. See also George Hunsinger, "Where the Battle Rages: Confessing Christ in America Today," *dialog* 26 (1987), pp. 264–274.

2

FOUNDATIONS

The end of the Enlightenment ideal of knowledge

In 1639 and 1640, in the countryside near the small Dutch town of Santpoort, René Descartes was writing his *Meditations on First Philosophy*. The news of Europe must have reached even his quiet corner of north Holland. As the Thirty Years War, in which Descartes had fought as a young man, dragged on, a Swedish army overran Saxony and took Prague. An army of Scots Covenanters captured Edinburgh, and Charles I, unable to defeat them, agreed to abolish episcopacy in Scotland. Galileo's scientific masterpiece, the *Dialogues on Two New Sciences*, had been published the year before in Holland, smuggled out of Italy. Six years earlier, the Inquisition had threatened him with the instruments of torture because of his support of Copernican astronomy. He had remained under house arrest ever since. When Galileo was arrested, Descartes had been about to publish a masterly summation of the new science of the day, but he put it away when he heard the news, and it remained unpublished. In September of 1640, Descartes's only child, an illegitimate daughter named Francine, died of a fever at the age of five.[1]

Descartes's surviving correspondence tells us little about either the state of his mind or the progress of his writing during those years. But we know something of what was going on in his world, and we have his *Meditations*, published in 1641. New scientific theories were challenging the most basic assumptions about the natural world—even the earth no longer remained stable beneath humanity's feet. Quarrels about religious authority divided Europe and had helped to provoke a generation of bloodshed—by some estimates over a third of the population of Germany died of battle or resulting disease and famine before the war was over.[2] The growth of capitalism was producing conflict between the traditional power of the aristocracy and the rising influence of middle-class merchants. The traditional securities of natural world, religious faith, and social order all seemed uncertain. As John Donne had written a generation earlier:

> And new Philosophy calls all in doubt,
> The Element of fire is quite put out;
> The Sun is lost, and th'earth, and no mans wit
> Can well direct him where to look for it.
> . . . .
> 'Tis all in peeces, all cohaerence gone;
> All just supply, and all Relation:
> Prince, Subject, Father, Sonne, are things forgot,
> For every man alone thinkes he hath got
> To be a Phoenix.[3]

The Phoenix, rising newborn out of its own ashes, is not a bad symbol for Descartes's project in the *Meditations.* In the midst of intellectual chaos, he proposed to find certainty by beginning with universal doubt:

> It is some time ago now since I perceived that, from my earliest years, I had accepted many false opinions as being true, and that what I had since based on such insecure principles could only be most doubtful and uncertain; so that I had to undertake seriously once in my life to rid myself of all the opinions I had adopted up to then, and to begin afresh from the foundations, if I wished to establish something firm and constant in the sciences.[4]

To avoid error, Descartes concludes, "I must avoid believing things which are not entirely certain and indubitable"[5] and find something which is, something that can provide the "foundation" for an edifice of certain knowledge. After all, "Archimedes, in order to take the terrestrial globe from its place and move it to another, asked only for a point which was fixed and assured. So also, I shall have the right to entertain high hopes, if I am fortunate enough to find only one thing which is certain and indubitable."[6]

Descartes has become a kind of mythical figure—the Father of the Enlightenment[7]—and philosophers tend to read their own agendas back into his work, creating either a Descartes in their own image or a father figure they can attack with Freudian gusto. The complexity of his work permits many different interpretations, and even undergraduates in their first course in philosophy do not need to read many pages beyond the opening of the *Meditations* before they begin to identify the points Descartes failed to doubt. Nevertheless, with all their ambiguities and apparent inconsistencies, the *Meditations* did set out a project and a starting point for much of the Enlightenment:

Test everything you believe by submitting it to doubt.

Discover what passes the test, what is "clearly and distinctly" evident, independent of any other beliefs.

That will provide a secure foundation for an edifice of knowledge.[8]

If such rules provided an agenda for modern philosophy, then one reason for talking these days about "postmodern philosophy" is that the project they define no longer makes sense to many philosophers.[9] "We cannot begin with complete doubt," C. S. Peirce wrote back in 1868. "We must begin with all the prejudices which we actually have when we enter upon the study of philosophy. These prejudices are not to be dispelled by a maxim, for they are things which it does not occur to us *can* be questioned. . . . Let us not pretend to doubt in philosophy what we do not doubt in our hearts."[10] The person who doubted *everything,* Ludwig Wittgenstein insisted again and again, would not be able to *ask* any questions, would not be able to think at all. Only in the context of assuming *some* things can we question *other* things. In Wittgenstein's inversion of one of Descartes's favorite images, "I have arrived at the rock bottom of my convictions. And one might almost say that these foundation-walls are carried by the whole house."[11]

But such reference to the end of "modern philosophy" jumps ahead of the story. Descartes had set the goal of seeking a foundation for knowledge, but modern philosophy soon divided between empiricists who looked for that foundation in bare, uninterpreted sensations and rationalists who sought it in logically unchallengeable first truths.

John Locke stated a classic early form of the empiricist view:

> Let us then suppose the mind to be, as we say, white paper, void of all characters, without any ideas:—How comes it to be furnished? . . . First, our Senses, conversant about particular sensible objects, do convey into the mind several distinct perceptions of things. . . . And thus we come by those *ideas* we have of *yellow, white, heat, cold, soft, hard, bitter, sweet,* and all those which we call sensible qualities.[12]

We start with a blank sheet of paper. Experience prints on that paper the data that serve as the basis of our knowledge. As empiricists pursued that line of thought, with Descartes's goal of a secure foundation for knowledge in mind, they realized that they had to distinguish between those basic experiences and the interpretations we place on them. Obviously we sometimes misinterpret our experience. So we need to penetrate behind interpretation to basic sensations we know by direct observation.[13] The logical positivists, the principal inheritors of the empiricist tradition early in this century, insisted that a statement can be *meaningful* only if we can know how to go about *verifying* it.[14] "The act of verification in which the path to the solution finally ends is always of the same sort: it is the occurrence of a definite fact that is confirmed by observation, by means of immediate experience."[15] Logical positivism thus represents the most consistent empiricist version of Descartes's project: If we need a foundation for knowledge, and that foundation is to be experience, then there must be immediate experience which we can know directly, prior to interpretation. As the great logical positivist Rudolf Carnap put it many years later, "We assumed that there was a certain rock bottom knowledge, the knowledge of the immediately given, which was indubitable. Every other kind of knowledge was supposed to be firmly supported by this basis and therefore likewise decidable with certainty."[16]

Unfortunately, contemporary psychologists, physicists, and philosophers have generally come to agree that there is no such thing. In the jargon usually used to make this point, all observations are "theory-laden." What we see is shaped by what we already know, by other things we see, and by what we expect. That uninterpreted bare impression proves an illusion; as even Carnap eventually admitted, "there is no sharp line between observable and non-observable predicates."[17]

Some quite ordinary experiences illustrate the point. Draw two checkerboard patterns, one with red and white squares, the other with red and black squares. Use the same red paint in both patterns. Yet as we look at the two checkerboards, we "see" the red in the red-and-white pattern as the darker of the two. Even when we "know the trick," the appearance remains. Even more simply, we can measure the two lines:

and establish that they are the same length, but the one on the right still "looks" longer.

In a widely cited experiment, the psychologists Jerome Bruner and Leo Postman showed in a particularly vivid way that, in their words, "the perceptual effect of a stimulus is necessarily dependent upon the set or expectancy of the organism."[18] They flashed playing cards in front of their experimental subjects for periods from a fraction of a second to a full second. But they slipped among the cards an occasional oddity, such as a red five of clubs or a black ace of diamonds. All the subjects correctly identified all the "normal" cards when shown them for .4 second, but even when shown the "anomalous" cards for a full second, they often made mistakes. They "saw" the card as a five of clubs and somehow didn't register that it was red, or sometimes they would "see" it as brown or purple. One poor subject finally blurted out, "I don't know what the hell it is now, not even for sure whether it's a playing card."[19] The subjects were not color-blind, or drunk, but the context of their expectations shaped what they saw before them.

Artists and art historians, of course, knew all this a long time ago. We learn how to draw with perspective as children, and we would say, "Well, you can just see that the back corner of the box looks shorter than the front corner, so that's the way you draw it." Yet artists generally did *not* draw it that way until the time of the Renaissance. To be sure, this example raises complicated issues, for artists can know about perspective and choose not to use it if they have different assumptions about what it means to represent reality. Nevertheless, it does seem that drawing how a box "looks"—which seems like a task of reproducing direct experience—in fact has to be learned. E. H. Gombrich cites the case of Jehudo Epstein, who was brought up a strictly orthodox Jew in a Polish ghetto and came to adulthood virtually without having seen or drawn pictures. When he then tried to draw, he could produce nothing that satisfied him—until someone gave him a book on perspective, which came as a revelation to him.[20] It is as if we have to learn how to see, as if the great artist John Constable was right to say, "The art of seeing nature is a thing almost as much to be acquired as the art of reading Egyptian hieroglyphs."[21]

"But the scientist," someone might interrupt, "surely the scientist does gather uninterpreted data." In fact, nothing could be further from the truth. The untrained observer watching a cloud chamber or observing cells through a microscope soon learns how much training is required before one can see what the scientist sees. As the philosopher of science N. R. Hanson remarked, "Were a physicist in an ordinary laboratory situation to react to his visual environment with purely sense-data responses—as does the infant or the idiot—we would think him out of his mind. We would think him *not* to be seeing what was around him."[22] Hanson may be a bit too hasty about infants and idiots—their capacity to see uninterpreted sense-data seems unlikely too—but he is right about scientists. The great physicists of our century seem to agree, from Ludwig Boltzmann ("In my opinion we cannot utter a single statement that would be a pure fact of experience"[23]) to Niels Bohr ("Any experience . . . makes its appearance within the frame of our customary points of view and forms of perception"[24]).

All this exposes the falsity of what the American philosopher Wilfred Sellars called the Myth of the Given. Suppose I want to claim, "I am now seeing a red circle." I might try to defend this as a bare, uninterpreted sensation I can know independent of anything else: "Maybe my memory of earlier red circles is false; maybe I'm hallucinating, and there's no red circular object out there. All I'm saying is that I now see this red circle, and I know that independent of any theory or any other sensations."

Sellars disagreed. Think about how babies learn to recognize colors and shapes. Gradually they realize they can distinguish red things from orange things from yellow things and sort out long-thins from short-fats. The point is: they have to *learn* such categories, they have to develop ideas of different colors and shapes, and indeed the very idea of sorting things according to color and shape, before they can *recognize* anything as a "red circle." "The coming to see something as red is the culmination of a conceptual process which is the slow building up of a multi-dimensional pattern of linguistic responses."[25] "Even such simple concepts as those of colors are the fruit of a long process of publicly reinforced responses."[26] Therefore, Sellars concludes, "one is not in a position to be perceptually aware of any fact, however minimal, unless one has a whole system of concepts."[27] Even knowing "Red here now" means having concepts of redness, of color, of time, of space, and so on—a rather complicated apparatus. "And to admit this requires an abandonment of the traditional empiricist idea that observational knowledge 'stands on its own feet.' "[28] We cannot build knowledge on a foundation of uninterpreted sense-data, because we cannot know particular sense-data in isolation from the conceptual schemes we use to organize them.

The other way to pursue the Enlightenment project was to begin with unquestionable first principles—rationalism instead of empiricism. This was in fact the route Descartes himself chose. In his most famous argument, having succeeded in doubting everything else, he finds he cannot consistently doubt his own existence as a thinking thing, for, even if he doubts, still *he* is doubting; even if he is deceived, still *he* is deceived. "So that, having thought carefully about it, and having scrupulously examined everything, one must then, in conclusion, take as assured that the proposition: *I am, I exist*, is necessarily true, every time I express it or conceive of it in my mind."[29] "In this first knowledge," Descartes reflects, "there is nothing except a clear and distinct perception of what I affirm which indeed would not be sufficient to assure me that my assertion is true, if it could ever be found to be false. And consequently it seems to me that I can already establish as a general rule that all the things we conceive very clearly and distinctly are true."[30]

Later philosophers would vary their lists of clear and distinct truths and search for alternative ways of defining the quality such truths possess, but the dream of finding somehow self-evident truths offered another way of providing knowledge with a secure foundation. Unfortunately, this strategy has not fared better than the empiricists' search for interpretation-free, immediate sense experience.

The simplest line of attack against it comes from looking at nearly every rationalist's favorite example of first principles: the five postulates of Euclid's geometry.[31] Euclid assumed five principles at the start of his system, claims such as "All right angles equal one another" and "A straight line can be drawn from any point to any other point." From these, plus some axioms and definitions, he derived his whole system of geometry. If you asked Euclid how he knew the truth of some geometrical theorem, he could prove it for you, starting with the postulates. If you asked how he knew the truth of the postulates, he might have said something like, "Well, just think about it; isn't it clear that

that *has* to be true?"[32] And, to be honest, his postulates do seem obviously true. They survived essentially unchallenged for about two thousand years. So this seems to be the perfect example of a system based on a secure foundation, and a great deal of modern philosophy sought to model its method on Euclid.

There was for a long time a bit of nervousness about Euclid's fifth postulate. Euclid's own way of stating it is a bit complicated,[33] so it is usually stated in the form of the "parallel postulate": "From a point not on a line, one and only one line can be drawn parallel to the given line." Partly just *because* it seemed a bit more complicated, a number of mathematicians tried—always unsuccessfully—to derive it from some combination of the first four postulates.[34] In the 1820s the Russian Nikolai Lobachevsky and the Hungarian Farkas Bolyai independently worked out a geometry alternative to Euclid's. If you assume that *more than one* line can be drawn through that point parallel to the given line, then you get a geometrical system in which the sum of the angles of a triangle is always less than two right angles and the ratio of the circumference of a circle to its diameter is always greater than pi. The system is just as internally consistent as Euclid's, and the differences might be so small that there is no way of checking one system against another by empirical measurement.

In the 1850s the German G. F. B. Riemann took another tack and assumed that *no* straight line parallel to the original line could be drawn through a point not on the line. The sum of the angles of a triangle is always greater than two right angles, the ratio of the circumference of a circle to its diameter is always less than pi. You can draw more than one straight line between two points, and a straight line *cannot* be extended infinitely in any direction. Again, the system is internally consistent, and there was at least no obvious empirical way of checking it.

Einstein's theory of relativity, however, seemed to offer support for Riemann's geometry. According to Einstein, if we connect three points within a gravitational field with light rays, then the sum of the internal angles of the resulting triangle will be greater than two right angles. Moreover, each light ray will travel along a path such that there is no path between those two points that one could measure with fewer lengths of a measuring rod—and yet there is more than one such path between any two points. So Riemann seems to be right.

On the other hand, if one says that gravitational fields bend light rays and distort the length of any possible measuring rods, then Euclid's geometry still holds for straight lines—it just turns out that the figure we were considering is not really a triangle, and its sides are not really straight lines. It is odd to think of a gravitational field working this way—but then it is arguably odd to reject Euclidean geometry. There may be arguments in favor of one strategy or the other, but there is no way of settling the question in isolation. To quote Hans Reichenbach:

> We can no more say that Einstein's geometry is "truer" than Euclidean geometry than we can say that the meter is a "truer" unit of length than the yard. . . . Properties of reality are discovered only by a combination of the results of measurement with the underlying coordinative definition. . . . [According to Einstein,] a three-dimensional non-Euclidean geometry results in the neighborhood of heavenly bodies, if we define the comparison of length by transported rigid rods. But . . . it could just as well be said that in the neighborhood of a heavenly body a universal field of force exists which affects all measuring rods, while the geometry is Euclidean. . . . These considerations indicate what is meant by *relativity* of geometry.[35]

There is no way of identifying one right answer. We have to choose among the advantages and disadvantages of each way of thinking about the problem.

The example of geometry seemed worth such discussion partly because it was for so long *the* favorite example of rationalist philosophers but also because it so nicely illustrates the conclusions many contemporary philosophers have reached more generally. "Our statements about the external world," the great Harvard philosopher Willard Van Orman Quine has written, "face the tribunal of sense experience not individually but only as a corporate body."[36] Even if we take something like Euclid's fifth postulate, we cannot judge it in isolation, either by empirical test or by some criterion of intuitive self-evidence. On the face of it, the postulate does seem reasonable, but in order to preserve it, we have to give up something else that also seems reasonable. We can do that, but we then have to face a different set of consequences, and we have to look at connections all through our system.[37] Quine provides a fine metaphor:

> The totality of our so-called knowledge or beliefs, from the most casual matters of geography and history to the profoundest laws of atomic physics or even of pure mathematics and logic, is a man-made fabric which impinges on experience only along the edges. . . . A conflict with experience at the periphery occasions adjustments in the interior of the field. . . . But the total field is so underdetermined by its boundary conditions, experience, that there is much latitude of choice as to what statements to reevaluate in the light of any single contrary experience.[38]

If I hear that a friend is in China and then see her on the street, the most natural conclusion is that the report of her visit was false. But perhaps she *was* in China and has unexpectedly returned early. Or perhaps I have just seen her identical twin sister, previously unknown

to me. Or perhaps, under the pressure of reading too much philosophy, I have begun to hallucinate. Similarly, if the triangle formed by
light rays in a gravitational field does not fit Euclidean geometry,
perhaps Euclidean geometry is wrong. But then again, perhaps the
light rays are bent and it is not really a triangle. Quine's point is that
we can always solve the problem in more than one way. Since a solution at one point will always have consequences elsewhere, we cannot
decide single questions in isolation. If I want to save any particular
point badly enough, I can adjust other beliefs, other elements in the
system, in order to do so. Any argument one way or the other will have
to consider implications throughout the system of my beliefs. "The
lore of our fathers is a fabric of sentences. . . . It is a pale grey lore,
black with fact and white with convention. But I have found no substantial reasons for concluding that there are any quite black threads
in it, nor any white ones."[39]

Many philosophers have long argued, however, that some truths are
necessarily true, and it might seem that such truths would stand on their
own. Maybe they could provide the kind of foundation for knowledge
of which the rationalists dreamed. As tough-minded philosophers have
chipped away at supposed examples of necessary truths, the most
plausible surviving candidates have been matters of definition. Kant
established a distinction between analytic and synthetic truths: matters
of definition and matters of fact.[40] If I say, "All Swedes are stubborn,"
this is a *synthetic* truth, a matter of fact to be tested out empirically by
interviewing Swedes—or their relatives and neighbors. But if I say,
"All bachelors are unmarried," this is an *analytic* truth, a matter of
definition. I do not need to take surveys of bachelors to check it out;
being unmarried, we might say, is *part of what we mean* by the word
"bachelor." Synthetic truths depend on empirical investigation and
face all the problems already noted, but—so it might seem—analytic
truths stand fast. After all, how can things change if that is how I have
defined the word?

Wittgenstein, in his discussion of "family resemblances," and
Quine, in his attack on the "dogmas of empiricism," have both raised
questions about the distinction between analytic and synthetic judgments. Suppose, for instance, I define a "mammal" as a "warm-
blooded animal with hair which bears live young." Then an explorer
returns from Australia with a platypus. In so many ways, it resembles
other mammals—but it lays eggs. I might say, "Well, it's very like a
mammal—but not quite." But then again I might say, "Let's change
our definition of 'mammal.'" My original definition brought together
a group of qualities that seemed to belong together, but in the face of
the platypus, that way of classifying things may seem cumbersome and
artificial. It may seem most natural to say, "I guess I was wrong in
thinking that no mammals lay eggs."

So is "bearing live young" a part of the definition of "mammal" or an empirically discovered quality? Originally, we probably would have called it part of the definition, but later empirical evidence leads us to change our minds. Odd as it seems, an empirical discovery (the platypus) leads us to change something some philosophers would have called a definition, an "analytic truth." Hilary Putnam recalls:

> Quine once compared the question, "Which sentences in physical theory are definitions?" to the question, "Which places in Ohio are starting places?" *No* place in Ohio is a "starting place" *in itself;* it all depends on what journey you wish to take. Similarly, *no* sentence in physical theory is a "definition" in itself; it may be convenient in one context to call one sentence a definition and a second sentence a theorem or an empirical consequence, and convenient in a different context to call the second sentence the definition and the first sentence the theorem or the empirical consequence.[41]

What we *cannot* do is to find some point that is uniquely certain by definition, guaranteed to hold regardless of any empirical discoveries, independent of any other elements in our system. If we determinedly save one element as unchallengeable, it is only because we choose to do so.

A famous example from the logical foundations of mathematics illustrates the point. Much of the modern theory of the foundations of mathematics involves thinking about "classes." Yet Bertrand Russell showed early in this century that thinking about classes in its most natural form leads to a paradox. A class is just a specified collection of something or other: the class of all the chairs in this room; the class of all apples; the class of all people; the class of all classes. Every apple is a "member" of the class of all apples; every class is a "member" of the class of all classes. Now some classes are members of themselves. "The class of all classes" is itself a class. "The class of all things referred to in this book" is itself used in this book (I just did it). But other classes are not members of themselves: "the class of all apples" is not itself an apple; "the class of all people" is not itself a person.

Consider *the class of all classes which are not members of themselves.* Is it a member of itself? Well—if it is, then it isn't, but if it isn't, then it is. Answering the question either way leads to a contradiction. Gottlob Frege had based his whole philosophy of mathematics on the theory of classes, so that when Russell sent this puzzle to him in a letter, Frege wrote back that the very foundations of mathematics were shaken.[42]

Russell resolved the paradox by developing the "theory of types." Simply stated, he distinguished first-order classes (classes of apples, people, and so on) from classes of classes. They are, he said, simply different sorts of things, different types—call them classes$_1$ and classes$_2$. According to the theory of types, then, a class$_1$ could only be a member of a class$_2$, no class could possibly be a member of itself, and so the paradox does not arise.[43]

Ernst Zermelo, Quine, John Von Neumann, and others found alternative ways around the paradox. But each of these "solutions" involves problems of its own—as does Russell's theory of types. To take Russell's theory as an example: As we think about the idea of classes, the theory of types does not come naturally to mind. The idea of a class that is a member of itself seems reasonable enough, and the rule forbidding such classes seems correspondingly artificial. If someone asks, "Why should we accept the theory of types?" the best answer says something like, "Well, because otherwise we fall into Russell's paradox." "But aren't there other ways of avoiding the paradox?" "Yes, but they involve arbitrary assumptions too." "So how do you decide which is the best way to go?" "Experts in logic can see one solution as less arbitrary or more decisive than another. But it's the kind of thing about which people can disagree, and, in fact, they do."

Quine has argued that comparing the various proposed solutions to Russell's paradox always involves a kind of trade-off: the more certain you want to be that you have buried the paradox once and for all, the more complex, artificial, and counterintuitive a solution you need.[44] In the end, we have to choose. If our definitions in mathematics or logic lead to problems, we may decide to change them, but we always have more than one choice. "The same proposition may get treated at one time as something to test by experience, at another as a rule of testing."[45] We cannot preserve even a class of analytic truths free from empirical consequences, truly independent of other elements in the way we see the world.

But all this implies a dead end for Descartes's project, and with it the Enlightenment dream. We cannot find a starting point firmly established on its own, on which we could construct the rest of our system of knowledge. Sellars' attack on the Myth of the Given showed how all experience is theory laden. Quine's attack on the dogmas of empiricism shows that even definitions may need to be altered because of their consequences elsewhere in a system. And on these issues, most of the most influential "analytic philosophers" today are the intellectual descendants of Wittgenstein, Sellars, and Quine.[46]

It does seem that Wittgenstein was right: when we find the foundations, it turns out they are being held up by the rest of the house. If theologians try to defend their claims by starting with basic, foundational truths that any rational person would have to believe or observations independent of theory and assumption, they are trying to do something that our best philosophers tell us is impossible—not merely for religious beliefs but for any beliefs whatever. It makes no sense to demand that Christians undertake such a self-limiting discipline as the price of entry into contemporary intellectual conversation.

NOTES

1. John Cottingham, *Descartes* (Oxford: Basil Blackwell, 1986), p. 14.

2. E. A. Beller, "The Thirty Years War," in *The New Cambridge Modern History*, vol. 4 (Cambridge: Cambridge University Press, 1970), p. 357. Beller cites the estimates from Günther Franz, *Der dreissigjährige Krieg und das deutsche Volk* (Jena, 1943; reprint, Stuttgart: G. Fischer, 1961), p. 53, that the population of Germany decreased by 40 percent in the countryside and 33 percent in the cities.

3. John Donne, "An Anatomie of the World: The First Anniversary," in John Donne, *Complete Poetry and Selected Prose* (New York: Random House, 1941), p. 171.

4. René Descartes, *Discourse on Method and the Meditations*, trans. F. E. Sutcliffe (Harmondsworth: Penguin Books, 1968), p. 95.

5. Ibid.

6. Ibid., p. 102.

7. See part 1 of Jeffrey Stout, *The Flight from Authority* (Notre Dame, Ind.: University of Notre Dame Press, 1981).

8. The philosophical literature on foundationalism has grown vast and involves many technical issues I cannot discuss here. For good introductions, see William P. Alston, "Two Types of Foundationalism," *Journal of Philosophy* 73 (1976), pp. 165–185; Ernest Sosa, "The Foundations of Foundationalism," *Nous* 14 (1980), pp. 547–564; and Ernest Sosa, "The Raft and the Pyramid," *Midwest Studies in Philosophy* 5 (1980), pp. 3–25. For my relatively nontechnical purposes, foundationalism can be defined as "the doctrine that knowledge constitutes a structure the foundations of which support all the rest but themselves need no support" (Alston, "Two Types of Foundationalism," p. 165). Ronald F. Thiemann has traced the parallel story of foundationalism in theology in *Revelation and Theology: The Gospel as Narrated Promise* (Notre Dame, Ind.: University of Notre Dame Press, 1985), pp. 9–46.

9. "Postmodern" has become a cliché used to mean so many different things that it sometimes seems to mean nothing at all. I had intended never to use the word in this book, but it turned out to be helpful in three or four specific contexts.

10. Charles Sanders Peirce, *Collected Papers*, vol. 5 (Cambridge, Mass.: Harvard University Press, 1934), p. 265.

11. Ludwig Wittgenstein, *On Certainty*, #248, ed. G. E. M. Anscombe and G. H. von Wright and trans. Denis Paul and G. E. M. Anscombe (New York: Harper & Row, 1969), p. 33.

12. John Locke, *An Essay Concerning Human Understanding* (Oxford: Clarendon Press, 1894), pp. 121–123.

13. Carl Hempel, "The Empiricist Criterion of Meaning," in A. J. Ayer, ed., *Logical Positivism* (Glencoe, Ill.: Free Press, 1959), p. 109.

14. A. J. Ayer, *Language, Truth and Logic,* 2nd ed. (New York: Dover Books, 1957), p. 35.

15. Moritz Schlick, "The Turning Point in Philosophy," trans. David Rynin, in Ayer, *Logical Positivism,* p. 56.

16. Rudolf Carnap, "Intellectual Autobiography," in Paul Arthur Schilpp, ed., *The Philosophy of Rudolf Carnap* (La Salle, Ill.: Open Court Publishing Co., 1963), p. 57. When Carnap wrote this, he no longer held such a view.

17. Rudolf Carnap, "Testability and Meaning," in Herbert Feigl and May Brodbeck, eds., *Readings in the Philosophy of Science* (New York: Appleton-Century-Crofts, 1953), p. 63.

18. Jerome S. Bruner and Leo Postman, "On the Perception of Incongruity: A Paradigm," *Journal of Personality* 18 (1949), p. 206.

19. Ibid., p. 214.

20. E. H. Gombrich, *Art and Illusion* (Princeton, N.J.: Princeton University Press, 1960), p. xii; citing Jehudo Epstein, *Mein Weg von Ost nach West* (Stuttgart, 1929).

21. John Constable, "Lecture at Hampstead, 1836"; quoted in C. R. Leslie, *Memoirs of the Life of John Constable,* ed. Jonathan Mayne (London: Phaidon Press, 1951), p. 327. The experience of blind people who suddenly receive their sight also seems relevant here. In order to distinguish a triangle from a square, for instance, they sometimes have to count the vertices one by one, as they would have when recognizing shapes by touch. They cannot immediately "see" the shape. See Anton Ehrenzweig, *The Hidden Order of Art* (Berkeley and Los Angeles: University of California Press, 1967), p. 13.

22. N. R. Hanson, *Patterns of Discovery: Inquiry Into the Conceptual Foundations of Science* (Cambridge: Cambridge University Press, 1958), p. 22.

23. Ludwig Boltzmann, *Populäre Vorlesungen,* p. 286; quoted in Paul K. Feyerabend, *Philosophical Papers,* vol. 1 (Cambridge: Cambridge University Press, 1981), p. 13.

24. Niels Bohr, *Atomic Theory* (Cambridge: Cambridge University Press, 1934), p. 1; quoted in Feyerabend, *Philosophical Papers,* vol. 1, p. 22.

25. Wilfred Sellars, *Science, Perception and Reality* (New York: Humanities Press, 1963), p. 90.

26. Ibid., p. 176.

27. Wilfred Sellars, "The Structure of Knowledge," in Hector-Neri Castañeda, ed., *Action, Knowledge, and Reality: Critical Studies in Honor of Wilfred Sellars* (Indianapolis: Bobbs-Merrill Co., 1975), p. 314.

28. Sellars, *Science, Perception and Reality,* p. 168. Sellars also makes a more technical logical argument. The attempt to base knowledge on a "foundation" of uninterpreted sensation, he says, involves three claims:

1. " 'John senses a red sense-content *s*' entails 'John knows that *s* is red.' " This simply says that sensation leads to knowledge; without such an assumption, empiricism collapses.

2. "The ability to have some sense contents is unacquired." This says that there *are* immediate sense-data, prior to any interpretations. If one denies this assumption, then one has to *learn* how to sense, and particular sensations presuppose a network of concepts and therefore cannot be "foundational."

3. "The ability to know facts like '*s* is red' *is* acquired." Having such knowledge implies having the concepts in which to express and understand what one

knows. Newborn infants pretty clearly do *not* already have such concepts—therefore, they must be acquired later.

As Sellars points out, though, these three claims are logically inconsistent. If A is unacquired, and having A entails having B, then B would have to be unacquired too. So logical consistency demands giving up one of these three claims. Sellars concludes that we have to give up No. 2; that means denying the Myth of the Given and admitting that we have to learn even how to sense that *s* is red. And that implies that there are no basic sense-data that could serve as foundations for all other knowledge while themselves not dependent on anything else. (Ibid., pp. 130–132.)

29. Descartes, *Discourse on Method and the Meditations,* p. 103.

30. Ibid., p. 113.

31. The story that follows is clearly presented in Stephen F. Barker's article on "Geometry" in *The Encyclopedia of Philosophy,* vol. 3, pp. 285–290. For another good summary, see Gottfried Martin, *Kant's Metaphysics and Theory of Science,* trans. P. G. Lucas (Manchester: Manchester University Press, 1955), pp. 16–20.

32. In fact, the text of Euclid says only, "Let the following be postulated" (*The Thirteen Books of Euclid's Elements,* trans. Thomas L. Heath, 2nd ed., vol. 1, p. 154; New York: Dover Books, 1956).

33. "That, if a straight line falling on two straight lines make the interior angles on the same side less than two right angles, the two straight lines, if produced indefinitely, meet on that side on which are the angles less than the two right angles" (ibid., p. 155).

34. A series of such efforts represented Kant's only forays into pure mathematics. See Jaakko Hintikka, "Kant's Theory of Mathematics Revisited," in J. N. Mohanty and Robert W. Shahan, eds., *Essays on Kant's Critique of Pure Reason* (Norman, Okla.: University of Oklahoma Press, 1982), p. 203.

35. Hans Reichenbach, *The Philosophy of Space and Time,* trans. Maria Reichenbach and John Freund (New York: Dover Books, 1958), p. 35. Yet another alternative would be to say that geometry describes purely mathematical objects and not the physical world, so that such physical considerations are irrelevant to evaluating geometry. This too has both advantages and disadvantages.

36. Willard Van Orman Quine, *From a Logical Point of View,* 2nd rev. ed. (New York: Harper & Row, Harper Torchbooks, 1963), p. 41.

37. I have used the geometrical example because it admits of fairly easy explanation. Similar problems have arisen with many other fields in mathematics. For a theologian's reflections on such questions, see Helmut Peukert, *Science, Action, and Fundamental Theology,* trans. James Bohman (Cambridge, Mass.: MIT Press, 1984), pp. 39–40.

38. Ibid., pp. 42–43. "Our system of statements has such a thick cushion of indeterminacy, in relation to experience, that vast domains of law can easily be held immune to revision on principle. We can always turn to other quarters of the system when revisions are called for by unexpected experiences. Mathematics and logic, central as they are to our conceptual scheme, tend to be accorded such immunity, in view of our conservative preference for revisions which disturb the system least; and herein, perhaps, lies the 'necessity' which the laws of mathematics and logic are felt to enjoy" (Willard Van Orman

Quine, *Methods of Logic,* p. xiii; London; Routledge & Kegan Paul, 1952). Quine is here making two radical claims: "necessity" is a matter of *degree* (some beliefs are *nearer* the center of our system), and it is a matter of *choice* (we *decide* what we want to preserve come what may).

39. Willard Van Orman Quine, "Carnap on Logical Truth," in Schilpp, *The Philosophy of Rudolf Carnap,* p. 406.

40. Immanuel Kant, *Critique of Pure Reason,* trans. F. Max Müller (Garden City, N.Y.: Doubleday & Co., Anchor Books, 1966), pp. 7–10. For Kant, even the postulates of geometry were still synthetic: they did more than restate the definitions of geometrical terms.

41. Hilary Putnam, *Realism and Reason* (Cambridge: Cambridge University Press, 1983), p. 37.

42. "Let *w* be the predicate: to be a predicate that cannot be predicated of itself. Can *w* be predicated of itself? From each answer its opposite follows" (Russell to Frege, 16 June 1902, in Jean van Heijenoort, *From Frege to Gödel: A Source Book in Mathematical Logic,* p. 125; Cambridge, Mass.: Harvard University Press, 1967). Russell stated the paradox in terms of classes in "Mathematical Logic as Based on the Theory of Types," *American Journal of Mathematics* 30 (1908), p. 222. "Your discovery of the contradiction caused me the greatest surprise and, I would almost say, consternation, since it has shaken the basis on which I intended to build arithmetic" (Frege to Russell, 22 June 1902, in van Heijenoort, *From Frege to Gödel,* p. 127).

43. "'Whatever involves *all* of a collection must not be one of the collection'; or, conversely: 'If, provided a certain collection had a total, it would have members only definable in terms of that total, then the said collection has no total'" (Russell, "Mathematical Logic as Based on the Theory of Types," p. 225).

44. Willard Van Orman Quine, *Mathematical Logic,* rev. ed. (Cambridge, Mass.: Harvard University Press, 1951), pp. 164–166.

45. Wittgenstein, *On Certainty,* #94, p. 15.

46. Most but not all. I think I have done a fair if hasty summary of one trajectory in modern philosophy. I think it is even fair to describe this as the dominant tendency, but I should make it clear that *some* contemporary philosophers do not accept these conclusions. It should also be noted that Quine does not accept all the implications of Sellars' work and vice versa. Richard Rorty has diagnosed a kind of failure of nerve at work: "It is as if Quine, having renounced the conceptual-empirical, analytic-synthetic, and language-fact distinctions, were still not quite able to renounce that between the given and the postulated. Conversely Sellars, having triumphed over the latter distinction, cannot quite renounce the former cluster. . . . Each of these two men tends to make continual, unofficial, tacit, heuristic use of the distinction which the other has transcended" (Richard Rorty, *Philosophy and the Mirror of Nature,* pp. 171–172; Princeton, N.J.: Princeton University Press, 1979). Quine indeed seems increasingly inclined to refer to bare empirical data in a way hard to fit together with the rest of his philosophy. See Hilary Putnam, "Misling," *London Review of Books* 10 (21 April 1988), p. 12.

3

SCIENCE

The waning of claims to unique rationality

The Harvard philosopher Hilary Putnam tells how one morning he summarized for his students issues like those discussed in the preceding chapter. "I asked the class," he reports, " 'If this is the predicament we are in, what justifies us in supposing that our theories and judgments are true?' A student raised his hand and gave me precisely the answer I expected: 'Well, it seems to work for scientists.' "[1]

As he indicates, Putnam was not surprised. Scientists' accomplishments make it hard for most people in our society to take philosophical puzzles about knowledge seriously when it comes to science. The planes fly, the medicines cure, the bombs explode. Perhaps we have an unwarranted belief in science's ability to solve all our problems, epistemological or otherwise, but it is hard not to be impressed.

As chapter 1 indicated, many people today therefore urge religion to try to be more like science—or else condemn it for failing to do so. Science, they say, can provide a way of objectively finding out the truth, independent of the assumptions of any particular tradition. Science, therefore, does not have to wrestle with problems of pluralism: there is *one* scientific method, and, properly applied, it generates one set of conclusions given the currently available evidence. Measured against such a standard, religious thinking seems thoroughly muddled.

Some of those who make such appeals to science simply have not come to terms with the arguments I tried to summarize in the preceding chapter. They still think that knowledge—scientific knowledge, anyway—can have foundations in pure data or indubitable first principles. I hope I have shown the untenability of such positions. Some recent philosophers of science, however, beginning with Karl Popper, have claimed that, even without any belief in "secure foundations" for knowledge, science remains a uniquely objective, rational activity.[2]

The foundations of Descartes's edifice having crumbled, Popper claimed he could rescue science from the rubble.

He began to see how to do it, he says, as a seventeen-year-old student in Vienna just after World War I, when he was struggling with the question of what set science apart from what seemed to him the confusion and polemic of so many books about politics and psychology. One day he was reading a popular account Einstein had written about his theory of relativity. At one point Einstein said, "If the red shift of spectral lines due to the gravitational potential should not exist, then the general theory of relativity will be untenable."

Popper had found what he was looking for:

> Here was an attitude utterly different from the dogmatic attitude of Marx, Freud, Adler, and even more so that of their followers. Einstein was looking for crucial experiments whose agreement with his predictions would by no means establish his theory; while a disagreement, as he was the first to admit, would show his theory to be untenable.
> This, I felt, was the true scientific attitude.[3]

Ideologues of one sort or another look only for evidence to *support* their prejudices. Scientists too start with hypotheses—by making "bold conjectures"—but then they actively search for data that would *falsify* them. If they find such data, then *they give up the hypotheses.* That is what makes them scientists.

This emphasis on "conjectures and refutations" frees us from the need to establish an unchallengeable starting point or observations free from theory.

> The empirical basis of objective science has thus nothing "absolute" about it. Science does not rest upon solid bedrock. The bold structure of its theories rises, as it were, above a swamp. It is like a building erected on piles. The piles are driven down from above, into the swamp, but not down to any natural or "given" base; and if we stop driving the piles deeper, it is not because we have reached firm ground.[4]

Scientists can start anywhere, with any kind of guess or hunch, but science is nevertheless not like religious faith, political propaganda, or popular prejudice. Scientists keep testing their claims and throwing out the ones that fail, and therefore science does make progress, and it is a uniquely "rational" activity.

Popper's theory explains one of the oddest features of the history of science. Sooner or later, it seems, every great scientific theory gets superseded. If science is seeking to "find the truth," then it seems one long story of failure. But if science advances precisely by refuting one conjecture after another, then the falsification of theories is just what marks its success.[5]

Popper's theory, however, suffers from problems of its own. His central concern is to preserve the point he saw when reading Einstein as a seventeen-year-old: science is not like propaganda and politics, because scientists can define decisive experiments that would refute their theories, and they go out and perform those experiments—and then accept the results, even if that means giving up their theory. That makes science objective and rational in a special way, for scientists, unlike many of the rest of us, accept experimental refutations and do not cling to old theories out of loyalty or prejudice.

The idea of a decisive experiment that refutes a theory is therefore crucial to Popper's whole enterprise, but the practice of science turns out to be more complicated than that. Remember from the preceding chapter how Quine argued that we can never consider one claim in isolation. We have to look at the whole "web" of our beliefs, and there is always more than one solution to a particular problem. Popper has always resisted Quine's conclusions, and with good reason, for they imply that "refuting" a theory is never such a clear-cut business as Popper needs to claim.

Medieval astronomers, for instance, thought that the planets revolve suspended on crystalline spheres. Galileo claimed to have refuted this hypothesis. Through his telescope, he said, he could see moons revolving around Jupiter, and these moons did not bump into Jupiter's crystalline sphere. Therefore, there was no crystalline sphere. Unfortunately, one could see these moons only through the newly invented telescope, and the belief that telescopes gave observers an accurate but magnified view of objects presupposed some theories about optics. Further, not everyone with a telescope could initially reproduce Galileo's results. Even Galileo admitted that the telescope produced some optical illusions, and he had no theory that explained how to distinguish illusions from realities in telescopic observation.[6] Galileo's opponents could—and did—defend the crystalline spheres by denying the reliability of observations made through a telescope. As the Mathematician asks Galileo in Bertolt Brecht's dramatization of the story, "But has it occurred to you that an eyeglass through which one sees such phenomena might not be a too reliable eyeglass?"[7]

It is not impossible to make good arguments for Galileo's position. Galileo himself made some, and, given subsequent developments, we are in a position to make even more. But those arguments cannot appeal to a single decisive experiment or discovery that, in isolation, settles the question. They all involve, just as Quine has taught us they would, weighing the consequences of giving up some belief against the consequences of various strategies for holding on to it, considering the whole issue in the context of all the things we believe. As Popper himself admits, "In point of fact, no conclusive disproof of a theory can ever be produced, for it is always possible to say that the experimental results are not reliable or that the discrepancies which are asserted to exist between experimental results and the theory are only apparent and that they will disappear with the advance of our understanding."[8] But if that is so, then it is never quite clear when a theory has been "refuted."

Furthermore, anyone who has done scientific research knows that the data almost never exactly fit the theory. The smooth curve on a scientist's graph summarizes a scattered array of points. Yet we often judge that the results fit the prediction "close enough" to save the theory. But how close is close enough? In some parts of spectroscopy, "reasonable agreement" means agreement to 6–8 digits. In the theory of solids, two digits is rather good; in the theoretical study of stellar magnitude, agreement to the right power of ten is often taken as reasonable.[9] Results that would seem a decisive refutation in one field count as supporting evidence in another, and such judgments cannot be made in isolation from a whole set of assumptions.

Moreover, *any* theory, particularly in its early stages, will face data that do not quite fit in place; a hard-line falsificationism would never let science get off the ground. Take an example: In 1815 an Edinburgh physician named William Prout proposed that all elements were composed of hydrogen and that their atomic weights therefore ought to be integral multiples of the atomic weight of hydrogen. Shortly afterward, the Swedish chemist Jöns Berzelius and others came up with some counterexamples; assigning 1 as the atomic weight of hydrogen yields atomic weights of 103.5 for lead, 35.45 for chlorine, and 68.7 for barium. Only in the twentieth century did chemists find that these elements had different isotopes. The atomic weight of each isotope was an integral multiple of hydrogen, and the anomalous elements appear in nature as mixtures of different isotopes. "Thus, the very phenomena which had early constituted anomalies for Prout's hypothesis became positive instances for it."[10] Indeed, "the hypothesis thrown out so lightly by Prout, an Edinburgh physician, in 1815, has, a century later, become the corner-stone of modern theories of the structure of atoms."[11] But take Popper's method in simplest form, and the theory would have been "falsified" and discarded.

To be sure, Popper himself regularly qualifies his position and insists that one must know when to keep working at a theory as well as when to abandon it.[12] But he is much less clear about the criteria for such judgments. At minimum the clean-cut lines of "falsification" grow blurred. He sometimes makes the process of falsification sound quite mathematical:

> Assuming that the truth-content and the falsity-content of two theories t_1 and t_2 are comparable, we can say that t_2 is more closely similar to the truth, or corresponds better to the facts, than t_1, if and only if either
> > (a) the truth-content but not the falsity content of t_2 exceeds that of t_1,
> > (b) the falsity-content of t_1, but not its truth-content, exceeds that of t_2.[13]

But what can such an analysis really mean? Given the ways in which theories shape how we judge the accuracy of data, how can one quantify the "truth-content" or "falsity-content" of two theories? How can one know how soon to give one up and adopt another? Popper wanted to claim that science is special because of the way a decisive experiment can refute a hypothesis. That would make scientific judgments "objective," because once the theory has been falsified, any rational, responsible scientist will abandon it. But if decisive experiments prove hard to find, and themselves always presuppose possibly controversial assumptions, then Popper's project breaks down.

His student Imre Lakatos has sought to produce a more sophisticated version of Popper's approach by focusing on the "research program" instead of the individual theory. Lakatos acknowledges that *any* theory will predict some data correctly and face anomalies from other data. Those anomalies challenge scientists sympathetic to the theory to try to explain them—they thus generate a research program. Newton's theories worked fairly well, for example, but they did not quite fit at many points—so Newtonians started trying to figure out the reasons for those discrepancies. In the most famous case, a discrepancy in the orbit of Uranus led to the prediction and then discovery of the planet Neptune. Here was a research program working at its best: the problems in the theory led to questions that generated new discoveries.

Sometimes, however, research programs reach a dead end. The original theory does not suggest new experiments; the anomalies remain unsolved.[14] According to Lakatos, science is an empirical activity, a rational activity, to the extent that scientists pursue productive research programs and give up on ones that have reached such dead ends. Unlike Popper, in other words, Lakatos admits that one can appropriately keep working within a theory even in the face of data that seem to contradict it—as long as those aberrant data generate interesting new questions and experiments that keep a productive research program going.[15] Yet he preserves Popper's essential point—the objective rationality of science—because scientists try out research programs but forthrightly give them up when they are no longer productive.

Just as it turned out to be hard to specify when a theory had been refuted, however, so it proves hard to set the objective criteria for knowing when a research program has reached a dead end. A new research program, Lakatos admits, may need to be "sheltered for a while from a powerful established rival"[16] to see whether it can produce successes in spite of an unpromising start. Sometimes, on the other hand, a research program slides into a "degenerating trough" and falls on bad times only to emerge later with new successes.[17] Indeed, sometimes one "may rationally stick to a degenerating programme until it is overtaken by a rival and even after."[18] "But," in the words of one of Lakatos' critics, "once this concession is made, the tough-minded action-guiding force of his methodology dissipates."[19] Indeed, another critic says, it seems that "Lakatos has gradually reduced the extent to which his methodology issues in advice to scientists, until finally he denies that he gives any advice worth speaking of at all."[20] We expected that Lakatos was going to show us how sometimes it is rational to keep working at a research program and sometimes it isn't—and good scientists continue as long as it does remain rational, and not a moment longer. But if "scientific method" can provide the scientist no concrete advice about when a research program should be abandoned, then one decision seems as rational—or irrational—as another, and the case for science's distinctive rationality seems to have disappeared.[21]

Another of Popper's former students, Paul Feyerabend, admits this conclusion—indeed, he revels in it. "There is hardly any difference," Feyerabend has written, "between the members of a 'primitive' tribe who defend their laws because they are the laws of the gods . . . and a rationalist who appeals to 'objective' standards, except that the former know what they are doing while the latter does not."[22] In his historical studies, most notably of Galileo, Feyerabend argues that science has "advanced" through the use of all kinds of sophistry: "Galileo uses *propaganda.* He uses *psychological tricks* in addition to whatever intellectual reasons he has to offer."[23] But Feyerabend does not offer such analysis as criticism. Quite the contrary. He thinks that we progress by challenging traditional views and standard assumptions, and anything that makes people take notice of such a challenge is fair enough:

> Given any rule, however "fundamental" or "necessary" for science, there are always circumstances when it is advisable not only to ignore the rule, but to adopt its opposite. For example, there are circumstances when it is advisable to introduce, contradict, and defend ad hoc hypotheses, or hypotheses which contradict well-established and generally accepted experimental results, or hypotheses whose content is smaller than the content of the existing and empirically adequate alternative, or self-inconsistent hypotheses, and so on.[24]

The only general principle is what Feyerabend calls the principle of proliferation: "Invent, and elaborate theories which are inconsistent with the accepted point of view."[25]

If someone were to protest that as a result science seems no more rational than magic or witchcraft, Feyerabend would cheerfully agree. He notes the general claim that modern Western science has at least produced better "results" than its rivals and asks for the evidence and argument. Who has ever run a controlled experiment to show that scientific medicine is more effective than the medicine of the Nei Ching or than traditional Hopi medicine? And how would one judge "effectiveness" anyway? To the mystic who experiences that he can free himself from his body and rise to the direct contemplation of God, merely getting a man to the moon does not seem particularly impressive.[26] Obviously most modern scientists would want to challenge the mystic's claim—but, Feyerabend argues, their challenges would presuppose the beliefs of modern science they mean to defend.

Feyerabend does not hesitate to press the practical (or perhaps wildly impractical) implications of such views. He deplores the degree to which "science" has exercised a kind of imperialism in modern education: "While the parents of a six-year-old can decide to have him instructed in the rudiments of Protestantism, or in the rudiments of the Jewish faith, or to omit religious instruction altogether, they do not have similar freedom in the case of the sciences. Physics, astronomy, history *must* be learned; they cannot be replaced by magic, astrology, or by a study of legends."[27] In a truly free society, he insists, "everyone should have a chance to make up his own mind and to live in accordance with the social beliefs he finds most acceptable. The separation between the state and church must therefore be complemented by the separation between state and science."[28] Scientists will try to resist such pluralism, and political force will sometimes be necessary to get them to give up their current intellectual monopolies—as the Chinese Communists did when they forced the introduction of folk medicine on reluctant, Western-trained physicians and substantially improved medical care in China in the process.[29] He urges that, if we mean to take democracy seriously, ordinary citizens have to become involved in the decisions about the value of science:

> "State Colleges and Universities" are financed by taxpayers. They are therefore subjected to the judgment of the taxpayers *and not* to the judgment of the many intellectual parasites who live off public money. If the taxpayers of California want their universities to teach Voodoo, folk medicine, astrology, rain dance ceremonies, then this is what the universities will have to teach.[30]

So much for science's claims to intellectual superiority.

Yet the exact position of Feyerabend, like that of an electron in contemporary quantum theory, is difficult to determine. He certainly believes that too many scientists have come to take too much for granted, and they need some shaking up. He really does think modern Western science could learn from various traditions of folk medicine. And he believes that epistemological liberation is best served by challenging dominant ways of thinking—so that just as the scientific challenge to traditional religion was a progressive force in the seventeenth century, so we may now need challenges to an entrenched scientific establishment.

On the other hand, although the subtitle of his book *Against Method* was "an anarchistic philosophy of science," Feyerabend has more recently denied that he advocates anarchism as some sort of "method" for science:

> I do not say that epistemology should become anarchic, or that the philosophy of science should become anarchic. I say that both disciplines should receive anarchism *as a medicine.* Epistemology is sick, it must be cured, and the medicine is anarchy. Now medicine is not something one takes all the time. One takes it for a certain period of time, *and then one stops.* . . . There may, of course, come a time when it will be necessary to give reason a temporary advantage and when it will be wise to defend *its* rules to the exclusion of everything else. . . . I do not think that we are living in such a time today.[31]

Indeed, in his most recent book, he denies the appropriateness of *any* single approach to science:

> There are no elements that occur in every scientific investigation but are missing elsewhere. . . . The most we can do . . . is to enumerate rules of thumb, give historical examples, present case studies containing divergent procedures, demonstrate the inherent complexity of research. . . . Listening to our tale, scientists will get a feeling for the richness of the historical process they want to transform.[32]

It would be too simple to classify such a remark as either "more radical" or "less radical" than other things Feyerabend has written. He here denies his earlier "anarchism," but he still rejects Popper's dream of distinguishing science from other forms of inquiry—there is not even something called "*the* scientific method."

There are rules of thumb to be followed, Feyerabend says, and a rich tradition within which science does its work. In chapter 7, I will argue that tradition and pragmatic judgment can provide a broader definition of what counts as "rational" or "a good argument." I wish that Feyerabend consistently made the kind of argument I will try to make there: that we ought to expand our concept of what "rationality" means. Instead, he often accepts rather narrow definitions of the "rational" and then seems to celebrate irrationality.

Two reasons come to mind. First, his onetime teacher Popper may still shape his image of rationality. And if being "rational" means being like Popper, then Feyerabend says the hell with it. Second, he just cannot resist the chance to shock—*Against Method* must be the only book that contains an index entry for "wicked remarks." And praising irrationality does catch the reader's attention.

In pursuing this radical strategy, however, Feyerabend opens himself up to some of the standard charges made against strong forms of relativism.[33] He gleefully demolishes standards of judgment, ways of objectively determining that one theory is "better" than another. Then he talks about the circumstances under which it is "advisable" to break the usual rules of scientific method. Advisable for what purpose? He defends his own approach on the grounds that his stodgy opponents stifle progress, while his own openness encourages the imagination that leads us toward . . . well, toward what? Truth? How would he define the term? Progress? How would he recognize it? He seems to have undercut the grounds on which he could argue even for his own conclusions.[34]

The historian of science Thomas Kuhn has cast his case in rhetoric far milder than Feyerabend's, but he too sometimes seems to reject "rationality" rather than expanding our definition of what it means to be rational—a better way of making the point he really wants to make. Kuhn is worth considering not only because of his influence—he often seems to be the only philosopher of science whom people outside the field have read—but also because both the strengths of his work and his occasional inconsistencies focus the real issues in contemporary philosophy of science with particular clarity.

Kuhn's first concern has been to trace how science develops, and in particular to make a radical distinction between the kind of progress that occurs during periods of "normal science" and the "paradigm shifts" that occur during scientific revolutions. Any field of inquiry, he says, begins in a very chaotic phase. Investigators share few common assumptions, and every writer has to begin by defining a basic approach. At some point, however, one piece of scientific work stands out so impressively that others in the field adopt it as a "paradigm"—they agree to accept its assumptions, and they begin to clarify its details and pursue the questions it left unanswered.[35] Newton's physics and Darwin's theory of evolution provide obvious examples.

There follows a period of "normal science" in which scientists make measurable progress precisely because they leave the basic assumptions of the paradigm unchallenged and engage in "puzzle solving"— working out the details of the overall view. Physicists try to produce more accurate predictions of planetary orbits using Newtonian principles; biologists try to figure out the paths of evolution. Some of Kuhn's critics object to this picture of normal science. They say he seems to be describing an uncritical, utterly pedestrian activity.[36] Kuhn insists, however, that it is just the methods of normal science—the willingness to put aside certain kinds of fundamental questions and get on with solving particular puzzles—that distinguish natural science from other disciplines and make its vaunted progress possible.

Any paradigm always lives with anomalies, Kuhn admits—they provide some of the puzzles that normal science seeks to solve. But at some point in the life of a paradigm, the persistent anomalies may build to the level of a crisis, and, usually about the same time, someone offers an alternative paradigm, embodying a quite different set of assumptions, definitions, and problems. If the new paradigm can solve the problems that led to the crisis in the old one, produces greater quantitative precision, predicts phenomena unsuspected under the old paradigm, and generates a quasi-aesthetic sense that the new way of looking at things is neater, more suitable, or simpler, then the scientific community, or some particular branch of it, will gradually shift to this new model for its activities, and a scientific revolution will have taken place—though a good many of the adherents of the old paradigm will probably die off rather than undergo conversion.[37]

Such scientific revolutions, however, are not just larger-scale versions of the changes that take place within normal science. During a period of normal science, the accepted paradigm provides clear rules for measuring success and advance. But in a shift between paradigms such rules themselves are open to question. Philosophers have borrowed from mathematics the word "algorithm" to mean a mechanical method for solving a problem that leads to a clear solution. Thus, for instance, there is an algorithm for calculating square roots—you just plug in the right numbers and crank out a repetitive process to get the answer. By extension, we might say there is an algorithm for deciding which jar has the most beans in it—you empty out the jars and count the beans in each—or for most problems within normal science. Kuhn wants to say, however, that there is no algorithm, no mechanical procedure, for choosing between scientific paradigms. He has written of paradigm shifts as like a "conversion experience," "a decision . . . that . . . can only be made on faith,"[38] and claimed that conflicting paradigms are "incommensurable."

Kuhn's critics have attacked him with considerable passion. Imre Lakatos, for instance, wrote that Kuhn made science utterly "irrational, a matter for mob psychology."[39] Part of the problem lies in some of the claims and terms of the original edition of *The Structure of Scientific Revolutions.* In more recent works, Kuhn says he has clarified what he originally meant. Others think he has retreated from his earlier position. In any event, it is clear that he had said some things that were at least open to misinterpretation.

A key issue concerns that term "incommensurability." To many of Kuhn's critics, it implied the belief that it is simply impossible to translate one scientific paradigm into language that could be understood by the adherents of a different paradigm. You really just cannot say in the language of Galilean-Newtonian physics what "natural motion" meant to an Aristotelian physicist—the two ways of looking at the world create "incommensurable" terms. The critics then go on to point out that Kuhn himself succeeds quite well in describing earlier scientific paradigms in twentieth-century terms. In so doing, they say, he refutes his own claim.

This debate turns in part on the analogy between comparing scientific paradigms and translating from one language to another, so perhaps some remarks on the process of translation will help clarify the issues. In a famous essay, Donald Davidson has attacked the idea of a language utterly untranslatable into our own. Suppose Martians land on earth and begin to make complicated noises and gestures. Someone suggests that they are speaking the Martian language but that it is just completely incommensurable with our own. We literally cannot begin to translate from one to the other. Someone else, however (perhaps having read Davidson just before the Martians landed), hypothesizes that the Martians are not speaking a language at all: they are just making random noises, like the sounds a tree makes in the wind— sounds that lack any intended meaning and are certainly not the tree's "language." At this point, the defender of the "untranslatable language" thesis has an insurmountable problem, a problem that shows the fallacy of that position. As Davidson puts it, "Nothing . . . could count as evidence that some form of activity could not be interpreted in our language that was not at the same time evidence that that form of activity was not speech behavior."[40] If I want to claim that the Martians have a language at all, I will need to make arguments such as, "See, they make that funny clicking sound to show they are pleased," or, "They seem to mean 'water' by that high-pitched squeal." In short, I will have to try to translate their language into ours. If I make no efforts at translation, I will have no evidence that they are speaking a language at all.

Similarly, if I hold that earlier scientists had a theory at all, and were not just mumbling incoherently, I will have to begin "translating" their views into terms that make sense to us. Kuhn, of course, never really meant to deny this. In seizing on the word "incommensurability," he led some philosophers to hear him making a far stronger claim than he intended.[41] After all, he knows one can describe a different way of looking at the world—he has spent much of his scholarly career doing so. (One thinks of Samuel Johnson's retort when asked if he believed in infant baptism: "Believe in it? Why, I've seen it done!")

Kuhn had a more modest claim to make but nonetheless an important one. Again, the analogy of translation helps make the point.[42] Of course we can translate from French to English, but we also recognize that translation always loses something. And the choice of what to lose often comes down to a matter of personal judgment. One translation catches more of the original to one person's ear but not to another's. Or perhaps one translation preserves a more literal sense of the original, while another better preserves the original's crispness of style. One has to make a choice, and there is no method of mathematical calculation that can generate the "right" answer to that judgment. We say, sometimes, that translation is an "art" rather than a "science."

Kuhn's point about incommensurability is that when it comes to choices between paradigms, *science* is an "art" rather than a "science" too. There are, he writes, "many reasons for choosing one theory rather than another. . . . These are, furthermore, reasons of exactly the kind standard in philosophy of science: accuracy, scope, simplicity, fruitfulness, and the like."[43] But one theory may be simpler while another is more accurate—Copernicus' theory, for instance, at one stage seemed simpler than Ptolemy's but was initially less accurate—and we cannot rank accuracy and simplicity on the same scale. Moreover, judgments of what counts as "simpler" may themselves vary from one person to another.[44]

Or again, in the eighteenth century the oxygen theory could account for observed weight relations in chemical reactions, as the phlogiston theory could not, but the phlogiston theory could explain why metals were more alike than the ores from which they came, and the oxygen theory could not. Which success was more important? There was no way to quantify their relative importance and come up with an inarguable answer.[45] The defenders of a new paradigm "when arguing in its defense can nonetheless provide a clear exhibit of what scientific practice will be like for those who adopt the new view of nature. That exhibit can be immensely persuasive, often compellingly so. Yet, whatever its force, the status of the circular argument is only that of persuasion. It cannot be made logically or even probabilistically compelling for those who refuse to step into the circle."[46] If that is what "incommensurability" means, then scientific paradigms do indeed seem incommensurable.

The beliefs of different religious traditions, of course, also seem in that sense "incommensurable," and in subsequent chapters I will propose that theology should understand its own task as doing what Kuhn says a new scientific paradigm does: exhibiting what intellectual practice will be like for those who adopt it, with whatever persuasive force that exhibit may carry. It does not follow that natural science is "just like" religion or indeed just like any other discipline. (Kuhn is generally quite clear about this, and his occasional references to "faith" and "conversion" can be misleading.) Chapter 9 will return to these issues and discuss some of the differences.

On the other hand, what sets science apart is *not* that decisions between scientific theories get made by some objective, calculative procedure by which one can prove what is right or wrong and clearly establish that anyone who does not accept it is just irrational. Popper had hoped to preserve such an ideal of science even in the absence of "foundations" for knowledge through the method of falsification.

Lakatos sought to follow his example. I have tried to argue that they failed.

Good arguments *can* be offered in favor of or against a theory or a research program. Feyerabend and Kuhn, however, seem to me to make a persuasive case that (1) those arguments will in turn always rest on assumptions that can be challenged and (2) their results can often not be quantified, so that deciding among theories will always involve factors more like aesthetic judgment than like adding up a column of numbers.

That need not mean, however, that any opinion is as good as any other or that no one can ever compare radically different points of view. Chapter 2 argued that there is no demonstrably certain foundation on which we can erect an edifice of knowledge. This chapter has maintained that the methods of science do not provide a uniquely rational and objective way of discovering truth. Yet people can still talk with one another and persuade one another with good arguments— even if their differences are even more fundamental than those which divide the adherents of different scientific paradigms. The next chapter will consider how such conversation can occur even with people who stand quite outside the Western scientific tradition. To see that, we need to turn from the philosophy of science to anthropology.

NOTES

1. Hilary Putnam, "Liberation Philosophy," *London Review of Books* 8 (20 March 1986), p. 3.

2. At least Popper and his students brought these issues into the mainstream of the philosophy of science. In different ways, Pierre Duhem and Michael Polanyi anticipated many of the arguments that will be surveyed in this chapter.

3. Karl R. Popper, "Autobiography," in Paul Arthur Schilpp, ed., *The Philosophy of Karl Popper* (La Salle, Ill.: Open Court Publishing Co., 1974), pp. 28–29. The passage from Einstein appears in Albert Einstein, *Relativity: The Special and the General Theory* (London: Methuen, 1920), p. 132, though I have quoted Popper's slightly different translation of the German original. The example is not without irony; Einstein often elsewhere expressed considerable doubt about the role of particular experiments in forming or falsifying theories.

4. Karl R. Popper, *The Logic of Scientific Discovery* (New York: Basic Books, 1959), p. 111.

5. Karl R. Popper, *Conjectures and Refutations* (New York: Harper & Row, Harper Torchbooks, 1968), p. 28.

6. Paul K. Feyerabend, *Farewell to Reason* (London: Verso, 1987), p. 287.

7. Bertolt Brecht, *Galileo*, in Bertolt Brecht, *Seven Plays*, ed. Eric Bentley (New York: Grove Press, 1961), p. 353.

8. Popper, *The Logic of Scientific Discovery*, p. 50.

9. Thomas S. Kuhn, *The Essential Tension: Selected Studies in Scientific Tradition and Change* (Chicago: University of Chicago Press, 1977), p. 185.

10. Larry Laudan, *Progress and Its Problems: Towards a Theory of Scientific Growth* (Berkeley and Los Angeles: University of California Press, 1977), p. 31.

11. Frederick Soddy, *The Interpretation of the Atom* (London: J. Murray, 1932), p. 50.

12. Popper, "Autobiography," in Schilpp, *The Philosophy of Karl Popper*, p. 32.

13. Popper, *Conjectures and Refutations*, p. 233.

14. Imre Lakatos, "The History of Science and Its Rational Reconstructions," *Boston Studies in the Philosophy of Science* 8 (1972), p. 100.

15. As Lakatos points out, this oversimplifies Popper, who *sometimes* conceded this point. Lakatos actually worked out complicated theories of various stages of Popper's development on such issues. A completely accurate history would probably describe a debate here between Lakatos and some stages of Popper against other stages of Popper, rather than just Lakatos against Popper.

16. Imre Lakatos, "Falsification and the Methodology of Scientific Research Programs," in Imre Lakatos and Alan Musgrave, eds., *Criticism and the Growth of Knowledge* (Cambridge: Cambridge University Press, 1970), p. 157.

17. Ibid., p. 164.

18. Lakatos, "The History of Science and Its Rational Reconstructions," p. 104.

19. W. H. Newton-Smith, *The Rationality of Science* (London: Routledge & Kegan Paul, 1981), p. 92.

20. Alan Musgrave, "Method or Madness," *Boston Studies in the Philosophy of Science* 39 (1976), p. 474. Lakatos says he will give "criteria of progress and stagnation within a programme and also rules for the 'elimination' of whole research programmes" (Imre Lakatos, *Philosophical Papers*, vol. 1, p. 112; Cambridge: Cambridge University Press, 1978); he talks about "objective reasons" for switching from one program to another (p. 69), but then he admits (p. 113), "It is very difficult to decide . . . when a research programme has degenerated hopelessly or when one of two rival programmes has achieved a decisive advantage over the other."

21. Paul Feyerabend made just this point by dedicating his book *Against Method* (London: Verso, 1978) to "Imre Lakatos, Friend and fellow-anarchist"; Lakatos was really an "anarchist" about scientific method too.

22. Paul K. Feyerabend, *Science in a Free Society* (London: Verso, 1983), p. 82.

23. Feyerabend, *Against Method*, p. 81.

24. Ibid., pp. 23–24.

25. Paul K. Feyerabend, *Philosophical Papers*, vol. 1 (Cambridge: Cambridge University Press, 1981), p. 105.

26. Paul K. Feyerabend, *Philosophical Papers*, vol. 2 (Cambridge: Cambridge University Press, 1981), p. 29.

27. Feyerabend, *Science in a Free Society*, p. 74. When one critic suspects Feyerabend of overdramatizing and tries to call his bluff by asking, "If *he* had a child diagnosed with leukemia would he look to his witchdoctor friends or to the Sloan Kettering Institute?" Feyerabend replies, "I can assure him that

I would look to my 'witchdoctor friends' to use his somewhat imprecise terminology *and so would many other people in California* whose experience with scientific medicine has been anything but encouraging. . . . Numerous women reluctant to have their breasts amputated as their doctors advised them went to acupuncturists, faithhealers, herbalists and got cured. Parents of small children with allegedly incurable diseases, leukemia among them, did not give up, they consulted 'witchdoctors' and got cured. How do I know? Because I advised some of these men and women and I followed the fate of others" (Paul K. Feyerabend, "Reply to Tibbetts and Halliangadi," *Philosophy of Social Science* 8 [1978], p. 184). This argument, I suppose, either supports Feyerabend's case about science or else confirms some popular prejudices about California.

28. Feyerabend, *Against Method*, p. 299.

29. Ibid., pp. 51, 220.

30. Feyerabend, *Science in a Free Society*, p. 134.

31. Ibid., p. 127.

32. Feyerabend, *Farewell to Reason*, p. 281.

33. I will have more to say about these in chapter 6.

34. Roger Trigg poses the dilemma nicely: "Feyerabend . . . wishes to retain the concept of knowledge and the notion of *improving* our knowledge. But if nothing is true, there is nothing to know, and certainly nothing further to find out" (Roger Trigg, *Reason and Commitment*, p. 113; Cambridge: Cambridge University Press, 1973).

35. As Kuhn himself had admitted, he uses "paradigm" in a bewildering number of different ways; one sympathetic reader has identified at least twenty-one (Margaret Masterman, "The Nature of a Paradigm," in Lakatos and Musgrave, *Criticism and the Growth of Knowledge*, pp. 61ff.). Kuhn has subsequently concluded that his original distinction between pre-paradigm science and normal science was drawn too sharply (Thomas S. Kuhn, *The Structure of Scientific Revolutions*, 2nd ed., p. ix; Chicago: University of Chicago Press, 1970). He now prefers to talk, at least in some contexts, of a "disciplinary matrix," but he still believes that even if we can "dispense with the term 'paradigm,' " we cannot dispense with "the concept that led to its introduction" (Kuhn, *The Essential Tension*, p. 319).

36. " 'Normal' science, in Kuhn's sense, exists. It is the activity of . . . the not-too-critical professional: of the science student who accepts the ruling dogma of the day. . . . In my view the 'normal' scientist, as Kuhn describes him, is a person one ought to be sorry for" (Karl R. Popper, "Normal Science and Its Dangers," in Lakatos and Musgrave, *Criticism and the Growth of Knowledge*, p. 52).

37. Kuhn, *The Structure of Scientific Revolutions*, pp. 152–155. Kuhn quotes a famous remark by Max Planck: "A new scientific truth does not triumph by convincing its opponents [but] because its opponents die, and a new generation grows up that is familiar with it" (Max Planck, *Scientific Autobiography and Other Papers*, trans. F. Gaynor, pp. 33–34; New York: Philosophical Library, 1949).

38. Kuhn, *The Structure of Scientific Revolutions*, pp. 150, 157.

39. Lakatos, "Falsification and the Methodology of Scientific Research Programs," in Lakatos and Musgrave, *Criticism and the Growth of Knowledge*, p. 178.

40. Donald Davidson, *Inquiries Into Truth and Interpretation* (Oxford: Clarendon Press, 1984), p. 185.

41. Here and elsewhere I think it relevant that Kuhn's training was in physics and the history of science, not in philosophy. I do not mean that he is philosophically inept, but he does sometimes use terms in ways different from their standard use among philosophers.

42. In response to Hilary Putnam's charge that it is "totally incoherent" to say that some of Galileo's terms are incommensurable with our own and then go on and describe them (Hilary Putnam, *Reason, Truth, and History*, p. 115; Cambridge: Cambridge University Press, 1981), Feyerabend appeals to this analogy, reminding us that we can learn to operate in a foreign language, discovering the appropriate context for using various words, as infants learn their first language, without being able to "translate" into our first language. (Feyerabend, *Farewell to Reason*, pp. 265–266.)

43. Thomas S. Kuhn, "Reflections on My Critics," in Lakatos and Musgrave, *Criticism and the Growth of Knowledge*, p. 261.

44. Ludwig Boltzmann concluded that judgments of "simplicity" are to some degree subjective: "It may be doubtful and in a sense a matter of taste which representation satisfies us most. By this circumstance science loses its stamp of uniformity. We used to cling to the notion that there could be only one truth, that error was manifold but truth one. From our present position we must object to this view" (Ludwig Boltzmann, "Essay 16" from *Populäre Schriften*, trans. Paul Foulkes, in Brian McGuinness, ed., *Ludwig Boltzmann: Theoretical Physics and Philosophical Problems*, p. 106; Dordrecht: D. Reidel Publishing Co., 1974).

45. Kuhn, *The Essential Tension*, pp. 322–323.

46. Kuhn, *The Structure of Scientific Revolutions*, p. 94.

4

WITCHCRAFT

Dialogue across boundaries
in anthropology and philosophy of religion

Between 1926 and 1930 the English anthropologist Edward Evans-Pritchard spent about twenty months living among the Azande, a tribe of the southern Sudan. Evans-Pritchard was an interesting character: he chose a career in anthropology when the field scarcely existed in Britain, and, although his father had been a Church of England clergyman and virtually all his fellow anthropologists were agnostics or atheists, he converted to Roman Catholicism.[1] The book he wrote on the basis of those twenty months of fieldwork, *Witchcraft, Oracles and Magic Among the Azande,* is an anthropological classic.

It has also become a central text for a good many debates about how (or whether) we can judge what is "rational" in a culture very different from our own, and these debates have had an important impact on contemporary philosophy of religion. Evans-Pritchard believed some Zande beliefs to be irrational. Some of his critics have maintained that these beliefs made perfectly good sense in the context of Zande society, and Evans-Pritchard had no right to judge them in any other context. In chapters 2 and 3 I have been claiming that there is no single universal standard for judging what is rational; it might seem that I support Evans-Pritchard's critics and indeed favor some kind of radical relativism. But in fact I think there are ways of making judgments even about a culture's most basic beliefs—it just turns out that those ways involve reflection within a tradition and comparisons among particular traditions made by people who can never claim to stand outside their own tradition or to occupy some uniquely "objective" point of view.

Evans-Pritchard's work on the Azande provides a good starting point for understanding many of the issues involved here. The Azande believed that life's unexpected misfortunes—from a pot that breaks in the fire to a toe stubbed on a root that then fails to heal—are caused by witchcraft. Witches inherit their powers, though they grow with age and use. The autopsy of a witch will reveal "witchcraft substance," a black organ in the intestinal region. Obviously, a Zande wanted protection against witchcraft. Fortunately, witch doctors could free one from a witch's power, and the poison oracle could identify the witch who was the source of one's misfortune (as well as answer many other questions).

To work the poison oracle, the Azande took a red powder made from a particular kind of plant and fed it to a chicken. Then they asked "the oracle" a question. Sometimes the bird died, sometimes it lived, and this revealed the answer.[2] The question, incidentally, was always asked twice, and in opposite ways, so that one bird had to die and the other live to get a consistent answer.

At times the poison oracle yielded contradictory answers, or subsequent events refuted it. Though a witch's son ought to have inherited the powers, sometimes the autopsy of the son of a known witch revealed no "witchcraft substance." None of this shook Zande faith. To be sure, the Azande themselves mistrusted witch doctors. They thought the great majority "liars whose sole concern is to acquire wealth."[3] But if one practitioner's magic proved to be a fraud, that only meant one had to be more careful in choosing an authentic witch doctor next time. Besides, it could be hard to check out a witch doctor: they often gave vague answers, and their assertions usually concerned witchcraft, which one could not observe directly. A Zande had a better chance of getting a straight answer from the poison oracle, for he[4] could frame the question himself and receive a "yes" or "no" response. But the Azande had a range of explanations handy if the answer proved contradictory or subsequent events disconfirmed it. Perhaps the wrong variety of poison was gathered by mistake, or the person performing the ritual broke some taboo, or the whole enterprise was foiled by witchcraft, sorcery, or the anger of ghosts. Or perhaps the poison was too old and had lost its efficacy or was improperly administered.[5]

In just the way a philosopher like Quine would have predicted, in other words, there was always more than one way to explain the data, and Evans-Pritchard could never get a Zande to admit that a particularly awkward case showed that the poison oracle did not work or that witches did not exist after all.

> Azande do not consider what their world would be like without witch-doctors any more than we consider what it would be like without physicians. Since there is witchcraft there are naturally witch-doctors. There is no incentive to agnosticism. All their beliefs hang together, and were a Zande to give up faith in witch-doctorhood he would have to surrender equally his belief in witchcraft and oracles. . . . In this web of belief every strand depends on every other strand, and a Zande cannot get out of its

meshes because this is the only world he knows. The web is not an external structure in which he is enmeshed. It is the texture of his thought and he cannot think his thought is wrong.[6]

As a good anthropologist, Evans-Pritchard "tried to adapt" himself to their culture by living the life of his hosts, "as far as convenient, and by sharing their hopes and joys, apathy and sorrows." He even consulted their oracles concerning decisions about his daily life and confessed, "I found this as satisfactory a way of running my home and affairs as any other I know of."[7] As a result, he admitted, "I, too, used to react to misfortunes in the idiom of witchcraft, and it was often an effort to check this lapse into unreason."[8] Still, he had no doubt that it *was* unreason:

> It is an inevitable conclusion from Zande descriptions of witchcraft that it is not an objective reality. The physiological condition which is said to be the seat of witchcraft, and which I believe to be nothing more than food passing through the small intestine, is an objective condition, but the qualities they attribute to it and the rest of their beliefs about it are mystical. Witches, as Azande conceive them, cannot exist.[9]

Evans-Pritchard came to like his hosts. They were successful farmers, hunters, and craftsmen who on many matters displayed "intellectual ingenuity and experimental keenness."[10] Reading sometimes between the lines, one senses his impatience with their belief in witchcraft. To him, it all seemed not only wrong but stupidly wrong, somehow irrational. When we read, for instance, Aristotle's biology, we find a good many points where we want to say that he made a mistake. Yet we might also say that, given the information and equipment available to him (the lack of microscopes and so on), he made a reasonable, intelligent guess. Evans-Pritchard did not feel that way about the Azande. He thought the evidence clear enough, right in front of them, that their beliefs about witchcraft fell apart, and poison oracles did not work. Yet somehow the Azande could not "perceive the futility of their magic."[11]

The British philosopher Peter Winch has criticized Evans-Pritchard's conclusions. Evans-Pritchard, he says, was judging the Azande by the standards of modern science, but their beliefs and practices need to be understood—and evaluated—in terms of their own culture. And in those terms, they make good sense. In a famous article, Kai Nielsen in turn criticized Winch as a "Wittgensteinian fideist" who believes that no culture—or religion—can be criticized from "outside" its own life and practices. A good many philosophers and anthropologists have chosen up sides between Winch and Nielsen, and the resulting debate has had a significant impact on discussions about the philosophy of religion.

As the term "Wittgensteinian fideist" implies, those on Winch's side have been influenced by their reading of the works of Ludwig Wittgenstein. (I will argue later in this chapter that in important respects they seem to misread what he had to say.) Before the argument proceeds any further, then, something needs to be said about Wittgenstein's views.

To oversimplify the work of a very great philosopher rather drastically: In his early work[12] Wittgenstein shared the logical positivists' commitment to tough-minded standards for what is meaningful. Language, he thought, functions by picturing the world. The world is made up of facts, or states of affairs, and language is made up of propositions. A proposition is true if the elements in it are arranged so that they correctly picture the elements in the corresponding state of affairs. Propositions, therefore, are either objectively true, if the picture is an accurate one, or objectively false, if it is not. Any use of language that does not fit this model is not meaningful.

Beginning in the 1930s, however, Wittgenstein realized that this was too simple a picture of how language works. We use language, after all, to ask questions, give orders, express hopes, conjure up dreams— in all kinds of ways that the model of "picturing the facts" does not describe. The best generalization to be made about how language works is that the *meaning* of an utterance is *the way it is used.* [13] Suppose, for example, someone from a completely different culture who has learned English attends his first American baseball game and reacts in horror to the crowd's cries of "Kill the umpire!" We say, "No, no, you misunderstand," and he replies, "But does not 'kill' mean 'put to death'? That is how my dictionary defines it." We respond, "Well, yes, literally that is what it means. But the crowd doesn't really mean that. This is just a traditional way of expressing anger at a bad call, of letting off steam. Everyone in the stands would be horrified if someone actually did kill the umpire." We have explained the *meaning* of the crowd's calls, not by offering an alternative translation, but by showing how those words are *used* in their social context.

Language can be used, of course, in a great many different ways. Wittgenstein introduced the idea of "language games" in part to make precisely that point. Just as we use a ball in different ways in soccer, baseball, and tennis, so we use language in different ways in different "language games"—in giving an order, reporting an event, lying, testing a hypothesis, and so on.[14] Philosophers go astray when they try to impose one set of rules on all forms of language. It makes no sense for scientists to condemn poets because their statements cannot be empirically tested, for instance, just as it makes no sense for a soccer fan to condemn basketball players for picking up the ball with their hands—that would be judging by the rules of the wrong game. Yet, Winch argued, this is what Evans-Pritchard is trying to do when he judges Zande beliefs about witchcraft according to his own Western standards.[15]

Another example may illustrate the point more clearly. In his work on some neighbors of the Azande, the Nuer, Evans-Pritchard reported that, when one of the women of the tribe gave birth to twins, the Nuer said that they were birds.[16] Our first reaction may well be that this is crazy: twins aren't birds, they're human beings. The Nuer were indeed just being irrational. But then we learn more about Nuer life and customs. The Nuer were very poor and lacked cattle or other sources of animal milk. Mothers who gave birth to twins often could not supply them with adequate nourishment. Moreover, a very structured kinship system played a large role in the way the Nuer organized their life and understood their world, and the birth of twins produced two people to occupy only one slot in the kinship structure, which undercut a good many of the Nuer's basic social assumptions. As the anthropologist Victor Turner puts it:

> There are two things that can be done about twinship in a kinship society. Either you can say, like the little boy on first seeing a giraffe, "I don't believe it," and deny the social existence of the biological fact; or else, having accepted the fact, you can try to cope with it. If you try to cope, you must make it, if you can, appear to be consistent with the rest of your culture.[17]

The Nuer kinship system had a place for only one human at each birth, but the Nuer recognized that multiple births are the norm among birds. They thought of birds as "people of the above" or "children of God," and they said the same things about twins.[18]

A full analysis of these Nuer customs would involve much more detail, and a good bit of empathetic imagination besides, but perhaps even these few comments make the relevant point. As we learn the problems the birth of twins created in Nuer society and the meaning of "birds" for them, we at least begin to understand why they might say, "Twins are birds." We start to see the rules of the "game" they were playing and see how these "moves" made sense in the context of that game. At least it does not seem quite so crazy as it did at first. Similarly, if we understood more about why the Azande consulted the poison oracle, and where that practice fit in their life together, we might start to see the point of it all. The disturbing possibility emerges, then, that the better we understood any activity's context, the less crazy it would seem, so that, if we only understood enough, we would never judge *any* belief established within the practices of a given society to be "irrational."

Winch makes a similar point about religion. A religion represents a particular social context—to use a term Wittgenstein occasionally employs, it is a "form of life."[19] Within such a form of life, Christians, for instance, can assert appropriately Christian sentences about God and correct the errors in sentences that break Christian rules. Condemning religious language because we cannot find "evidence" for its claims or it somehow fails to conform to the rules of scientific language, however, is, according to Winch, just another instance of condemning a basketball player for failing to follow the rules of soccer:

> Criteria of logic are not a direct gift of God, but arise out of, and are only intelligible in the context of, ways of living or modes of social life. It follows that one cannot apply criteria of logic to modes of social life as such. For instance, science is one such mode and religion is another; and each has criteria of intelligibility peculiar to itself. So within a science or religion actions can be logical or illogical. . . . But we cannot sensibly say that either the practice of science itself or that of religion is either illogical or logical.[20]

If I set out to be a historian, you can argue that I have been a bad historian if I fail to respect the rules of doing history—if, for instance, I simply invent some documentary evidence. If I am writing a historical novel, however, I am playing a different game, with a different set of rules, and inventing conversations out of whole cloth may be part of my job. To judge how well I am following the rules, you have to know what game I am playing. And there are no rules for judging what game to play. There are no overarching rules according to which you can say that writing historical monographs is more or less rational than writing historical novels. Analogously, if the Azande are engaged in witchcraft, we need to understand the rules of that game and judge them accordingly. Evans-Pritchard, however, is either judging them by the rules of a different game—the game of Western science—or else illegitimately condemning the game they have chosen to play.

Kai Nielsen attacked the views of Winch and others as "Wittgensteinian fideism," a position he summarized in three theses:

1. "Religious concepts can only be understood if we have an insider's grasp of the form of life of which they are an integral part."

2. "Forms of life taken as a whole are not amenable to criticism; each mode of discourse is in order as it is, for each has its own criteria and each sets its own norms of intelligibility, reality, and rationality."

3. "There is no Archimedean point in terms of which a philosopher (or, for that matter, anyone else) can relevantly criticize whole modes of discourse or, what comes to the same thing, ways of life, for each mode of discourse has its own specific criteria of rationality/irrationality, intelligibility/unintelligibility, and reality/unreality."

For the Wittgensteinian fideist, Nielsen says, "religion is a unique and very ancient form of life with its own distinctive criteria. It can only be understood or criticized, and then only in a piecemeal way, from within this mode by someone who has a participant's understanding. . . . Philosophy cannot relevantly criticize religion; it can only display for us the workings, the style of functioning, of religious discourse"—

and the same could be said of Zande witchcraft.[21] As some Wittgensteinians have written, "objectivity and rationality must be things that
we forge for ourselves as we construct a form of collective life";[22] "the
concepts of truth and meaning . . . can legitimately be applied only
within systems of thought and institutions" so that "all cultures . . .
must be understood from within in their own terms."[23]

Wittgensteinian fideism is one of those odd positions which sometimes seem not to have any adherents. When Nielsen and others define
the position, most of those they might seem to be describing quickly
respond, "But I don't believe *that* at all."[24] It's a complicated business,
and no doubt there is defensiveness on one side and oversimplification
on the other. *Some* so-called Wittgensteinian fideists really do seem to
want to free religious assertions from challenge from outside faith.[25]
Others qualify their positions more carefully.[26]

For my immediate purposes, it is fortunately not necessary to sort
out whether there really are any Wittgensteinian fideists in the sense
Nielsen and others have described. Even if it is a caricature, Nielsen's
account of fideism does help clarify the issues by describing one possible extreme view. One might set out a triangle of possibilities on some
issues in the philosophy of religion.[27] At the vertices of the triangle are
three positions:

1. ATHEISM. Religious beliefs should be judged by universal standards of rationality. They fall short of those standards and are therefore irrational.

2. NATURAL THEOLOGY. Religious beliefs should be judged by
universal standards of rationality. Following those standards, we can
make good arguments for the existence of God and other religious
claims.

3. FIDEISM. There are no general criteria of rationality, and religious beliefs can be judged only in the context of the form of life
associated with them. Within a given form of life, of course, the associated beliefs always make good sense.

I want to argue in favor of a position somewhere in the middle of
that triangle—or, rather, in the middle of the line connecting natural
theology and fideism. After chapters 2 and 3, it will not be surprising
that I do not believe there is some universal standard of rationality
against which we can measure other cultures or some standpoint outside all cultures from which such judgments could be made. At the
same time, I also do not think that it is always impossible to judge a
culture's practices as being irrational or that any culture's beliefs are
as good as any other's. I think the same claims apply to the case of
different religious traditions. Let me try to define a middle ground.

The Wittgensteinian emphasis on the importance of use and social
context for understanding meaning implies rather persuasively that we
cannot understand, and therefore cannot judge, a single utterance in

isolation. If the Nuer say, "Twins are birds," or the Azande say, "The poison oracle can determine the identity of a witch," we need to know a good bit about their whole societies before we can even begin to understand what this means. If we want to make criticisms, then, we need to criticize a whole context of social practices, and that gets difficult.

Suppose, for instance, we try to make a case that some cultures, by virtue of their technological superiority, are "more advanced" than others and that therefore their beliefs must be "more rational." In his *Civilisation* series, for example, Kenneth Clark describes the idyllic society of Tahiti as Captain Cook found it but then remarks that "the very fragility of those Arcadian societies—the speed and completeness with which they collapsed on the peaceful appearance of a few British sailors followed by a handful of missionaries—shows that they were not civilisations in the sense of that word which I have been using."[28] Perhaps Lord Clark could have defended that specific, qualified claim, but any generalization of such an argument moves nervously close to the worldview of the old British colonial ditty:

> Whatever happens, we have got
> The Gatling gun, and they have not.[29]

It seems a risky business to claim that if "we" conquered "them"— whether by imperialist armies or Coca-Cola advertisements—then "our games" are somehow proven superior: risky not only because it implies the harsh gospel that power makes truth but also because, given the possibility that our culture will collapse in nuclear devastation or ecological crisis where another might have lived at peace with nature, one could at best claim that the jury is still out.

Indeed, such comparing of cultures always seems to risk cultural imperialism on the one side and the worst kind of romanticism on the other. Consider our own society and a preliterate tribal culture. Of course we value modern medicine, greater opportunities of education, and all the rest. Yet they seem to come at the price of a kind of alienation from knowing one's place in an ordered cosmos—what Max Weber called the disenchantment of the world.[30] After arguing for the superiority of Western science, the British anthropologist Robin Horton admits that he himself lives in traditional Africa—for many reasons, but among them "the discovery of things lost at home. An intensely poetic quality in everyday life and thought, and a vivid enjoyment of the passing moment—both driven out of sophisticated Western life by the quest for purity of motive and faith in progress."[31] Near the end of John Boorman's film *The Emerald Forest,* with its no doubt romanticized view of an Amazonian tribe, we see the tribe huddled together in a cave during a rainstorm, listening with rapt attention as their new chief tells the tribal stories. It is hard not to wish, however briefly, that we could share such moments.

We cannot, of course, and we would not be happy there even if we could, but that is not the point either. Given *our* upbringings, we prefer our society—if it came to that, we would take good plumbing and central heat at the price of alienation. But the products of another society might have another view. As Charles Taylor notes:

> The Renaissance sage had a different ideal from the modern scientific researcher's. From our point of view within this culture, we may want to argue that our science is clearly superior. We point to the tremendous technological spin-off it has generated in order to silence many doubters.
>
> But a defender of relativism might retort that this begs the question. We are the ones who value technological control; so to us our way of life is clearly superior. But the sage didn't value this, but rather wisdom. And this seems to be a quality we're rather short of. . . . So . . . the Renaissance sage . . . would still be scoring higher by *his* criteria, even as we are by ours.[32]

Such debates are not simply the games of intellectuals. In many parts of the third world the transition to "modern" agriculture or forestry is wreaking ecological devastation, and the collapse of the world of tribal society drives people to the shantytowns on the edges of vast cities where their life seems worse than that of their ancestors by nearly any standard.[33] We want, of course, "the best of both worlds": the advantages of technology without its problems. But in social and cultural practice the advantages and the disadvantages seem all tied together, and the total score on balance is sometimes very difficult to determine even for those who think they have clear criteria for judgment. At least we have to say of the argument from technological superiority what Kuhn said about arguments between scientific paradigms: we cannot settle the question by mathematical calculation, and the debate involves appeals to values that different participants may weigh differently.

Drawing on ideas from Karl Popper, Robin Horton has proposed a different way of making cross-cultural comparisons, based on the distinction between "open" and "closed" societies. Traditional cultures like the Azande, Horton says, remain unaware of alternatives to their own way of looking at things; indeed, they refuse to consider such alternatives even when they encounter them. "It is this difference we refer to when we say that traditional cultures are 'closed' and scientifically oriented cultures 'open.' . . . Absence of any awareness of alternatives makes for an absolute acceptance of the established theoretical tenets, and removes any possibility of questioning them."[34] In one sense, therefore, Horton claims we are more "rational" than the Azande, not merely by our standards but by a criterion that holds across cultures: we are willing to consider their point of view and learn from it; they are not willing to do the same with ours.

At least three questions arise about this argument. First, African tribes like the Azande had usually encountered either Christianity or Islam, sometimes both. At some levels, they no doubt understood their British colonial administrators better than most of those administrators understood tribal culture. As Isak Dinesen wrote after living many years in Africa:

> The lack of prejudice in the Native is a striking thing for you expect to find dark taboos in primitive people. It is due, I believe, to their acquaintance with a variety of races and tribes, and to the lively human intercourse that was brought upon East Africa, first by the old traders of ivory and slaves, and in our days by the settlers and big-game hunters. Nearly every native, down to the little herd boy of the plains, has in his day stood face to face with a whole range of nations as different from one another, and to him, as a Sicilian to an esquimo: Englishmen, Jews, Boers, Arabs, Somali, Indians, Swaheli, Masai and Kawirondo. As far as receptivity of ideas goes, the Native is more a man of the world than the suburban or provincial settler or missionary, who has grown up in a uniform community and with a set of stable ideals. Much of the misunderstanding between white people and the Natives arises from this fact.[35]

Horton's contrast between "open" and "closed" societies is at least too simple and maybe just wrong.

Second, Horton makes use of what might be called the Horton-Popper Preemptive Strike argument. It works like this: I announce that I am willing to take your point of view seriously. If you are not willing to do the same, then I am "open" and you are "closed," so it turns out that I do not have to take your point of view seriously. After all, you represent a closed, irrational society. In a game like this, whoever makes the first move always wins.[36] Horton seems to be claiming that we should feel free to reject out of hand cultures that reject other cultures out of hand, and there is something very odd about such an argument. A *really* "open" society might, one would have thought, be willing to try to learn even from more "closed-minded" neighbors— indeed, that would be one of the marks of its openness.

Third, as the passage quoted from Charles Taylor suggested, the claim that "open" is better than "closed" is itself a culturally relative judgment, and the Zande tribesman or the Renaissance sage could at least make a case that a certain sense of community and security about one's place in the world have greater value than technological advance and cultural pluralism and can be achieved only by refusing to question certain of the values of one's own culture—that the disenchantment of the world is too high a price for the possibility of technological and social innovation.

Neither the argument from technological superiority nor Horton's case for the "open" society, in other words, provides us with a clear, objective criterion for judging the rationality of one society over another. Does that leave us with radical relativism? Not necessarily.

Wittgenstein's talk of language games again provides some help. Wittgensteinian fideists sometimes seem to treat language games as if they were isolated entities: one culture has its rules, another has its rules; science one set, religion another—and never the twain shall meet.[37] Wittgenstein's own references to language games, however, were deliberately unsystematic. He talked about any kind of reporting as a language game,[38] but also about the particular language game of reporting a dream[39] or the particular language game of talking about colors.[40] Language games, in other words, can overlap, and one can be a subcategory of another. He used the term as a heuristic device to remind us of the many different ways language can work,[41] but the boundaries between language games are like the limits of the term "language game" itself, which, he says, "is *not* a closed frontier. For how is the concept of game bounded? What still counts as a game and what no longer does? Can you give the boundary? No."[42]

And so it is with cultures. The anthropologist often consciously seeks out the vanishing culture in an effort to preserve it before "the modern world" destroys it, so that "the anthropologist's odyssey upriver or to the back country to situate fieldwork where 'they still do it'" becomes the standard opening chapter of ethnographic narratives.[43] Such "salvage anthropology" serves a valuable function, but, taken as a general model, it risks implying that "real" cultures are those unaffected by interactions with other societies and that the culture in transition, half shaped by modernity, is somehow "impure," a less appropriate subject of anthropological investigation. In New Guinea, Margaret Mead explained in a letter to a friend, she avoided studying those groups which had been "badly missionized." Bronislaw Malinowski did not think the reasons why many Trobriand Islanders had become Christians were worthy of anthropological study. *"The* culture" was of course what survived from the time before contact with Christianity—even if most of the local inhabitants now lived a complex and interesting life in which tribal traditions, Christianity, and modern secularism mixed together in intriguing ways. As James Clifford, an anthropologist who has taken the lead in asking hard questions about such approaches, puts it, "Anthropological culture collectors have typically gathered what seems 'traditional'—what by definition is opposed to modernity."[44] As a result, their accounts make "culture" sound much more self-contained and static than in fact it is.[45]

Clifford Geertz picks up Wittgenstein's image of a culture as a growing city, with narrow, twisting streets in the old town and planned avenues in the suburbs, and remarks, "Anthropologists have traditionally taken the old city for their province, wandering about its haphazard alleys trying to work up some rough sort of map of it, and have only lately begun to wonder how the suburbs, which seem to be crowding in more closely all the time, got built, what connection they have to the old city . . . and what life in such symmetrical places could possibly be like."[46]

At the beginning of his study of Zande witchcraft, for instance, Evans-Pritchard mentioned that he was "working on behalf of the [British colonial] Government and mainly at their expense." He dedicated the book to the British District Commissioner and hoped that it "will be of service to political officers, doctors, and missionaries in Zandeland."[47] Yet, that having been said, the interaction between British rulers and Zande tribesmen virtually disappears from the narrative. The rest of us, therefore, sometimes get left with the impression that questions about the relative value of Zande witchcraft and Western science arise only in the philosopher's study. But they came up, one suspects, often enough even in Zandeland.[48]

One of the most obvious facts about cultural beliefs, after all, is that they change. One of the ways they change is through the interaction of different cultures. Evans-Pritchard's British ancestors believed in witches too; they even hanged them. But the British, whatever their faults these days, no longer hang witches. Africans who grew up in traditional tribal culture sometimes move to the city and, while retaining some of their traditional beliefs, discard others. Europeans like Robin Horton find some traditional African patterns of life deeply appealing and begin to adopt them. Such changes do not imply the discovery of the Archimedean point from which one judges one view objectively truer than another. Rather, they indicate that different sets of assumptions overlap, that most probably contain some internal inconsistencies, and that reflection and conversation can lead us, starting where we are, to move to someplace a bit different. We share enough in common so that I can see your point, and it leads me to question something I have always believed, to think that maybe your way of looking at it (or maybe a way different from yours but also different from my former view) makes more sense. Wittgensteinians who want to leave things "just as they are," to respect cultural practices as they exist, need to acknowledge that criticizing cultural practices and moving on to new ones is itself a widespread cultural practice. It will not do simply to say, "When in Rome, do as the Romans do," if it turns out that the Romans themselves are questioning traditional Roman patterns of behavior.[49]

An anthropologist, visiting a culture for twenty months, seeking out the oldest members of the tribe, concludes that these people have a tightly bounded worldview impervious to change. Another anthropologist, visiting fifty years later, notices that all sorts of customs and beliefs have changed radically. As Kai Nielsen has remarked:

> Once there was an ongoing form of life in which faeries and witches were taken to be real entities, but gradually as we reflected on the criteria we actually use for determining whether various entities, including persons, are or are not part of the spatio-temporal world of experience, we came to give up believing in faeries and witches. That a language game was played, that a form of life existed, did not preclude our asking about the coherence of the concepts involved and about the reality of what they conceptualized.[50]

I need not make some ultimate judgment about the technological superiority of your culture, or its greater openness, in order to learn from you, for I am making an *immanent* critique of my own previous assumptions, letting your ideas evoke questions implicit in my own previous views, in the course of the conversation (and my conversation partner may even be my own skeptical side). To use a favorite image of the anthropologist Claude Lévi-Strauss, in such conversations we function like *bricoleurs,* the odd-job men who squirrel away tools and bits of string for possible future use. As Lévi-Strauss explains the *bricoleur*'s methods:

> The rules of his game are always to make do with "whatever is at hand," that is to say with a set of tools and materials which is always finite and is also heterogeneous because what it contains bears no relation to the current project, or indeed to any particular project, but is the contingent result of all the occasions there have been to renew or enrich the stock or to maintain it with the remains of previous constructions or destructions.[51]

For good *bricoleurs,* the bits and pieces inherited from their own tradition often suffice for the task of raising questions about that tradition and moving on to a new way of looking at the world. Such a style of inquiry can provide a way of thinking about rationality that respects authentic pluralism—it does not force us all to share the same assumptions, but it finds ways we can talk with one another. I want to pursue such possibilities and their implications for theology in subsequent chapters, but first it may help clarify the character of the middle ground of *bricolage* to contrast it with efforts to rescue the Enlightenment ideal of universal rationality on the one hand and some forms of radical relativism on the other.

NOTES

1. See the brief biography in T. O. Biedelman, *A Bibliography of the Works of E. E. Evans-Pritchard* (London: Tavistock Publications, 1974), pp. 1–3; and E. E. Evans-Pritchard, "Religion and the Anthropologists," *Blackfriars* 41 (1960), p. 110.

2. E. E. Evans-Pritchard, *Witchcraft, Oracles and Magic Among the Azande* (Oxford: Clarendon Press, 1937), p. 260.

3. Ibid., p. 183.

4. Women almost never consulted the poison oracle.

5. Evans-Pritchard, *Witchcraft, Oracles and Magic Among the Azande,* p. 330. One might argue that such ad hoc excuses show that the Azande are being irrational, but the issue is at least very complex. Barry Barnes imagines a Martian anthropologist visiting Britain who discovers to his amazement that the local inhabitants believe that sexual intercourse induces pregnancy: "When women fail to procreate after many years of active intercourse, excuses are propounded. The male 'semen' may have lacked 'potency,' or the female may have been a pathological specimen. At times completely *ad hoc* ideas are invoked, 'psychological tension' for example or 'fear of childbirth' may be interfering with the normal process. The British never see that these cases are evidence of the randomness of conception" (Barry Barnes, *About Science,* pp. 147–148; Oxford: Basil Blackwell, 1985). Trying to explain why this case is different from the Zande explanations of the failures of the poison oracles, one realizes just how many assumptions get involved in the argument.

6. Evans-Pritchard, *Witchcraft, Oracles and Magic Among the Azande,* pp. 194–195. Laura Bohannan reports the remark made to her by an old man of a West African tribe: "We believe you when you say your marriage customs are different, or your clothes and weapons. But people are the same everywhere; therefore, there are always witches" (Laura Bohannan, "Miching Mallecho, That Means Witchcraft," in John Middleton, ed., *Magic, Witchcraft, and Curing,* p. 53; Garden City, N.Y.: Natural History Press, 1967).

7. Evans-Pritchard, *Witchcraft, Oracles and Magic Among the Azande,* p. 270.

8. Ibid., p. 99.

9. Ibid., p. 63.

10. Ibid., p. 338.

11. Ibid., p. 475.

12. Ludwig Wittgenstein, *Tractatus Logico-Philosophicus,* trans. D. F. Pears and B. F. McGuinness (London: Routledge & Kegan Paul, 1961). The original German text was first published in 1921.

13. "For a *large* class of cases—though not for all—in which we employ the word 'meaning' it can be defined thus: the meaning of a word is its use in the language" (Ludwig Wittgenstein, *Philosophical Investigations,* #43, trans. G. E. M. Anscombe; Oxford: Basil Blackwell, 1968).

14. Wittgenstein, *Philosophical Investigations,* ## 123, 249, 630. For a more complete list of Wittgenstein's examples of language games, see G. P. Baker and Peter M. S. Hacker, *An Analytical Commentary on the "Philosophical Investigations"* (Oxford: Basil Blackwell, 1980), pp. 97–98.

15. Like Thomas Kuhn, Winch has spent a good bit of time denying that his original statement had implications as radical as many read into it. For the original essay, see Peter Winch, "Understanding a Primitive Society," in Bryan R. Wilson, ed., *Rationality* (Oxford: Basil Blackwell, 1970), pp. 78–111; for subsequent qualifications, see Winch, "Comment," in Fred R. Dallmayr and Thomas A. McCarthy, eds., *Understanding and Social Inquiry* (Notre Dame, Ind.:

University of Notre Dame Press, 1977), esp. pp. 207–208; Peter Winch, *Ethics and Action* (London: Routledge & Kegan Paul, 1972), p. 3; and Peter Winch, *Trying to Make Sense* (Oxford: Basil Blackwell, 1987), esp. p. 198.

16. E. E. Evans-Pritchard, *Nuer Religion* (Oxford: Clarendon Press, 1956), pp. 130–131.

17. Victor Turner, *The Ritual Process: Structure and Anti-Structure* (Ithaca, N.Y.: Cornell University Press, 1969), p. 49.

18. Ibid., pp. 46–47. Clifford Geertz's references to "thick description" involve a similar approach to understanding a different culture. See Clifford Geertz, *The Interpretation of Cultures* (New York: Basic Books, 1973), p. 6.

19. The term "form of life," which has become central to many discussions of Wittgensteinian fideism, actually appears only five times in the *Philosophical Investigations:* ##19, 23, and 241, and pp. 174 and 226.

20. Peter Winch, *The Idea of a Social Science* (London: Routledge & Kegan Paul, 1958), pp. 100–101.

21. Kai Nielsen, "Wittgensteinian Fideism," *Philosophy* 62 (1967), pp. 191–193. In addition to Winch, Nielsen mentioned G. E. Hughes, Norman Malcolm, Stanley Cavell, J. M. Cameron, and Robert Coburn. D. Z. Phillips and Paul Holmer have often been cited since.

22. David Bloor, *Wittgenstein: A Social Theory of Knowledge* (New York: Columbia University Press, 1983), p. 3.

23. F. A. Hanson, *Meaning in Culture* (London: Routledge & Kegan Paul, 1975), p. 22.

24. See, e.g., D. Z. Phillips, *Belief, Change, and Forms of Life* (Atlantic Highlands, N.J.: Humanities Press International, 1986), p. x.

25. How else, for instance, to read this passage from Norman Malcolm: "*Within* a language-game there is justification and lack of justification, evidence and proof, mistakes and groundless opinions, good and bad reasoning, correct measurements and incorrect ones. One cannot properly apply these terms to a language-game itself. . . . In this sense religion is groundless; and so is chemistry. Within each there are advances and recessions of insight into the secrets of nature or the spiritual condition of humankind and the demands of the Creator, Savior, Judge, Source. Within the framework of each system there is criticism, explanation, justification. But we should not expect that there might be some sort of rational justification of the framework itself" (Norman Malcolm, *Thought and Knowledge,* pp. 208–209; Ithaca, N.Y.: Cornell University Press, 1977).

26. To make matters even more complicated, D. Z. Phillips, who (though Nielsen's original article did not mention him) is often cited as the classic Wittgensteinian fideist, sometimes seems to be saying that religion does not make claims about some independently existing God at all. In prayer, he says, we "tell" something "to God," but telling God "is a kind of 'telling' such that having understood the telling, it is misleading to ask whether the person told is present or not" (D. Z. Phillips, *The Concept of Prayer,* p. 74; London: Routledge & Kegan Paul, 1965). Indeed, it is just wrong to think that "in addition to all the many human consciousnesses there is another consciousness which is the consciousness of God" (Phillips, *Belief, Change, and Forms of Life,* p. 73). A Christian's belief in the Last Judgment "is not a conjecture about the future,

but, as it were, the framework, the religious framework, within which he meets fortune, misfortune, and the evil that he finds in his own life and in life about him" (D. Z. Phillips, *Faith and Philosophical Enquiry*, p. 113; New York: Schocken Books, 1971).

Nielsen and others sometimes criticize the fideists as defenders of a traditional orthodoxy they are trying to preserve from any possibility of challenge. But in passages like these, Phillips can sound more like a reductionistic social scientist. Religious beliefs, it seems, cannot be challenged from outside a form of life because they are *about* that form of life—and not about some transcendent God. I think there are probably left-wing and right-wing Wittgensteinian fideists. It is sometimes hard to know which is which; that seems to me part of the problem.

27. Gary Gutting sets out this "three-sided polemic" in his *Religious Belief and Religious Skepticism* (Notre Dame, Ind.: University of Notre Dame Press, 1982), p. 5.

28. Kenneth Clark, *Civilisation* (London: John Murray, 1969), p. 275.

29. Quoted in Charles Taylor, *Philosophical Papers*, vol. 2 (Cambridge: Cambridge University Press, 1985), p. 150.

30. See, e.g., Max Weber, "Science as a Vocation," in *From Max Weber: Essays in Sociology*, trans. and ed. H. H. Gerth and C. Wright Mills (New York: Oxford University Press, 1946), pp. 139–140.

31. Robin Horton, "African Traditional Thought and Western Science," in Wilson, *Rationality*, p. 170.

32. Charles Taylor, "Rationality," in Martin Hollis and Steven Lukes, eds., *Rationality and Relativism* (Oxford: Basil Blackwell, 1982), p. 100. This passage does not represent Taylor's final view.

Feyerabend makes a similar point: "If I have a friend then I shall want to know lots of things about him but my curiosity will be limited by my respect for his privacy. Some cultures treat Nature in the same respectful-friendly way. Their whole existence is arranged accordingly, and it is not a bad life, neither materially nor spiritually. Indeed one asks oneself if the changes resulting from more intrusive procedures are not at least in part responsible for the ecological problems and the pervasive feeling of alienation we are facing today. But this means that the transition from non-science to science (to express a highly complex development in terms of a simple alternative) is progressive only when judged from inside a particular form of life" (Paul K. Feyerabend, *Farewell to Reason*, p. 155; London: Verso, 1987).

As Hugh Lacey points out, modern physics can explain the flight of an arrow, but only by considering it purely as a projectile obeying the laws of mechanics and ignoring its relation to the archer and victim and its status as a culture artifact. Some cultures would have felt this didn't count as a very good explanation. (Hugh Lacey, "The Rationality of Science," in J. Margolis, M. Krausz, R. M. Burian, eds., *Rationality, Relativism, and the Human Sciences*, pp. 142–143; Dordrecht: Martinus Nijhoff, 1986.)

33. Feyerabend addresses this issue with characteristic forcefulness: "Many so-called 'Third World problems' such as hunger, illness and poverty seem to have been caused rather than alleviated by the steady advance of Western civilization" (Feyerabend, *Farewell to Reason*, p. 4). Yet we discourage the

preservation of alternative cultures. Indeed, "much of the spiritual misery of the remnants of non-Western cultures in the United States is due to the uninformed intellectual fascism of most of our leading philosophers, scientists, philosophers of science" (Paul K. Feyerabend, "Reply to Tibbetts and Halliangadi," *Philosophy of Social Science* 8 [1978], p. 185).

34. Horton, "African Traditional Thought and Western Science," in Wilson, *Rationality*, pp. 153–154.

35. Isak Dinesen, *Out of Africa* (New York: Vintage Books, 1972), p. 54. Horton has since conceded the oversimplification in his original position. See Robin Horton, "Tradition and Modernity Revisited," in Hollis and Lukes, *Rationality and Relativism*, p. 211.

36. Ernest Gellner quotes an unnervingly similar passage from, of all people, Lévi-Strauss: "This attitude of mind, which excludes . . . 'savages' . . . from human kind, is precisely the attitude more strikingly characteristic of those same savages." As Gellner points out, the second reference to "savages" is not in quotation marks. Lévi-Strauss seems in the odd position of saying that people who call other people "savages" ought to be called savages—an oddly self-referential position (Ernest Gellner, "Concepts and Society," in Wilson, *Rationality*, p. 30, quoting from the chapter on "The Ethnocentric Attitude" in Lévi-Strauss's *Race and Society*). In American academic circles, one hears this form of argument most often in connection with Marxists: "We are tolerant of other points of view. Marxists are intolerant of other points of view. Therefore, we cannot hire Marxists, because that might threaten our pluralism and tolerance." Sidney Hook made this case repeatedly.

37. Winch denies that this has ever been his position, but I am not sure. For his denials, see Winch, "Comment," in Dallmayr and McCarthy, *Understanding and Social Inquiry*, p. 254; and idem, *The Idea of a Social Science*, p. 101.

38. Wittgenstein, *Philosophical Investigations*, ##123, 363.

39. Ibid., p. 184.

40. Ludwig Wittgenstein, *Zettel*, trans. G. E. M. Anscombe (Berkeley and Los Angeles: University of California Press, 1967), #345.

41. See Wittgenstein, *Philosophical Investigations*, #5; Ludwig Wittgenstein, *The Blue Book*, in idem, *The Blue and Brown Books* (New York: Harper & Row, Harper Torchbooks, 1965), p. 17.

42. Wittgenstein, *Philosophical Investigations*, #98. In his early work, Wittgenstein's student Norman Malcolm seemed clear that a "form of life" would be something much smaller in scale than the totality of a religion—he offered the words, gestures, and actions involved in comforting someone as an example of a form of life (Norman Malcolm, *Knowledge and Certainty*, p. 119; Englewood Cliffs, N.J.: Prentice-Hall, 1963). In his *Memoir* of Wittgenstein, however, having admitted that Wittgenstein was not in any conventional sense religious, Malcolm cautiously added, "But I think that there was in him, in some sense, the *possibility* of religion. I believe that he looked on religion as a 'form of life' (to use an expression from the *Investigations*) in which he did not participate, but with which he was sympathetic" (Norman Malcolm, *Ludwig Wittgenstein: A Memoir*, p. 72; London: Oxford University Press, 1958). Recently, Malcolm flatly states, "Religion is a form of life; it is language embedded in action— what Wittgenstein calls a 'language-game' " (Malcolm, *Thought and Knowledge*,

p. 212). On my interpretation, Malcolm was gradually drifting away from Wittgenstein's use of "form of life." For a good discussion of all of this, see Fergus Kerr, *Theology After Wittgenstein* (Oxford: Basil Blackwell, 1986), pp. 29–30.

43. George E. Marcus, "Contemporary Problems of Ethnography in the Modern World System," in James Clifford and George E. Marcus, eds., *Writing Culture* (Berkeley and Los Angeles: University of California Press, 1986), p. 165. The classic version of this voyage—the best written and the funniest—is Lévi-Strauss's *Tristes Tropiques*.

44. James Clifford, *The Predicament of Culture* (Cambridge, Mass.: Harvard University Press, 1988), p. 232.

45. As Jeffrey Stout says, we need to think about cultures and languages diachronically rather than synchronically, to see how a culture can evolve new ways of talking in its own terms about something it has encountered in interaction with another culture. See Jeffrey Stout, *Ethics After Babel* (Boston: Beacon Press, 1988), p. 64. Victor Turner puts it vividly: "The culture of any society at any moment is more like the debris, or 'fall-out,' of past ideological systems, than it is itself a system, a coherent whole" (Victor Turner, *Dramas, Fields, and Metaphors*, quoted in Ihab Hassan, *The Postmodern Turn*, p. 120; Columbus, Ohio: Ohio State University Press, 1987).

46. Geertz, *The Interpretation of Cultures*, pp. 73–74.

47. Evans-Pritchard, *Witchcraft, Oracles and Magic Among the Azande*, pp. vii, 3.

48. "The people in my favorite Nigerian town drink Coca-Cola, but they drink *burukutu* too; and they can watch *Charlie's Angels* as well as Hausa drummers on the television sets which spread rapidly as soon as electricity has arrived. My sense is that the world system, rather than creating massive cultural homogeneity on a global scale, has replaced one diversity with another; and the new diversity is based relatively more on interrelations and less on autonomy" (Ulf Hannerz, "The World System of Culture: The International Flow of Meaning and Its Local Management" [manuscript], p. 6; quoted in Clifford, *The Predicament of Culture*, p. 17).

49. Ernest Gellner, "The New Idealism—Cause and Meaning in the Social Sciences," in Imre Lakatos, ed., *Problems in the Philosophy of Science* (Amsterdam: North-Holland Publishing Co., 1968), p. 385. Bernard Williams warns against the contradiction embedded in what he calls "the anthropologists' heresy." Many anthropologists want to say, he claims, that "right" means "right in a given society," but at the same time to say that it is wrong for people in one society to condemn or interfere with the values of another society. But if, in our society, we have traditionally defined it as "right" to condemn the customs of strangers, then such anthropologists seem required to acknowledge that this is "right for us." See Bernard Williams, *Morality* (Harmondsworth: Penguin Books, 1973), p. 34.

50. Nielsen, "Wittgensteinian Fideism," p. 208. "In seventeenth-century Scotland, for example, the question could not but be raised, 'But are there witches?' If Winch asks, from within what way of social life, under what system of belief was this question asked, the only answer is that it was asked by men who confronted alternative systems and were able to draw out of what confronted them independent criteria of judgment. Many Africans today are in the

same situation" (Alasdair MacIntyre, "The Idea of a Social Science," in Wilson, *Rationality*, p. 129).

51. Claude Lévi-Strauss, *The Savage Mind* (Chicago: University of Chicago Press, 1966), p. 17. Lévi-Strauss used the image of the *bricoleur* to distinguish characteristics he thought particular to "primitive" thought. Jeffrey Stout makes the case I am trying to argue: that we are all *bricoleurs*. See Stout, *Ethics After Babel*, pp. 74, 292.

5

LIBERALISM

Habermas and Rawls as defenders of the Enlightenment

At the end of the preceding chapter, I briefly introduced my own position. The lack of any universal criteria of rationality, I said, need not imply that there is no way to criticize the beliefs and practices of a particular tradition, if traditions contain within themselves reasons for questioning their own beliefs and practices and, in the natural course of things, encounter challenges from other traditions. In chapters 7 and 8, I will try to develop and defend those ideas, before returning in chapters 9 and 10 to their implications for the three questions mentioned in chapter 1. First, however, it seems only fair to take a look at the strongest available alternatives to such views.

On one side, writers such as Michel Foucault and Richard Rorty regard with suspicion even the modest claims I want to make for "progress" in conversation. Truth, Foucault says, is defined by those who have power, "produced only by virtue of multiple forms of constraint."[1] If the powerful establish fascism and everyone else lets them get away with it, Rorty says (quoting Jean-Paul Sartre), "fascism will be the truth of man."[2] On this account, a particular culture's beliefs and practices simply are what they are—what those in power make them—and it seems to make no sense to talk of their "advance" through self-criticism. I will consider where that kind of relativism leads us, and what kinds of arguments can be made for it, in chapter 6.

On the other side, John Rawls's *A Theory of Justice*[3] and the work of Jürgen Habermas seem to me the greatest contemporary efforts to rescue something like the Enlightenment dream. I have been arguing that we cannot evaluate the reasonableness of assertions, or even understand their meaning, in isolation from the values and practices of the culture in which they are made. So any comparative judgments about rationality will have to be made at the level of the general structures of society. In different ways, both Habermas and Rawls have claimed that there *are* objective standards for evaluating at least some features of the way a society is set up. Habermas is, he admits, "defending an outrageously strong claim in the present context of philosophical discussion: namely, that there is a universal core of moral intuition in all times and in all societies."[4] In *A Theory of Justice,* Rawls claimed to have found an Archimedean point for assessing the justice of any social system.[5] If either of those claims could be defended, then we would have a very sophisticated kind of objective starting point—a foundation, if you like—for evaluating the standpoints of different cultures after all. We might not have to depend, *bricoleur* fashion, on the string and wire collected from particular traditions.

Before we look at the work of Habermas and Rawls, a word about the title of this chapter seems in order. I am not using "liberal" in its usual political sense—the moderate left wing of the Democratic party in the United States or the Liberal party in Britain. Instead, by "liberal" I refer to a much broader tradition, beginning with the Enlightenment, of those, often suspicious of tradition, who believe that society should not try to find a common vision of the good toward which we could work together. Rather, they accept that we will always have different religious and ethical ideals, and we are socially united only in procedures that preserve our rights to pursue those different ideals without interference.[6] In that sense, Ronald Reagan and Margaret Thatcher are at least as much liberals as Edward Kennedy and David Steel.[7] Rawls is a political liberal in the more narrow sense, Habermas a heterodox Marxist, but they are both liberals in this broader sense.

Habermas is one of the most prolific philosophers of our time, and his views have changed substantially over the course of his career. Given a large and still growing body of work with a shifting point of view, one attempts quick summaries with caution. Still, at least two themes are clear enough: (1) Habermas wants to defend many of the ideals of the Enlightenment, in part as a bastion against the dangers of contemporary neoconservatism.[8] (2) His defense rests on analyzing the presuppositions of communication—the things we have to assume every time we communicate with one another.

Habermas began his career within the "Frankfurt school," led by neo-Marxists like Theodor Adorno, Max Horkheimer, and Herbert Marcuse, who drew on insights from Freud as well as Marx to analyze the ways in which an oppressive society distorts people's self-understanding. Just as a Freudian therapist helps patients to free themselves from the false consciousness that has constricted their lives, so some members of the Frankfurt school, including the young Habermas, hoped to undertake a social analysis that would emancipate people from the distorted vision that social oppression has imposed upon them. Realizing that you have been oppressed, after all, often represents the first step toward freedom.

The vindication of such an analysis is that the "patients" themselves recognize its validity, so that those it addresses "themselves must be the final judges of whether or not they are being coerced and whether or not they are free."[9] Unfortunately, if the oppression is pervasive enough, the distortion bad enough, then its victims may not even realize that they have a problem or be able to understand the call to emancipation. That possibility haunted the project of the Frankfurt school.[10] What does the analyst of a society do with a genuinely psychotic patient? For Germans, many of them Jews, writing in the 1930s and 1940s, the question was not a purely academic one. Even the analogy with a therapist breaks down. With an individual patient, one can at least appeal to social norms and say, "Don't you see you can't fit in, you can't adjust to the world around you, you must need some kind of help?" But if aberrant norms come to dominate a whole society, to what can one appeal?[11]

Beginning in the 1960s, Habermas therefore turned partially away from the views of his teachers. He sought a way to *prove* that a given society was engaged in distortion and oppression, whether the people in that society could recognize it or not. He claims that the *assumptions implicit in the process of communication* provide the starting point for making such judgments.

Whenever I speak, I am not only asserting a proposition, I am also performing a social action. To use the terminology of philosophers of language like J. L. Austin, my speech has both *locutionary* and *illocutionary* force.[12] A particularly explicit case makes the point: When the minister asks, "Do you, Mary, take this man, John, to be your lawfully wedded husband . . . ?" and Mary says, "I do," she is speaking a particular declarative sentence (locutionary force), but she is also performing an action—affirming the wedding vows (illocutionary force). If John and Mary were just joking around, or acting in a play, then "I do" might have the same locutionary force (the words would in a sense mean the same thing), but it would have a very different illocutionary force (the meaning of the action of saying those words would be very different).

Whenever we engage in conversation, Habermas argues, our remarks have the illocutionary force of seeking to persuade the others in the conversation.[13] If I say to you, "Richard Nixon was a bad President," I am not just making a comment, in a vacuum, about Mr. Nixon. I am implicitly urging, "Don't you agree with me?" That illocutionary act makes sense, however, only if I am not at the same time using force. Suppose I put a loaded gun to your head and then begin to argue, on moral grounds, why you ought to give me some of your money. Rather quickly, you would begin to feel there was something phony about my argument. If I really want to try to persuade you, I should put the gun down. As long as I hold the gun, my arguments are not merely annoying but somehow beside the point, inappropriate to the situation. In such a context, *making an argument at all* just does not make illocutionary sense. The very fact of entering into a discussion ought to imply that "no force except that of the better argument is exercised."[14]

Therefore, Habermas can claim to have found some values that transcend any particular culture. Anytime people are talking with one another anywhere, the mere fact that they are trying to persuade one another implies a commitment to what Habermas calls the "ideal speech situation," where everyone is free to say what he or she thinks, and force and constraint do not enter into the argument. That commitment in turn implies allegiance to some particular moral values: equality for all participants (so that everyone has a chance to be heard), tolerance of other points of view, a preference for persuasion over violence, and so on. In practice, of course, ideal speech situations are at least very rare: most of the time—maybe always—subtle or not so subtle forces exert pressure on participants in a conversation to stay out of trouble, to agree with the boss, or whatever.[15] Yet the ideal remains, and Habermas insists that to the extent that we fail to live up to it we are betraying standards presupposed as soon as we begin conversation—regardless of the customs of our particular society. Therefore, we can "rely on this intuitive knowledge whenever we engage in moral argument."[16]

Particularly in his more recent work, however, Habermas has not been willing to "rely" on this argument all by itself. And, in fact, such a purely formal argument based on the nature of conversation has some serious flaws. As Wittgenstein emphasized, we use language in a great many different ways. Sometimes we seek to make an argument that will convince any disinterested listener, but we also use language to give orders, to threaten, or to seduce by appealing to unconscious motivations. *Some* uses of language, Habermas properly points out, imply the moral values of the ideal speech situation—but that leaves open the question of whether those uses of language are morally superior to others.

For instance, when the Hebrew prophets spoke, or Hammurabi set out his code of laws, they were not inviting their listeners to treat them as equal partners in the conversation. They claimed special kinds of authority. Habermas, as a defender of Enlightenment values, thinks we are better off when we rule out that kind of appeal, when society gives up "mythological world views . . . which take on legitimating functions for the occupants of positions of authority" and allows only secular, open, liberal debate.[17] He may be right. But his argument presumes that some kinds of conversation—and the cultures that tend to foster them—are better than others; it does not follow from the nature of conversation itself.

Habermas has recognized that such a claim cannot be defended just by analyzing how language—any language whatever—works. He therefore turns from philosophical analysis to social scientific research to try to find support for his position. Specifically, he claims that Noam Chomsky's account of the way human beings learn language, Jean Piaget's analysis of how children develop the ability to think conceptually, and Lawrence Kohlberg's picture of the stages of moral reasoning all show empirically that human "speaking and acting runs through an irreversible series of discrete and increasingly complex stages of development; no stage can be skipped over, and each higher stage implies the preceding stage in the sense of a rationally reconstructible pattern of development."[18] The last stages are the best, so the argument goes, and in those last stages people have values like those implied in Habermas' ideal speech situation.

Since Kohlberg's research deals most directly with moral issues, it illustrates the argument most clearly. In a series of experiments, the first with teenaged boys in Chicago starting in the 1950s, this Harvard psychologist traced six stages in the development of moral reasoning. To oversimplify, children begin by thinking that whatever brings a reward is "right" and whatever elicits punishment is "wrong." They gradually learn to think that whatever wins the approval of their immediate peer group is "right" (stage 3). Then they advance to thinking that some fixed order of authority, law, and duty, whether social or religious, determines right and wrong (stage 4). Most adults never advance beyond that stage, but some (20 to 25 percent in some studies) move on to thinking about ethics in social-contract terms (stage 5): they now judge something right, not because law or tradition approves of it, but because their own reflection leads them to think it a good way to work out the conflicts of interests within a society. Finally, a few (5 to 10 percent) advance to a "morality of individual principles of conscience that have logical comprehensiveness and universality" (stage 6). Kant's ethics provides a classic example: one does the right because rational reflection leads one to conclude that it *is* the right, independent of personal benefit or social consequences.[19]

The six stages represent different *ways of reasoning* about moral questions, not necessarily different conclusions. Indeed, people at the same stage might reach opposite conclusions. For instance: is capital punishment right or wrong? A stage 3 person surrounded by advocates of capital punishment would favor it, but placed among opponents of capital punishment would oppose it—adopting in either event whatever values won support in his or her peer group. A stage 4 person would not just accept the values of the peer group but might say *either*, "The Bible says, an eye for an eye" *or*, "Jesus taught us to love our enemies"—either way appealing to a religious authority. And so on.

Kohlberg, in other words, was not claiming to be able to generate "the right answer" to moral questions. He did claim at least two things: (1) Some people, indeed some cultures, may never get beyond stage 3 or 4 or 5, but in every culture the *order* of the stages remains the same: no one who has been reasoning according to stage 5 ever regresses to stage 4, and so on.[20] (2) The higher-numbered stages not only always come later; they are morally better, not just according to the standards of some particular society but according to "universal human ethical values and principles."[21] The "ethically optimal" point of view of stage 6, of course, turns out to embody roughly the same ideals as Habermas' ideal speech community—the values of a secular, liberal, Enlightenment point of view.

Through the "values clarification" movement, Kohlberg's disciples have had a good bit of influence on American education. Seeing what it means in practice provides a good way of beginning to evaluate Kohlberg's proposal. Suppose, for instance, that a class of schoolchildren are discussing a story about a murder. When the teacher gets them talking about why killing is wrong, some of the children say, "Well, you know you wouldn't want somebody else to kill you, so you just figure that you shouldn't kill them." Others say, "God made every human being, and in the Bible God tells us that it's wrong to kill." A Kohlberg-trained teacher might identify the first group as stage 6 reasoners (Kantian reflection on moral principles) and the second group as stage 4 (appeal to authority—in this case the Bible as the commandment of God). Since stage 6 is "better" than stage 4, the teacher will try to direct the discussion so as to "raise" the stage 4 children to the stage 6 point of view—all the while insisting that this represents an "objective" way of teaching about values based on social scientific research.

That claim to objectivity of course represents one of the attractions of Kohlberg's position, for it seems to offer a way around problems of cultural relativism. Unfortunately, under examination the proposal falls into confusion. At one point Kohlberg proclaimed, "My evidence supports the following conclusions: There is a universal set of moral principles held by people in various cultures, Stage 6." A page or so later, however, he admitted, "Our two highest stages are absent in preliterate or semi-literate cultures."[22] Now, principles "absent" in many cultures are simply not "universal." Kohlberg had to fall back on his argument about order and development: stages 5 and 6 do not appear everywhere, but when they do appear, they always come after stage 4 and in some sense "grow out of" problems that emerged in thinking in stage 4 terms—and no one ever retreats from stage 5 or 6 back to stage 4.

Even granting that empirical conclusion, what is its moral force? Research in villages in Yucatán and Turkey showed no signs of stages 5 and 6.[23] Imagine then a contrast between Yucatán villagers and the tourists at the nearby resort of Cancún, many of them, let us assume, reasoning at stage 5 or 6. All the tourists, if only in childhood, went through a stage of accepting moral doctrines based on authority, but perhaps that kind of tradition-bound innocence is irrecoverable, and none of them will ever be able to go back to it. One can show how their present views developed out of questions and doubts about their earlier trust in authority. Still, one might make a case that the tourists' lives seem devoid of overarching moral purpose, that many of them drink too much and experiment with drugs, and that the simple piety of the villagers leads to a far healthier approach to moral values. Given the conceptual problems with contemporary secular ethics, the argument might run, it just does not provide a secure basis for the moral life for those who have turned away from "authority." I am not sure I actually believe that, but I do not find the claim absurd. My real point, however, is simply that the fact that stage 5, if it comes at all, always grows out of stage 4, and no one ever "regresses," does not *in itself* prove the superiority of the later stage.[24] We need not even appeal to the simple piety of Yucatán villagers: William Alston has pointed out that a good many sophisticated philosophers occupy Kohlberg's stage 4 or 5 rather than 6, and Kohlberg's kind of empirical research in itself cannot refute their positions.[25]

I do not want to overstate Kohlberg's importance to Habermas. But just as Habermas appeals to Kohlberg as a "heuristic guide and encouragement" for his own work,[26] so perhaps what is wrong with Kohlberg can provide a heuristic guide to what is wrong with Habermas. Like Kohlberg, Habermas believes in Enlightenment values—in questioning tradition, in free inquiry, in equality. He wants to claim that these are not *just* the values of the Enlightenment but universal human values, and in trying to make that case, he encounters all the problems about cultural relativism raised in the preceding chapter. As Thomas McCarthy, Habermas' finest interpreter, himself admits, "If . . . the structures of communicative action and discourse that Habermas singles out are to be found with significant frequency only in certain spheres of certain (Western) cultures at certain (modern) times, how then is it possible to defend the view that these structures are universal-pragmatic features of communication as such?"[27] If they are not characteristic of all communication, how can one argue that cultures which foster them are better than those which do not unless one smuggles one set of cultural values into the argument? Empirical research showing that some cultural styles always come later and "grow out of" others does not in itself establish their moral superiority.[28]

Habermas deeply fears the rise of neoconservative thought in the United States and West Germany. He sees the Enlightenment values of free inquiry and equality as a bulwark against the horrors of an irrationalism whose potential Germans know all too well.[29] He therefore wants to find a way of defending those values. But, as his teachers Adorno and Horkheimer warned, Enlightenment too can become totalitarian.[30] The values Habermas—or Kohlberg—wants to defend include openness and tolerance, but they seem not to include tolerance of the values of Hasidic Jews or the Amish, or radical feminist critiques of "male" styles of rationality, or ecologically motivated efforts to recover some of the relationship with nature characteristic of some preliterate societies.[31] As McCarthy has written in criticism of Habermas, "We have things to learn from traditional cultures as well as they from us, not only what we have forgotten and repressed, but something about how we might put our fragmented world back together again. This is not a matter of regression, but of dialogue—dialogue that is critical, to be sure, but not only on one side."[32] An authentic pluralism would allow that kind of dialogue. The firm conviction that Enlightenment values are better than all others, and that countervailing appeals to tradition are always part of the neoconservative menace, does not. Yet just that conviction seems to pervade much of Habermas' work.[33]

Similar problems arise in the case of John Rawls. Rawls's *A Theory of Justice* remains what one early review called it: "the most notable contribution" to "the tradition of English-speaking political philosophy" in our century.[34] Some indexes of recent published work in philosophy list more articles about Rawls than about Plato or Kant. No one can deny that Rawls wrote an important book.

In that book he tried to define "justice." To do so, he imagined a hypothetical situation he calls "the original position." Suppose we got together to set up the rules for our society. Since I teach at a college and like to watch football, I propose, "College teachers should be especially well paid, and city governments should provide football stadiums for NFL teams." My neighbor, a lawyer and an opera lover, says, "No, *lawyers* should be especially well paid, and city government should subsidize opera companies." At this point a supporter of Rawls interrupts and says, "But imagine you were setting up the rules of society from behind what I call 'the veil of ignorance.' That is, you did not know who you would be in society—did not know whether you would be a college teacher or a lawyer, an opera lover or a football fan. If you were forced to set out rules and procedures in such circumstances—what I call 'the original position'—you would not try to tilt things toward your own interests. How could you? You would not know what your own interests were. In such circumstances, then, you would think about what it means to be fair to everybody. The princi-

ples you would come up with under those circumstances provide a
good guide to what constitutes 'justice.' "[35]

After lengthy analysis, Rawls concludes that everyone in the original
position would choose two fundamental principles:

> First, each person is to have an equal right to the most extensive basic
> liberty compatible with a similar liberty for others.
>   Second, social and economic inequalities are to be arranged so that
> they are both (a) reasonably expected to be to everyone's advantage, and
> (b) attached to positions and offices open to all.[36]

Part of his argument for the second principle runs like this: Suppose
I am considering what salaries people should be paid. If I do not know
whether I will be a company president or a janitor, my instinct will be
to try to make salaries as equal as possible, so that, whatever position
I end up holding, I will at least be guaranteed a reasonable minimum
income. Still, I could justify some inequalities. Suppose, for instance,
we admit that physicians have to go through a long and arduous
training and that only people with special skills have the potential to
become physicians. People with the potential to pursue such a career
might well say, "Why should I do all this extra work, if I will not receive
any extra pay?" A society that paid physicians just the same as everyone else might therefore find itself without anyone to treat its medical
problems. But we all want someone around to try to cure us if we get
sick. Therefore (according to Rawls's principle 2.a., as just quoted),
paying physicians somewhat more than the rest of us—permitting that
economic inequality—is justified because it can be "reasonably expected to be to *everyone's* advantage."

Rawls develops a wide range of social principles through similar
sorts of reasoning, and thus he generates results like those sought by
Habermas: the values of a certain kind of tolerant Western liberalism,
defended as having a kind of universal status—these are what *any
rational person* would choose in the hypothetical original position.

One controversial aspect of this approach is that decisions about
justice get made in the absence of knowledge about what kind of life
one prefers or thinks morally best. After all, if I *knew* I was an opera
lover, I would vote for federal subsidies for opera companies. If I *knew*
I was a Presbyterian, I might favor preferential treatment for the Presbyterian Church. If I am to make judgments that everyone else would
accept as just, I have to make the kind of judgment I would make in
ignorance of my own preferences and moral or religious beliefs. "Justice . . . is not at the mercy, so to speak, of existing wants and interests.
It sets up an Archimedean point for assessing the social system."[37]
"That we have one conception of the good rather than another is not
relevant from a moral standpoint."[38]

Take one example of how this would work: If, behind the veil of ignorance, I do not know my own religious beliefs, then the only reasonable decision would be to opt for religious freedom; "persons in the original position . . . cannot take chances with their liberty by permitting the dominant religious or moral doctrine to persecute or to suppress others if it wishes."[39] John Knox might want to create a Calvinist society, but, behind the veil of ignorance, not knowing whether he would turn out to be a Catholic or a Calvinist, he could not take the chance that he would choose a view that would outlaw his own religious convictions altogether.

As a number of Rawls's critics have pointed out, this approach raises some problems. When Rawls invites me to think about what I would choose in ignorance of my moral and religious values, he assumes that there is an "I" capable of making moral choices somehow separate from what may be my most deeply held convictions, that those convictions are not part of my essential self.[40] If I believed, for instance, that theoretical inquiry represents the highest and best human activity, then I would want an ideal society to foster that good. If I thought that the highest human purpose is "to glorify God, and to enjoy him forever," then I would design a rather different society. In each case, I might want to set up an educational system and encourage communal practices that would inculcate and develop some habits and customs rather than others.

But in Rawls's original position, I *would not know* that I believed in some particular ideal of the good, and therefore I could not vote for social features that would foster it. At this point, I might legitimately protest, "Your original position made sense to me as a way of hypothetically putting aside my selfish interests. But now it seems to be serving a different purpose. I deeply believe in the dominant value of the life of the mind [or glorifying God], and looking for ways to direct society toward that end does not seem selfish to me. It is a highest good I wish for everyone. So a veil of ignorance that hides my passion for that good from me seems an unreasonable constraint on my choice of social values."[41]

Rawls could make two replies. First, he could remind us that he is developing "a theory of *justice.*" There are other virtues too, and our ideals of the good may have to come into consideration in thinking about them—but not when we are defining justice. It is fair for Rawls to remind us of the modesty of his project—he is writing about only one of the virtues—but on the basis of that analysis he does propose certain basic features that a society ought to have. Maybe there are other virtues too, but in important ways they can be fostered in a Rawlsian society only after the basic demands of justice have been satisfied first. Such a ranking of the virtues imposes a particular set of social priorities.[42]

Second, Rawls could reply that once we allow people to consider

their various beliefs about the good, we will never be able to agree on
how to set up a society. So we need a starting point neutral with respect
to theories of the good. Yet his solution to this problem seems not
really neutral at all but rather an attempt to impose aspects of *his* view
of the good on the rest of us. Whatever Rawls's own religious beliefs,
his worldview seems shaped not by classical Aristotelianism or Judaism
or Christianity so much as by a relatively secular Western liberalism.
He values tolerance, social equality, living peacefully together. Religious faith, or a communally shared idea of the human good, is not
central to *his* vision of the good life, and he has, it seems to me, little
tolerance for people who disagree with him. He writes, for instance,
of the "underlying fanaticism and inhumanity" of Ignatius Loyola, who
thought that all human activities ought finally to aim at the one goal
of serving the glory of God. Although such a view, Rawls says, "does
not strictly speaking violate the principles of rational choice . . . it still
strikes us as irrational, or more likely as mad."[43]

Rawls tends to make the argument here too easy for himself by
setting up a false dichotomy: either a society will be neutral with regard
to conceptions of an overarching good or else it will use force to
impose one vision on everyone.[44] Given that choice, we all instinctively
turn away from the use of force. Rawls never much explores the ways
in which education and the right kind of leadership might, without
oppression, begin to inculcate a common set of such values.

Social contract theorists whom he admires, such as Locke and Rousseau, Rawls admits, limited religious freedom too, but they did so
because of what they considered its observable potential danger to the
public order. Rousseau believed that those who thought their neighbors damned to hell would not treat them civilly, and Locke thought
that Catholics and atheists could not be relied on to observe the bonds
of a civil society. Therefore they favored limiting the religious freedom
of such folk. Rawls thinks Rousseau and Locke were wrong about who
can be trusted, but he seems willing to accept the form of their argument. If some religious positions did make their adherents less reliable
supporters of a just social order, then Rawls would favor efforts to
supplant those positions. On the other hand, he totally condemns
intolerance in Aquinas or the Protestant Reformers: in those cases, he
says, the suppression of liberty is based on "theological principles or
matters of faith," and that can never be justified.[45]

Such conclusions favor one view of the good over others. Religious
commitments might be altered for the sake of social justice, but never
vice versa. Whether Rawls's position on the highest human good is
right or wrong, he is not neutral. As Steven Lukes has written, "The
motivations, beliefs and indeed the very rationality of Rawls's 'individuals' are recognizably those of a sub-class of rather cautious,

modern, Western, liberal, democratic, individualistic men. . . . So in the end Rawls's Archimedean point for 'judging the basic structure of society' (necessarily) eludes him. . . . Justice is an essentially contested concept and every theory of justice arises within and expresses a particular moral and political perspective."[46]

Like Habermas' ideal speech situation, a Rawlsian liberal society manifests a number of admirable virtues—social justice and freedom from violence, for instance—and I do not mean to condemn it. But it represents one kind of ideal among others. Like any other kind of society, it also has characteristic flaws. Once even the *search* for a fundamental shared commitment to the good is ruled out,[47] then, as Michael Walzer has written, "A liberal nation can have no collective purpose."[48] "The liberal state," Walzer says, "is not a home for its citizens; it lacks warmth and intimacy."[49] Its citizens do not finally work together toward any ideal higher than the right to be left alone.

In *Habits of the Heart,* Robert Bellah and his coauthors have traced some of the consequences of such liberalism for contemporary America. When the question of the good must be left open, then "the ultimate ethical rule is simply that individuals should be able to pursue whatever they find rewarding," and "there is no moral common ground and therefore no public relevance of morality outside the sphere of minimal procedural rules and obligations not to injure," so that "Americans . . . are deprived of a language genuinely able to mediate among self, society, the natural world, and ultimate reality."[50] Such a nation is not a family or a *communitas* but a well-regulated marketplace. This is the sense in which Reaganism and Thatcherism are forms of liberalism, though certainly different from—and to my mind far less attractive than—Rawls's version.

There are trade-offs, in short, between the real virtues of a liberal society and social visions of common purpose and common ideal characteristic of different kinds of society and also in their way admirable. Just as Thomas Kuhn argued regarding choices between scientific paradigms, arguments can be made on one side or the other, but there is no mathematical way to measure all these values on the same scale and come up with an indisputable answer about which kind of society is best. A genuine pluralism, it seems to me, would welcome an ongoing conversation about such matters, a conversation among liberals, Loyolas, Maoists, Hasidim, Kierkegaardians, and anyone else who wanted to join—a conversation about how to preserve virtues characteristic of different social ideals, how, perhaps, to encourage various kinds of enclaves within a larger society. To be sure, some advocates of some of these points of view will not want to join the conversation, and some will try to subvert it by threats and violence. But some of those committed to social ideals that involve a shared tradition and shared visions *will* be willing to join the conversation. Neither Habermas nor Rawls seems willing to accept them as morally or rationally equal conversation partners.

Rawls's more recent work, to be sure, has rested his case on a somewhat different argument. "What justifies a conception of justice," he has now written, "is not its being true to an order antecedent to and given to us, but its congruence with our deeper understanding of ourselves and our aspirations, and our realization that, *given our history and the traditions embedded in our public life,* it is the most reasonable doctrine *for us.*"[51] Since the Reformation, Rawls explains, Western societies have not been able to agree on a common set of religious values or a common vision of the good.[52] Therefore, *for us,* a "workable conception of political justice . . . must allow for a diversity of doctrines and the plurality of conflicting, and indeed incommensurable, conceptions of the good affirmed by the members of existing democratic societies."[53] From Rawls's more recent perspective, justice and tolerance have no absolute priority over piety or the virtues of the contemplative life, and there is no purely conceptual reason for ruling out considerations about the good when designing a society. Our culture simply happens to be unable to agree on the good, and therefore the cultivation of tolerance and social justice is, in our situation, the best way to keep us from each others' throats and preserve for each of us at least some chance to pursue our own visions.

This shift makes Rawls's position more cautious and, to me, more intriguing. (The parallel, incidentally, with Habermas' shift from a priori arguments about the nature of language to empirical arguments about how reasoning has in fact developed is also intriguing.) But I think its consequences are more radical than he has yet acknowledged. Rawls, after all, originally argued in favor of certain principles of social justice: income should be unequally distributed only when such distribution serves the good of everyone, and so on. He has not given up *these* views, and indeed it is not clear what would be left of his distinctive position if he did. Yet one need look no farther than dramatic election victories by Ronald Reagan and Margaret Thatcher to suspect that the odds of securing agreement on such principles of progressive social democracy in our society are not very great either. Therefore, it seems to me, Rawls cannot simply appeal to our inability to agree on a conception of the good as a reason for giving up the effort to find one. In fact, we seem unable to agree about social justice either, but he is not giving up on that.[54]

Rawls remains committed to seeking agreement on justice and willing to give up on piety or the good because, as a particular kind of liberal, he finds justice more important. Fair enough. But those whose priorities lie elsewhere are not necessarily irrational or insane, any more than those who do not accept Habermas' ideals for communicative practice are necessarily primitive or backward. We may have lessons to learn these days from cultures more bound to shared ideals than our own. Modern secularists may be able to learn something from Christians deeply committed to their tradition. At least we should not formulate the rules of conversation about important questions in such a way as to rule out such possibilities. Habermas and Rawls seem to want to do just that. For all their commitment to tolerance and pluralism, these representatives of liberalism seem at crucial points advocates of a rather strong form of intellectual intolerance.

NOTES

1. Michel Foucault, *Power/Knowledge: Selected Interviews and Other Writings, 1972–1977*, ed. and trans. Colin Gordon and others (New York: Pantheon Books, 1980), p. 131.

2. Richard Rorty, *Consequences of Pragmatism* (Minneapolis: University of Minnesota Press, 1982), p. xlii.

3. John Rawls, *A Theory of Justice* (Cambridge, Mass.: Harvard University Press, 1971). I point to this book because, as I will explain later in this chapter, in more recent work Rawls has shifted his position.

4. Jürgen Habermas, *Autonomy and Solidarity*, ed. Peter Daws (London: Verso, 1986), p. 206.

5. Rawls, *A Theory of Justice*, pp. 261, 584. I confess that these are isolated references in a very big book and that elsewhere Rawls defends a method of "reflective equilibrium," in which we formulate a model and then test it against our initial intuitions, sometimes modifying the model to fit our intuitions but sometimes modifying particular intuitions as the model helps us see how they fit into an overall pattern (ibid., pp. 20–21, 579). This sounds quite compatible with the Quinean ideas I have developed in previous chapters, and, indeed, by way of William Werpehowski's appropriation of Rawls for theology, it has been a significant influence on my own thought. (See William Werpehowski, "Social Justice, Social Selves: John Rawls' *A Theory of Justice* and Christian Ethics"; diss., Yale University, 1981.) Rawls does insist, however, that his basic principles of justice have priority over any conception of the good in setting up a society—on that crucial issue at least, I will argue, the image of the Archimedean point is not a passing metaphor but a serious model of his project.

6. For a classic critique of such "liberalism," see Robert Mangabeira Unger, *Knowledge and Politics* (New York: Free Press, 1975).

7. The leader of the British Liberal party.

8. "Ever since the appearance of his first books published during the early 1960s, Jürgen Habermas has devoted his efforts more than any other contemporary philosopher toward making the tradition of the European Enlightenment fruitful for the thought and practice of the present" (Peter Bürger, "The Significance of the Avant-Garde for Contemporary Aesthetics," *New German Critique* 22 [1981], p. 19).

9. Raymond Geuss, *The Idea of a Critical Theory: Habermas and the Frankfurt School* (Cambridge: Cambridge University Press, 1981), p. 78.

10. See ibid., pp. 64–65.

11. The analogy with psychotherapy raises other problems too. As Paul Ricoeur points out, the "initial situation of the doctor-patient relationship has no parallel in ideology-critique [Habermas' approach]. In ideology-critique no one identifies himself or herself as the ill, as the patient, and no one is entitled to be the physician" (Paul Ricoeur, *Lectures on Ideology and Utopia*, p. 248; New York: Columbia University Press, 1986). See also Hans-Georg Gadamer, *Philosophical Hermeneutics*, trans. David E. Linge (Berkeley and Los Angeles: University of California Press, 1976), pp. 41–42.

12. See J. L. Austin, *How to Do Things with Words* (Cambridge, Mass.: Harvard University Press, 1962), pp. 98–107.

13. Jürgen Habermas, *Knowledge and Human Interests*, trans. Jeremy J. Shapiro (Boston: Beacon Press, 1971), p. 314.

14. Jürgen Habermas, *Legitimation Crisis*, trans. Thomas McCarthy (Boston: Beacon Press, 1975), p. 17.

15. Jürgen Habermas, "Wahrheitstheorien," in Helmut Fahrenbach, ed., *Wirklichkeit und Reflexion: Festschrift für Walter Schulz* (Pfullingen: Verlag Günther Neske, 1973), p. 258.

16. Jürgen Habermas, *The Theory of Communicative Action*, vol. 1, trans. Thomas McCarthy (Boston: Beacon Press, 1984), p. 19.

17. Jürgen Habermas, *Communication and the Evolution of Society*, trans. Thomas McCarthy (Boston: Beacon Press, 1979), p. 157. See also Habermas, *Legitimation Crisis*, pp. 17–24; Jürgen Habermas, *The Theory of Communicative Action*, vol. 2, trans. Thomas McCarthy (Boston: Beacon Press, 1987), pp. 46, 77. Habermas can seem remarkably insensitive to the kinds of issues I raised in the preceding chapter. He flatly says, for instance, "A modern observer is struck by the extremely irrational character of ritual practices" (ibid., p. 191).

18. Habermas, *Communication and the Evolution of Society*, pp. 73–74. See also ibid., p. 205; and Habermas, *The Theory of Communicative Action*, vol. 2, pp. 145, 174. He has shifted, he says, from claims about what is implicit in any speech act to claims about "the intuitions of competent members of *modern* societies" (Jürgen Habermas, "Reply to My Critics," in John B. Thompson and David Held, eds., *Habermas: Critical Debates*, p. 253; London: Macmillan & Co., 1982; emphasis added). The question then, of course, is why modernity is necessarily better.

19. Kohlberg shifted his position on these matters in a variety of ways. For still good brief accounts of the six stages, see Lawrence Kohlberg, "From Is to Ought: How to Commit the Naturalistic Fallacy and Get Away with It in the Study of Moral Development," in Theodore Mischel, ed., *Cognitive Development and Epistemology* (New York: Academic Press, 1971), pp. 164–165; and Lawrence Kohlberg, "A Cognitive-Developmental Approach to Moral Development," *The Humanist* 32 (1972), pp. 14–15. For his addition of a seventh stage, see Lawrence Kohlberg, *The Philosophy of Moral Development* (San Francisco: Harper & Row, 1981), p. 135. For his admission that we cannot set stages 5 and 6 in a clear hierarchy, see Lawrence Kohlberg, "A Reply to Owen Flanagan and Some Comments on the Puka-Goodpaster Exchange," *Ethics* 92 (1982), p. 53.

20. "All individuals in all cultures go through the same order or sequence of gross stages of development, though varying in rate and terminal points of development" (Kohlberg, "From Is to Ought," in Mischel, *Cognitive Development and Epistemology*, p. 175).

21. Kohlberg, "A Cognitive-Developmental Approach to Moral Development," p. 14. "I have successfully defined the ethically optimal end point of moral development" (Kohlberg, "From Is to Ought," in Mischel, *Cognitive Development and Epistemology*, p. 153).

22. Kohlberg, *The Philosophy of Moral Development*, pp. 127–128.

23. Kohlberg, "From Is to Ought," in Mischel, *Cognitive Development and Epistemology*, pp. 173–174.

24. For a fuller study of cultural bias in Kohlberg's work, see Elizabeth Simpson, "Moral Development Research: A Case of Scientific Cultural Bias," *Human Development* 17 (1975), pp. 81–106. Carol Gilligan has written a famous feminist critique of Kohlberg's work in "In a Different Voice: Women's Conceptions of Self and Morality," *Harvard Educational Review* 47 (1977), pp. 481–517. For articles reviewing many issues, see Sohan Modgil and Celia Modgil, eds., *Lawrence Kohlberg: Consensus and Controversy* (Philadelphia: Falmer Press, 1986).

25. If Kohlberg wants to make "pronouncements as to how people *ought* to reason . . . he will have to show that this sense of 'moral' . . . has itself some recommendation other than congeniality to his predilections" (William P. Alston, "Comments on Kohlberg's 'From Is to Ought,'" in Mischel, *Cognitive Development and Epistemology*, p. 277). Kierkegaard might be the most dramatic example of a sophisticated anti-Kohlbergian.

26. Habermas, *Communication and the Evolution of Society*, p. 205.

27. Thomas McCarthy, "Rationality and Relativism," in Thompson and Held, *Habermas: Critical Debates*, p. 65. "I find it quite hard to burden pre-dynastic Egyptians, ninth-century French serfs and early-twentieth-century Yanomamö tribesmen with the view that they are acting correctly if their action is based on a norm with which there would be universal consensus in an ideal speech situation. The notion that social institutions should be based on the free consent of those affected is a rather recent Western invention" (Geuss, *The Idea of a Critical Theory*, p. 66).

28. "Habermas's treatment of ritual and myth in primitive societies is too brief and overly formal to be persuasive, at least given the very strong claims he wants to make about the privileged status of modernity." He "has not attempted the kind of detailed historical and anthropological studies that would be necessary to make his proposed theory of social evolution really possible" (Stephen K. White, *The Recent Work of Jürgen Habermas*, pp. 32, 170 n. 2; Cambridge: Cambridge University Press, 1988). I am not sure I understand the kind of empirical research White has in mind.

29. See Jürgen Habermas, "Neoconservative Culture Criticism in the United States and West Germany," in Richard J. Bernstein, ed., *Habermas and Modernity* (Cambridge, Mass.: MIT Press, 1985), p. 90.

30. Theodor W. Adorno and Max Horkheimer, *Dialectic of Enlightenment*, trans. John Cumming (New York: Herder & Herder, 1972), pp. 6, 24. I am of course writing from a North American point of view. Richard Rorty makes the interesting point that German neoconservatives tend to base their arguments

on a historicist appeal to tradition, unlike their American counterparts' appeal to "universal and objective moral values" (Richard Rorty, "Thugs and Theorists," *Political Theory* 15 [1987], p. 574). Habermas' identification of the underlying intellectual danger would therefore seem less plausible on this side of the Atlantic.

31. See Andreas Huyssen, "The Search for Tradition: Avant-Garde and Postmodernism in the 1970s," *New German Critique* 22 (1981), p. 38.

32. Thomas McCarthy, "Rationality and Relativism," in Thompson and Held, *Habermas: Critical Debates*, p. 78.

33. "Having defined Marxism once and for all as 'progressive,' he has no choice but to label any other ideology as reactionary or conservative, regardless of what it might offer. And having experienced in his youth the Third Reich, he has no alternative but to look anxiously on *anything*—Myth, Romanticism, Wagner, Nietzsche, Heidegger, Derrida, Postmodernism, all capitalized in a certain slant of History—that may revive old nightmares" (Ihab Hassan, *The Postmodern Turn*, p. 224; Columbus, Ohio: Ohio State University Press, 1987).

An analogous point could be made in terms of rhetoric. As Stephen White puts it, "Habermas's . . . privileging of serious, straightforward, unambiguous usage can be seen as diverting our attention away from precisely those aspects of language which have the capability of sensitizing us to the oppressiveness of whatever categorical distinctions are dominating our thought and social interaction at any given historical period. Humor, irony, metaphor, and aesthetic expression in general are what give us breathing space and weapons in this ongoing struggle to prevent closure in the way we see ourselves, others and the world" (White, *The Recent Work of Jürgen Habermas*, p. 31).

At this point, as at many others, Paul Ricoeur seems much more helpful than Habermas.

34. "The Good of Justice as Fairness," *Time Literary Supplement*, 5 May 1972, p. 1505.

35. See Rawls, *A Theory of Justice*, pp. 12, 139, 252.

36. Ibid., p. 60. Rawls later states these principles in fuller form. The second becomes: "All social primary goods—liberty and opportunity, income and wealth, and the bases of self-respect—are to be distributed equally unless an unequal distribution of any or all of these goods is to the advantage of the least favored" (ibid., p. 303).

37. Ibid., p. 261; see also pp. 142–143, 206.

38. John Rawls, "Fairness to Goodness," *Philosophical Review* 84 (1975), p. 537.

39. Rawls, *A Theory of Justice*, p. 207.

40. Michael J. Sandel, *Liberalism and the Limits of Justice* (Cambridge: Cambridge University Press, 1982), p. 27; Bruce A. Ackerman, *Social Justice in the Liberal State* (New Haven: Yale University Press, 1980), p. 339; Unger, *Knowledge and Politics*, p. 87; and Alasdair MacIntyre, *Whose Justice? Which Rationality?* (Notre Dame, Ind.: University of Notre Dame Press, 1988), p. 133. Marxist critics of Rawls argue that people cannot really separate themselves from their class point of view enough to imagine themselves in a really neutral original position. See Richard Miller, "Rawls and Marxism," *Philosophy and Public Affairs* 3 (1974), pp. 181–184.

41. For a good statement of a similar point, see T. M. Scanlon, "Rawls' Theory of Justice," in Norman Daniels, ed., *Reading Rawls: Critical Studies on Rawls' A Theory of Justice* (New York: Basic Books, 1975), p. 170.

42. This is a crucial point where Rawls limits his theory of "reflective equilibrium." I take it Werpehowski would accept some of my criticisms of Rawls here. See William Werpehowski, "Political Liberalism and Christian Ethics," *The Thomist* 48 (1984), pp. 81–115.

43. Rawls, *A Theory of Justice*, p. 554. See also his suspicion of religiously based pacifism, ibid., p. 370.

44. See, e.g., John Rawls, "The Idea of an Overlapping Consensus," *Oxford Journal of Legal Studies* 7 (1988), p. 4.

45. Rawls, *A Theory of Justice*, p. 216.

46. Steven Lukes, *Essays in Social Theory* (London: Macmillan & Co., 1977), pp. 170–171.

47. "Liberalism assumes . . . that it is a natural condition of a free democratic culture that a plurality of conceptions of the good is pursued by its citizens" (John Rawls, "Social Utility and Primary Goods," in Amartya Kumar Sen and Bernard Williams, eds., *Utilitarianism and Beyond* (Cambridge: Cambridge University Press, 1982), p. 160.

48. Michael Walzer, *Radical Principles: Reflections of an Unreconstructed Democrat* (New York: Basic Books, 1980), p. 69.

49. Ibid., p. 68.

50. Robert N. Bellah and others, *Habits of the Heart: Individualism and Commitment in American Life* (Berkeley and Los Angeles: University of California Press, 1985), pp. 6, 141, 237.

51. John Rawls, "Kantian Constructivism in Moral Theory," *Journal of Philosophy* 77 (1980), p. 519, emphasis added.

52. John Rawls, "Justice as Fairness: Political not Metaphysical," *Philosophy and Public Affairs* 14 (1985), p. 230.

53. Ibid., p. 225.

54. When Rawls begins to address this question in a recent article, he moves to a very high level of abstraction. Having talked about the particular history of the West since the Reformation in arguing the impossibility of a common ideal of the good, he shifts to the hypothetical "thought-experiment" reasoning he used in *A Theory of Justice* to make the case for a viable "overlapping consensus" regarding social justice. But, once one appeals to that kind of argument, why not try to construct a scenario for the gradual emergence of a common ideal of the good life? See Rawls, "The Idea of an Overlapping Consensus," p. 18.

6

RELATIVISM

Foucault and Rorty as critics of modernity

No one in our time has exposed the hidden intolerances of Enlightenment liberalism and their dangers more skillfully than Michel Foucault and Richard Rorty.[1] If Habermas and Rawls represent the Enlightenment, Foucault and Rorty have inherited Nietzsche's mantle as its great contemporary critics. Having made similar criticisms myself, I might be expected to cite them as prestigious allies, but I find I have deep reservations about their conclusions. Foucault attacks every effort to claim that some theories are "true," some practices "good" so resolutely that his position finally seems self-refuting: he has no way of arguing, or even of explaining what it would mean to say, that his own views are better than those of his opponents. Rorty, on the other hand, having demolished the foundations of Enlightenment liberalism, turns out to think it can survive perfectly well without foundations and proves no more tolerant of genuine pluralism, of voices that might speak from outside the Western Enlightenment, than Habermas or Rawls. In their worst moments anyway, these two figures represent two unhappy forms of relativism: a tendency toward nihilism in which nothing can be defended as good or true, and a kind of self-satisfaction in which one retreats to "the way the world looks to us," refusing to make claims beyond that intellectual ghetto but finding it possible to live quite comfortably there.

In chapter 4, I began to argue for an approach in the philosophy of religion intermediate between natural theology, with its efforts to prove the truth by publicly acceptable criteria, and fideism, with its refusal to admit that argument can escape the confines of a particular tradition at all. Analogously, my philosophical sympathies lie between Rawls and Habermas on the one hand and Rorty and Foucault on the other. Having laid out my doubts about the first extreme in the preceding chapter, it is time to turn to the second, before exploring, in the next chapter, my own preference, somewhere in the middle.

To begin with Michel Foucault: In a series of studies of prisons, insane asylums, hospitals, and sexuality, Foucault sought to show that what counts as "innocent," "sane," or "normal" is not a matter of "objective truth" but depends on the realities of power in a given society.[2] Those who have the power define guilt, sanity, normality, and truth itself. "Truth isn't outside power, or lacking in power. . . . Truth is a thing of this world: it is produced only by virtue of multiple forms of constraint. And it induces regular effects of power. Each society has its regime of truth, its 'general politics' of truth."[3]

Foucault made this point with moral passion and, it would seem, for moral purposes. He characteristically took some contemporary institution with its associated beliefs and practices—the prison, the asylum—which seems to us, however in need it may be of modest reforms, somehow the only "rational" way to cope with a particular problem—in these cases, with criminals or the insane. Foucault would then work back in history until he came to a way of dealing with the problem so radically different that it strikes us at first as lunatic—heinous torture of criminals, for instance. Then he would show how, in its own context, this earlier practice made sense.[4] His readers find themselves wondering: If that way of doing things seems crazy to us, may ours not someday seem crazy too?

Foucault's *The Order of Things* begins with a marvelous passage that Jorge Luis Borges had "quoted" from an imaginary Chinese encyclopedia, which classified animals as "(a) belonging to the Emperor, (b) embalmed, (c) tame, (d) sucking pigs, (e) sirens, (f) fabulous, (g) stray dogs, (h) included in the present classification, (i) frenzied, (j) innumerable, (k) drawn with a very fine camelhair brush, (l) *et cetera*, (m) having just broken the water pitcher, (n) that from a long way off look like flies."[5] Now this sounds just crazy, but its very craziness raises the question of *why* something seems wrong with it, how we *should* judge systems of classification. Later in the book, Foucault shows how people in the Middle Ages and even in the sixteenth century ordered the elements of the world in part according to the language and contexts we use to describe them. To us the fact that "flowers" and "flies" both begin with an "fl" or that camels and wolves are both mentioned in the Bible would seem completely irrelevant to their classification, which, we would say, ought to be based solely on the physical characteristics of the objects themselves. But why? Is not what we call them one of their characteristics too? Our judgment about how to classify properly rests in part on all sorts of assumptions about the separation between the objective world and subjective observers, between the thing and the language that describes it—assumptions that embody one philosophical point of view among others.

We think that modern science has found somehow more "objective" criteria of classification, but Foucault raises doubts. In his introduction to the autobiography of a nineteenth-century hermaphrodite, for instance, he argues that earlier ages could accept hermaphrodites for what they were, while modern biological theories have "obstinately brought into play" the "question of a 'true sex' in an order of things where one might have imagined that all that counted was the reality of the body and the intensity of its pleasures . . . consequently limiting the free choice of indeterminate individuals."[6] *Our* regime of truth seems to lead to distortion; we cannot admit a hermaphrodite for what even our own instincts tell us he/she is.

Regimes of truth thus set up categories to define guilt, sanity, health, and even gender. Foucault brought his considerable powers of eloquence to the task of describing the torture inflicted on prisoners, inmates in mental asylums, and even medical patients. Then he reminded his readers that the horrors he described were undertaken in the name of science and rationality, in efforts to "cure" insanity, disease, and criminality.

Philosophy, Foucault argued, becomes an accomplice in such repression. When the oppressed begin to ask, "Why do things have to be this way? Who gave *them* the right to imprison and torture *us?*" philosophers have often provided the oppressors with arguments to show, supposedly, that the system of repression did not rest simply on the interests of those in power but grew out of universal, objective standards of right and wrong, sanity and madness, truth and falsity. If the criminal is objectively immoral, the madman objectively insane, the means of punishment objectively just, the means of cure objectively effective, then challenges to the system can only be "irrational."

When reason thus becomes the accomplice of repression, Foucault argues, it is time to challenge the claims of reason, time to show how the very definitions of what is rational grow out of the interests of the powerful.[7] But the nature of his project raises obvious questions. Foucault attacks the very idea of standards of "good" and "true" because they can serve to support systems of repression. But the moral force of his attack depends on our recognition that such repression is a bad thing. That in turn seems to require some standard by which we can judge that freedom is better than repression—really better, objectively better—just the kind of judgment Foucault set out to undermine. "This puts Foucault in the paradoxical position of being unable to account for or to justify the sort of normative political judgments he makes all the time."[8] As Charles Taylor has written, "Foucault's analyses seem to bring *evils* to light; and yet he wants to distance himself from the suggestion which would seem inescapably to follow, that the negation or overcoming of those evils promotes a good."[9] One can claim to promote the good only if one claims to know what the good

is—but that demands the kind of criteria Foucault thinks so dangerous.[10]

Foucault appears to offer two sorts of answers to such puzzles.[11]
Sometimes he says that we can all recognize individual cases of injustice and repression without the need of any general theory—so we
ought to get on with fighting against them. For instance, a basically
sympathetic American interviewer discussing prison reform finally
grew impatient and demanded, "If you're in the tradition of unmask-
ing the origins of moral codes and our ethical practices, then where
do you stand? How can you have any values at all?" He focused the
question by asking, in practical terms, what those convinced by Foucault should *do*. Foucault replied, "Well, if you want to do something,
why don't you start trying to make San Quentin less horrendous?"[12]
Where prisoners are subjected to all sorts of brutality, one does not
need a philosophical theory as the foundation of an argument to prove
this is evil. Indeed, what philosophical starting point could be more
certain than the injustice of San Quentin? So stop looking for theoretical justifications, Foucault seems to say, and get on with the business
of practical reform.

Foucault himself was active in the French Information Group of
Prisons, which exposed particularly egregious conditions and worked
for their improvement.[13] He often emphasized the value of "local
knowledges," the concrete ways of dealing with particular problems
that grow out of particular situations, and he urged intellectuals to
concentrate on the problems within their own institutions—universities, hospitals, asylums—rather than looking for overall theories about
the nature of justice or society itself.[14] General theories are part of the
problem, not part of the solution: they always provide the excuse for
refusing to listen to alternative voices, for imposing the "expert's"
authority on the rest of us. Foucault sought instead "an insurgency of
subjugated knowledges" in opposition to the "tyranny of globalizing
discourse," "the kind of theoretical coronation of the whole which I
am so keen to avoid."[15] The sick person and the nurse know things
about illness to which the medical theorist will not listen; the delin-
quent has knowledge denied the criminologist.[16] But the very social
structures and technical language of theoretical discourse prevent
their ideas from being heard. Therefore, Foucault urges, "Reject theory and all forms of general discourse. This need for theory is still part
of the system we reject."[17]

A pragmatic, case-by-case reformism, however, would not satisfy
him. The ultimate goal of the Information Group of Prisons, he explained,

> was not to extend the visiting rights of prisoners to thirty minutes or to
> procure flush toilets for the cells, but to question the social and moral

distinction between the innocent and the guilty. . . . Confronted by this penal system, the humanist would say: 'The guilty are guilty and the innocent are innocent. Nevertheless the convict is a man like any other and society must respect what is human in him: consequently, flush toilets!' Our action, on the contrary, isn't concerned with the soul or the man *behind* the convict, but it seeks to obliterate the deep division that lies between innocence and guilt.[18]

Foucault really meant to challenge those fundamental distinctions between innocence and guilt. When terrorists hijacked a planeload of American tourists, and the press attacked them for endangering the lives of the innocent, for instance, Foucault quoted with approval Jean Genet's remark: After all, are people who can afford such an expensive vacation really innocent?[19]

That kind of radical challenge, however, needs some justification. And this is where Foucault runs into problems. Perhaps we do not need a "theory" to defend the claim that convicts deserve flush toilets. But we can do without a theory here because almost everyone in our society shares some common intuitions on such matters. Common-sense reformism, however, cannot push on to very radical challenges to the structure of our society, since at that point we will *not* all share common intuitions. A good many people would not think those American tourists had much to feel guilty for. If one wants to argue that they *were* guilty, then one needs some account of the nature of our society and the character of moral judgments—one needs, in short, something that looks very like a "theory."

Stanley Rosen has argued persuasively that truly radical political programs are always undergirded by the kind of "globalizing discourse" that Foucault claimed to oppose, and that Foucault tried to have it both ways—to launch a general, radical attack without a general theory behind it—only "by invoking the pathos of the sentimental left, a pathos to which Foucault, as the sober, even ruthless analyst of power, has no right."[20] "Why is struggle preferable to submission? Why ought domination to be resisted?" another perceptive critic, Nancy Fraser, asks. "Only with the introduction of normative notions of some kind could Foucault begin to answer this question."[21] Foucault believed that general principles always turn into an excuse for oppression. But only by appealing to such principles, it seems, could he justify the kind of radical challenge to current forms of oppression that he wanted to make.

Richard Rorty shares Foucault's suspicions of globalizing discourse and theoretical foundations. At least in some moods, however, he seems uninterested in making radical criticisms of his society, and therefore he avoids some of the inconsistencies that afflicted Foucault—at the price, to be sure, of a different set of problems.

Rorty has contrasted two possible roles for a philosopher. For the first, the philosopher is "the cultural overseer who knows everyone's common ground—the Platonic philosopher-king who knows what everybody else is really doing whether *they* know it or not." For the second, the philosopher is simply "the informed dilettante, the polypragmatic, Socratic intermediary between various discourses. In his salon, so to speak, hermetic thinkers are charmed out of their self-enclosed practices. Disagreements between disciplines and discourses are compromised or transcended in the course of the conversation."[22] Plato represents the first model, Socrates the second.

Rorty thinks philosophy has gone badly wrong in choosing Plato rather than Socrates as its ideal. We should not look for ultimate foundations of truth and values; we should simply encourage the conversation, ask tough questions, and try to get people to listen to one another. For pragmatists like himself, Rorty explains,

> the Socratic virtues—willingness to talk, to listen to other people, to weigh the consequences of our actions upon other people—are *simply* moral virtues. They cannot be inculcated nor fortified by theoretical research into essence. . . . The conversation which it is our moral duty to continue is *merely* our project, the European intellectual's form of life. It has no metaphysical nor epistemological guarantee of success. Further (and this is the crucial point) we do not know what "success" would mean except simply "continuance." We are not conversing because we have a goal, but because Socratic conversation is an activity which is its *own* end.[23]

Take all the most radical consequences of the philosophies of Sellars and Quine, of Kuhn and Feyerabend's interpretations of science, and put them all together: philosophy has no secure starting point; science is not drawing closer to anything called "the truth." Still, the conversation goes on, and the conversation is worth continuing.

Philosophers, Rorty thinks, have often modeled themselves after scientists—or rather, after an inaccurate picture of scientists. Better to think of themselves as being like poets or novelists. Western literature is not trying to "get somewhere"; we do not worry whether Shakespeare is "closer to the truth" than Aeschylus, James Joyce closer than Shakespeare. So philosophy—or the enterprise that will follow when philosophy comes to an end—should not look for progress or "the truth" but should find ways to encourage the widest and most open discussion—for its own sake. We must give up "dreams of an ultimate community which will have transcended the distinction between the natural and the social, which will exhibit a solidarity which is not parochial because it is the expression of an ahistorical human nature,"[24] and pursue "simply the desire for as much intersubjective agreement as possible, the desire to extend the reference of 'us' as far as we can."[25]

The question, as Rorty himself acknowledges, is whether the Socratic virtues can be defended except by Platonic means.[26] Just as
Foucault's critics asked why one should work for prison reform unless
there is a standard by which some things are better than others, so a
reader of Rorty can wonder why the Socratic virtues *are* virtues, why
this particular conversation is worth continuing.

Rorty assures us that in a strong sense of "relativism" he is not a
relativist at all. No one, he says, except "the occasional cooperative
freshman" really believes "that two incompatible opinions on an important topic are equally good." Those attacked as "relativists" are
merely "those who say that the grounds for choosing between such
opinions are less algorithmic than had been thought."[27] "If one drops
the idea that there is a common ground called 'the evidence,' one is
still far from saying that one person's web is as good as another." Rorty
insists that his position should disturb only those "who insist on quick
fixes."[28]

Suppose then that a patient reader, without need of a quick fix, seeks
Rorty's way of determining *why* one answer is better than another.
Sometimes he offers the kind of case-by-case pragmatism to which
Foucault also appealed on occasion. In concrete situations, he argues,
we recognize that conversation is better than violence, that listening
is better than shouting an opponent down. No philosophical argument
to "prove" such convictions could begin with premises more convincing than these convictions are themselves. "If anyone really believed
that the worth of a theory depends on its philosophical grounding,
then indeed they would be dubious about physics, or democracy, until
relativism in respect to philosophical theories had been overcome.
Fortunately, almost nobody believes anything of the sort."[29] So why
look for theoretical grounding for beliefs in which we are already
confident?

In the case of Foucault, however, I suggested that such appeal to
beliefs we all share fails when one tries to engage in radical social
criticism. Criticism that never challenges widely held beliefs is not very
radical. If Foucault did not want to accept the general outline of his
society's views, he faced the awkward task of criticizing them while
lacking any way at all of arguing that his own position was to be
preferred to those he wanted to attack. Rorty faces a similar problem.
On the one hand, in a famous—or perhaps notorious—passage worth
quoting at length, he admits that his views imply

> that when the secret police come, when the torturers violate the innocent,
> there is nothing to be said to them of the form "There is something within
> you which you are betraying. Though you embody the practices of a
> totalitarian society, which will endure forever, there is something beyond
> those practices which condemns you."

He then quotes with approval Sartre's remark:

> Tomorrow, after my death, certain people may decide to establish fascism, and the others may be cowardly or miserable enough to let them get away with it. At that moment, fascism will be the truth of man, and so much the worse for us.

As Rorty concludes:

> There is nothing deep down inside us except what we have put there ourselves, no criterion that we have not created in the course of creating a practice, no standard of rationality that is not an appeal to such a criterion, no rigorous argumentation that is not obedience to our own conventions.[30]

Rorty denied he was a relativist of the sort who believes that one web of belief is as good as another. But if *fascism* could be "the truth of man" if only "certain people . . . decide to establish" it, then it is hard to imagine what webs of belief Rorty *would* find less satisfactory.

Such rhetorical flourishes, however, may not represent Rorty's considered position.[31] Elsewhere he seems to defend the particular conversation of our society, our culture, in ways that strongly oppose relativism. The Vietnam War, he argues, led American intellectuals to abandon Dewey's pragmatic liberalism in hopes of finding some external standpoint from which to criticize society as a whole. But any such project—for reasons I discussed in earlier chapters—is doomed to failure.[32] Rather than moving to radical relativism, however, Rorty proposes returning to Dewey's pragmatic American liberalism: "There seems no particular reason why, after dumping Marx, we have to keep on repeating all the nasty things about bourgeois liberalism which he taught us to say."[33] In fact, "We should be more willing than we are to celebrate bourgeois capitalist society as the best policy actualized so far."[34]

Such remarks raise at least two sorts of problems—call them philosophical and political. *Philosophically,* one wonders what "the best" means in this context. If it means only "the best from the bourgeois capitalist point of view," then Rorty's point is trivial: presumably everyone finds that his or her own practices are best or they would already have changed them. But if "the best" means "the best not merely from our point of view, but really and truly the best," then it seems to embody the kind of claim Rorty has undercut.[35]

Politically, Rorty's reluctance to criticize Western bourgeois capitalism raises another set of questions. He is in fact some sort of progressive democrat; he says that Dewey's brand of pragmatism, which he adopts as his own, is a "philosophical defense of political liberalism—a way of rendering social democratic politics acceptable."[36] He is, he says, "astonished, and alarmed" to find himself lumped together with the neoconservatives.[37] Yet in some passages he starts to *sound* like a neoconservative himself, or at least as if he were offering, in Richard Bernstein's phrase, "little more than an ideological *apologia* for an old fashioned version of cold war liberalism dressed up in fashionable 'post-modern' discourse."[38] When not in a radically relativistic mood, Rorty seems to propose that the values and practices of contemporary Western bourgeois liberal society are just so obviously better than anything else available that he cannot see what the problem is.

The issue is not really Rorty's political views—when he lays out one version of his "political *credo*,"[39] I find myself in general agreement—but the way he cuts off certain kinds of discussion. Of course he *claims* to favor the widest possible conversation, but in practice the story often turns out differently. Rorty's personal inclinations often seem those of an old-fashioned rationalist, dismissive of traditional religion, of attempts to retrieve something of value from Aristotle's ethics, of claims to rescue insights from preliterate cultures—in short, of all those who want to recover something of value they think the Enlightenment lost. His own political standpoint views Marxism and Reaganism with roughly equal horror. As it happens, I agree with his politics and not with his rationalism, but I would certainly be interested in talking with him about both. Unfortunately, his resolute refusal to enter into anything like "philosophical" discourse makes it very hard to do that when one is in serious disagreement. Given the ways in which he has undercut any basis for *arguing* about fundamental principles, he can only dismiss or ridicule his opponents. Jeffrey Stout maintains that the "pithy little formulae" in which Rorty makes his most extreme claims should not be taken as summarizing his position.[40] Fair enough. But if I am correct, then at least some of Rorty's rhetorical style follows from his central beliefs: sarcasm really is a perfectly appropriate response to opponents if real argument is impossible.

Rorty himself acknowledges the problem, and in a way that connects his views to those of John Rawls. As noted in the preceding chapter, Rawls wrestled with the question of how his kind of liberal society should respond to someone like Ignatius Loyola, who holds that all other goods ought to yield to the dominant good of serving the glory of God. Rorty discusses the same issues and admits that

> in finding a dialectical stance to adopt toward Nietzsche or Loyola we liberal democrats are faced with a dilemma. To refuse to argue about what human beings should be like seems to show a contempt for the spirit of accommodation and tolerance which is essential to democracy. But it is not clear how to argue for the claim that human beings ought to be liberals rather than fanatics without being driven back upon a theory of human nature, upon philosophy.[41]

But Rorty has devoted much of his work to showing that such a theory is not possible. Therefore, like Rawls, he simply refuses to argue with such folk:

> We heirs of the Enlightenment think of enemies of liberal democracy like Nietzsche or Loyola as, to use Rawls' word, *mad*. We do so because there is no way to see them as fellow-citizens of our constitutional democracy, people whose life-plans might, given ingenuity and good will, be fitted in with those of other citizens. They are not crazy because they have mistaken the ahistorical nature of human beings. They are crazy because the limits of sanity are set by what *we* can take seriously. This in turn is determined by our upbringing, our historical situation.[42]

Given the abuse of psychiatric hospitals as arenas of punishment for political dissidents in the Soviet Union and elsewhere, the rhetoric that dismisses one's political opponents as "crazy" seems a bit scary—particularly when the only argument is, *"People like us* can't take that seriously."

Rhetorically, the use of "we" is one of Rorty's favorite devices, welcoming his readers into the in-group of sensible liberals. As Bernstein points out, it is a potentially dangerous technique:

> The standard form of intolerance is one where some group takes itself to be the measure of what is "rational" and excludes some other group, whether we speak of *"we* Greeks (versus barbarians), or *we* white South Africans," or *"we* white males." So despite Rorty's manifest pleas for extending the principle of tolerance, the latent content of what he says can lead to the worst forms of intolerance *unless* he is prepared to distinguish (even locally and historically) pernicious and benign forms of ethnocentric appeals.[43]

But making such distinctions requires the kind of argument Rorty does not think can be defended.

Rorty's rhetoric is different from that of Rawls or Habermas, but he too is, as he says, very much one of the "heirs of the Enlightenment." That heritage contains much worth admiring, and of course in some ways we are all the Enlightenment's heirs. One aspect of the Enlightenment vision Rorty seems to share with the writers discussed in the preceding chapter, however, is an intolerance of points of view that consciously grow out of particular communities, draw significantly from the authority of tradition, bring to bear the radical criticisms of some feminists or Marxists, or otherwise reject central elements of Enlightenment rhetoric. He just cannot imagine, it seems, engaging such tradition-bound folk or such radicals in serious conversation. To that extent, he seems the enemy of real pluralism.

Foucault turned out to be unable to sustain an argument that any set of values is better than any other. Rorty joins forces with the defenders of the Enlightenment, albeit without the ability to make a

philosophical argument for his position. Neither, therefore, opens the
door to genuinely pluralistic conversation in which people from very
different starting points can debate and sometimes really reach conclusions. How to do that will be the topic of the next chapter.

NOTES

1. The figure most obviously absent from this chapter is Jacques Derrida.
Many of the same questions I discuss in connection with Foucault and Rorty
would arise in his case, and they deal more directly with the moral issues I
wanted to address. I felt that, if I were to say anything at all about Derrida,
I would, to be fair, have to say so much that this would turn into a very different
book.

2. These themes run throughout Foucault's work, but his development is
a complicated story. I will be concentrating on his later work.

3. Michel Foucault, *Power/Knowledge: Selected Interviews and Other Writings,
1972–1977*, trans. Colin Gordon and others (New York: Pantheon Books,
1980), p. 131.

4. Mark Poster, *Foucault, Marxism and History* (Oxford: Polity Press, 1984),
pp. 95–96.

5. Michel Foucault, *The Order of Things: An Archaeology of the Human Sciences*
(New York: Vintage Books, 1973), p. xv.

6. Michel Foucault, intro., *Herculine Barbin: Being the Recently Discovered Memoirs of a Nineteenth-Century French Hermaphrodite*, trans. Richard McDougall (New
York: Pantheon Books, 1980), pp. vii–viii.

7. See, e.g., Michel Foucault, "On the Genealogy of Ethics," in Paul A.
Rabinow, *The Foucault Reader* (New York: Pantheon Books, 1984), p. 343.
Hilary Putnam has made the nice point that Foucault makes many of the
arguments for relativism one finds in anthropologists, but most anthropolo-
gists want us to respect the alternative rationalities of other cultures, while
Foucault wants to undermine the apparent rationality of our own (Hilary
Putnam, *Reason, Truth, and History*, pp. 161–162; Cambridge: Cambridge Uni-
versity Press, 1981).

8. Nancy Fraser, "Michel Foucault: A 'Young Conservative'?" *Ethics* 96
(1985), p. 172.

9. Charles Taylor, *Philosophical Papers*, vol. 2 (Cambridge: Cambridge University Press, 1985), p. 152.

10. Foucault writes what seem devastating exposés of certain appalling
medical practices but then insists, "This book has not been written in favor
of one kind of medicine as against another kind of medicine, or against medicine and in favor of an absence of medicine. It is a structural study that sets
out to disentangle the conditions of its history from the density of discourse,
as do others of my works" (Michel Foucault, *The Birth of the Clinic*, trans. A. M.
Sheridan, p. xix; London: Tavistock Publications, 1973).

11. For readings of Foucault that emphasize these two different sides, see
David Hoy, "Power, Repression, Progress: Foucault, Lukes, and the Frankfurt
School," *Triquarterly* 52 (1981), pp. 43–63; and Hubert L. Dreyfus and Paul A.

Rabinow, *Michel Foucault: Beyond Structuralism and Hermeneutics* (Chicago: University of Chicago Press, 1982). For a good statement of the issue, see Fraser, "Michel Foucault: A 'Young Conservative'?" p. 167. Near the very end of his life, Foucault seems to have shifted his views on these issues yet again, rejecting radical relativism, denying that he had ever said that knowledge and power were equivalent, and insisting that political regimes need to take questions of truth seriously. See Michel Foucault, "Le souci de la verité," *Magazine Littéraire*, no. 207 (May 1984), p. 18; and Peter Dews, *Logics of Disintegration* (London: Verso, 1987), pp. 218–219.

12. Dreyfus and Rabinow, *Michel Foucault: Beyond Structuralism and Hermeneutics*, p. 264.

13. See Poster, *Foucault, Marxism and History*, p. 155.

14. Foucault, *Power/Knowledge*, pp. 126, 85.

15. Ibid., pp. 81–83, 88.

16. Ibid., p. 82.

17. Michel Foucault, *Language, Counter-Memory, Practice*, trans. Donald F. Bouchard and Sherry Simon (Ithaca, N.Y.: Cornell University Press, 1977), p. 231.

18. Ibid., p. 227.

19. Ibid. Similarly, Foucault argues that in the time of Shakespeare and Cervantes madness and sanity remained "permeable," so that the madman could give us insights into a higher sanity. Modern psychiatry has drawn the lines more sharply, and Foucault wants to question its conclusions (Dews, *Logics of Disintegration*, pp. 181–182. See Michel Foucault, *Histoire de la folie à l'âge classique*, pp. 41–47; Paris: Editions Gallimard, 1972).

20. Stanley Rosen, *Hermeneutics as Politics* (Oxford: Oxford University Press, 1987), pp. 189–190.

21. Nancy Fraser, "Foucault on Modern Power: Empirical Insights and Normative Confusions," *Praxis International* 1 (1981), p. 283.

22. Richard Rorty, *Philosophy and the Mirror of Nature* (Princeton, N.J.: Princeton University Press, 1979), p. 317.

23. Richard Rorty, *Consequences of Pragmatism* (Minneapolis: University of Minnesota Press, 1982), p. 172.

24. Richard Rorty, "Solidarity or Objectivity?" in John Rajchman and Cornel West, eds., *Post-Analytic Philosophy* (New York: Columbia University Press, 1985), p. 4.

25. Ibid., p. 5.

26. Rorty, *Consequences of Pragmatism*, p. 172.

27. Ibid., p. 166.

28. Richard Rorty, "Pragmatism Without Method," in Paul Kurtz, ed., *Sidney Hook: Philosopher of Democracy and Humanism* (Buffalo, N.Y.: Prometheus Books, 1982), p. 263.

29. Rorty, *Consequences of Pragmatism*, p. 168.

30. Ibid., p. xlii.

31. Jeffrey Stout says that a "charitable" reading of Rorty must not give too central a place to his "pithy little formulae" (Jeffrey Stout, *Ethics After Babel*, p. 246; Boston: Beacon Press, 1988).

32. Richard Rorty, "Postmodern Bourgeois Liberalism," *Journal of Philosophy* 80 (1983), p. 588.

33. Rorty, *Consequences of Pragmatism*, p. 207.

34. Ibid., p. 210. Rorty adds, cryptically: "while regretting that it is irrelevant to most of the problems of most of the population of the planet."

35. Rorty has declared that "justification is relative to time and place and truth is not," and I therefore find it puzzling that he could agree with Sartre that under certain conditions fascism could be the *truth* for man. See Richard Rorty, "Realism and Reference," *The Monist* 59 (1976), p. 323.

36. Richard Rorty, "Le cosmopolitisme sans emancipation," *Critique* 41 (1985), p. 567.

37. Richard Rorty, "Thugs and Theorists," *Political Theory* 15 (1987), p. 565. He says he is reassured that he has "gotten as much flak from the right as from the left. . . . Had I not, I would have begun to fear that I had turned into a neo-conservative in my sleep, like Gregor Samsa" (ibid., p. 575 n. 5).

38. Richard J. Bernstein, "One Step Forward, Two Steps Back," *Political Theory* 15 (1987), p. 556. Other critics have been similarly pointed. Rorty is sometimes, David Tracy says, "an elegant spokesperson for the leisured classes" (David Tracy, *Plurality and Ambiguity*, p. 85; San Francisco: Harper & Row, 1987). Stanley Rosen writes, "Rorty's pleas for tolerance must strike the ears of the postmodern revolutionary as the posturing of an American Colonel Blimp" (Rosen, *Hermeneutics as Politics*, p. 187).

39. Rorty, "Thugs and Theorists," pp. 565–567.

40. Perhaps a contrast with Paul Feyerabend will make the point clearest. Rorty's analyses of epistemology lead, on the theoretical level, to conclusions much like Feyerabend's philosophy of science. But in practice, Feyerabend really does think we can learn from all sorts of people Rorty would dismiss as dangerous lunatics.

41. Richard Rorty, "The Priority of Democracy to Philosophy," pp. 31–32. I am quoting here from a widely circulated manuscript text. The essay will appear in Merrill Peterson and Robert Vaughan, eds., *The Virginia Statute of Religious Freedom* (Cambridge: Cambridge University Press, forthcoming). One assumes that "fanatics" is a descriptive term here; it is never very clearly defined.

42. Rorty, "The Priority of Democracy to Philosophy," p. 27. Later in the same essay, Rorty writes, "We do not conclude that Nietzsche or Loyola are [sic] crazy because they hold unusual views on certain 'fundamental' topics; rather, we conclude this only after extensive attempts at an exchange of political views have made us realize that we are not going to get anywhere" (ibid., p. 34). But what was the nature of those "extensive attempts"? James Cone has written of his impatience with white theologians who seem to be saying, "Unless you black people learn to think like us white folks, using our rules, then we will not listen to you" (James Cone, *God of the Oppressed*, p. 8; New York: Seabury Press, 1975). Rorty sometimes seems to make a parallel move. The Chinese or tribal people or Martians, he says, might make contributions to this ongoing conversation, but only "if they succeed in adapting themselves to our typically Western social-democratic aspirations" (Rorty, "Le cosmopolitisme sans emancipation," p. 570). But that really does lead us back to our starting point: anybody who doesn't think like "us" is crazy.

43. Bernstein, "One Step Forward, Two Steps Back," p. 550.

7

CONVERSATION

A pluralism open to voices of tradition

Now comes the hard part. It is easy to criticize appeals to some universal standard of rationality, appeals that seem to assume that the Enlightenment dream survives intact. It is easy to criticize various forms of radical relativism—the Wittgensteinian fideists' image of cultures as self-contained worlds that cannot interact, Foucault's self-destructive refusal to admit to taking a moral stand, Rorty's appeals to "what *we* can take seriously" as the standard of sanity. It is more difficult to describe a middle ground—in part because defense always comes harder than criticism, in part because the middle ground needs to be unsystematic, ad hoc, a work of *bricolage,* and any quick summary risks turning in spite of itself into a general theory. As Stanley Rosen has remarked, it is hard to offer a "coherent philosophical defense of moderation as moderation, or what might be called 'good-natured and liberal muddling through.' "[1]

Yet that middle ground should not seem all that exotic or mysterious, for we live most of our lives there. I will want to argue that a good many of our conversations about religion take place there, but the scope of such a middle ground is hardly confined to religious discussion. We meet, you and I, and begin a conversation. We soon discover that we are both Presbyterians, or liberal Democrats, or believers in "string theory" in contemporary physics, or whatever. Things begin to move more quickly, for we realize that we share a whole set of beliefs, and our conversation can assume them as common ground, as we go on to argue from there. Trying to prove matters that seem perfectly natural to both of us would seem odd and out of place, acting, as Aristotle says, "just like some students of philosophy, whose conclusions are more familiar and believable than the premises from which they draw them."[2]

On other occasions, we may discover that I am a religious believer, and religion has just never made any sense to you. Or that you are a defender of the current South African government. Or that I still share Einstein's doubts about much of quantum mechanics. We take a deep breath, realizing that, if the conversation is to continue, we will both at least have to take several steps back before we can find any common ground.

In either event, though, we need not appeal to *universal* principles, principles that the other person must share with us or we would dismiss that person as crazy or irrational. For instance, in arguing with a white South African Nationalist, I might first feel that we were separated by a veritable chasm. But we both stand, it turns out, in the tradition of Reformed Christianity. We share some assumptions about God's relation to creation, about an image of God present in all people. It would be bizarre to appeal to such principles in conversation with an atheist or a Buddhist, though in many ways I might feel I have more in common with them than with a South African Nationalist. These theological tenets are simply beliefs that these two persons, otherwise very different, happen to share. Still, they might provide a place for this particular conversation to begin.[3]

Beginning a conversation does *not* require suspending all our previous beliefs or agreeing to appeal only to premises that would be accepted by any "sane" person. Indeed, genuinely suspending all one's own beliefs—trying to wipe the slate clean—seems itself a recipe for insanity.[4] And the principle of appealing only to what would be accepted by any sane person seems, cases like Rawls and Rorty suggest, to lead to dismissing as "insane" those who do not share enough of our own cultural assumptions—the very opposite of tolerant pluralism.

This is not surprising. There may be—I am not sure—some beliefs general enough, or trivial enough, that no one has ever gotten round to doubting them. I cannot imagine an interesting conversation about substantive questions that began with such principles and nothing else. And I do not see the point of attempting such a conversation. If we found such a principle, maybe it *should* be questioned—some Newtonian assumptions about space and time, after all, would have been plausible candidates for such "universal" starting points until Einstein came along. Whether anyone has managed to doubt a given assumption really does not matter. You and I can admit that *we* begin with the assumptions *we* share, without making judgments about any proposition's special status or anyone else's sanity.[5]

Ever since Aristotle defined rhetoric as "the faculty of observing in any given case the available means of persuasion,"[6] rhetoricians have been making this kind of argument—often in spite of philosophers' suspicions. It is precisely when universal foundations come into question, when all the eternal verities have been discredited, Wayne Booth argues, that "rhetoric comes into its own" with a new set of questions:

> Who believes it? Why do they believe it? Do they *really* believe it? . . . What "rhetorical communities" can be discovered that may in fact unite seemingly warring factions, and what are the real conflicts that separate rhetorical communities based on conflicting assumptions?[7]

It is arguments like these that provide the lifeblood of democratic politics—building consensus, finding the common ground for a particular project.[8] By comparison, the insistence on finding principles that *all* sane people *must* share starts to look suspiciously totalitarian.

As Booth's analysis of rhetoric notes, rhetorical (or political) argument always takes place in some community—if only the ad hoc community of this particular conversation—and each community has a particular history. That history shapes the questions one asks, the assumptions one can make, and the arguments that will be persuasive. When we make decisions about public policy—on caring for the homeless, abortion, nuclear disarmament—then, as Alasdair MacIntyre points out, "the question posed in such actual debates is never: 'What code ought *I* as rational person to adopt?' but rather: 'How ought *we* as members of this particular community, sharing these particular beliefs, inheriting this particular moral tradition or traditions, to resolve this issue?' "[9]

Michael Walzer's *Spheres of Justice* offers many examples of how this kind of argument works in practice. Walzer rejects Rawls's attempt to find universally rational rules of justice.[10] To come up with those rules, after all, Rawls had to assume that people would put aside their beliefs about the good—the best kind of human life, the highest value in things—when designing the rules of distributive justice. Walzer protests that this does not make sense:

> Distributions can not be understood as the acts of men and women who do not yet have particular goods in their minds or in their hands. In fact, people already stand in a relation to a set of goods; they have a history of transactions, not only with one another but also with the moral and material world in which they live. Without such a history, which begins at birth, they wouldn't be men and women in any recognizable sense, and they wouldn't have the first notion of how to go about the business of giving, allocating, and exchanging goods.[11]

Walzer offers an example: Ancient Athens provided free public baths and gymnasiums for its citizens but did not provide anything like our unemployment insurance or social security. We provide the latter but not the former.[12] As Athenian society had developed, good physical condition was important to one's role as citizen-soldier, and the baths and gymnasiums were important centers of political discussion. *In that society,* therefore, it would have been unjust to close the gym-

nasiums to citizens who could not afford a substantial annual fee—it
would have made life considerably more difficult for them and significantly decreased their participation in the political debate of the community. It does not follow that contemporary American social
democrats should move public baths and gymnasiums to the top of
their political agenda. *As our society has developed,* providing such facili-
ties would generally seem an odd use of public resources:

> There are strong arguments to be made that, under given historical
> conditions, such-and-such a program should be adopted. But these are
> not arguments about individual rights, they are arguments about the
> character of a particular community. . . . Only its culture, its character,
> its common understandings can define the "wants" that are to be pro-
> vided for. . . . In a world of particular cultures, competing conceptions
> of the good, scarce resources, elusive and expansive needs, there isn't
> going to be a single formula, universally applicable.[13]

Our "rights," Walzer therefore insists, "follow from shared conceptions of social goods; they are local and particular in character."[14] In
one society, severe criminal penalties against the production or con-
sumption of wine might seem a heroic, if perhaps misguided, attempt
to bring alcoholism and drunken driving under control; in another
context, one would recognize it as part of a governmental attempt to
stamp out the Catholic Church.[15] To some people from developed
countries with pension plans in place, it can seem obvious that developing countries ought to discourage their citizens from having more
than one or two children. But in a society with high infant mortality
where one's children provide the only support in old age, having only
one or two children can, quite apart from anything else, exact a severe
practical hardship.

No universal principle dictates what is entailed by a "right" to drink
wine or have lots of children without some penalty; the consequences
of penalizing such activities depend on the practices and beliefs of a
given culture. Arguments about such matters, however, are neither
impossible nor utterly opaque to those who stand outside the culture
in question. If we take the time to learn enough about the relevant
context, we can all understand such arguments about ancient Athens,
Mexico in the 1920s, or a contemporary third world country—but we
do so by recognizing how the arguments work within a given tradition.

Such reference to tradition does not mean that our moral views
cannot change and develop. Quite the contrary: Alasdair MacIntyre
nicely defines a "tradition" as "an historically extended, socially embodied argument,"[16] and arguments, after all, do sometimes change
people's minds. A tradition is itself a pluralistic affair, and some values
or practices within a tradition often raise questions about other values
or practices: "If we say we believe this, then why have we always done

things this way?" "If we believe that everyone is endowed with life and liberty, then why do we permit slavery?" As Jeffrey Stout points out, the first abolitionists did not suddenly break through all cultural assumptions to see the Pure Moral Law which declares slavery to be wrong. They saw the incoherence of the particular arguments their compatriots had been making in favor of slavery and began to realize that some of their basic values implied opposition to it. They could criticize their own tradition while still standing within it.[17] The encounter with new situations or different traditions often provides the occasion for challenges to elements of one's own tradition. But we never question everything at once or in a vacuum; if we did, we would suddenly not be able to argue at all.[18]

The role of tradition in moral discourse may seem relatively uncontroversial, but MacIntyre goes on to argue that "Which scientific theory is better?" is as tradition-bound a question as "What is just?"[19] All the arguments I mentioned in chapters 2 and 3 come into play here: we cannot appeal to theory-neutral sense-data; we cannot find neat mechanical devices for choosing between theories. But, as noted in chapter 3, contrary to what Thomas Kuhn's rhetoric might sometimes suggest, we do not throw out the past and start from scratch in a "scientific revolution."

MacIntyre insists, in fact, that we can evaluate scientific theories only in the context of a tradition, a story about the history of science. We find a new theory persuasive when it enables us to tell a better story: to place the old theory in a narrative in which we can explain why people believed it and then show how it led to internal inconsistencies resolved by the new theory.[20] Conversely, a theory endures to the extent that it resists attempts to fit it plausibly into another theory's story.[21]

Consider two examples: Aristotle and Galileo. Suppose one asks: "Was Aristotle right? Do all things really have four causes: efficient, formal, material, and final?" Without some context, it is hard to know how even to think about giving an answer. One may not want to say, "Yes, there are four causes," but one does not want to say that Aristotle was wrong, exactly, either.

Reading Book Alpha of Aristotle's *Metaphysics,* however, does help us make a different sort of judgment. Aristotle looks at his predecessors and shows how each of them was trying to explain the cause of things but they meant different things by "cause." When Thales talked about water, he meant "the stuff everything was made from"; when Anaxagoras talked about Mind, he meant "the force that causes motion"; and so on. Aristotle suggests that all these are appropriate, but different, ways of thinking about the causes of things. As MacIntyre puts it, "Aristotle's peculiar achievement was first to provide a framework of thought within which both the achievements and the limitations of his predecessors could be identified and evaluated and, second, in so doing, to transcend those limitations."[22] We may still not be sure how to answer the question, "Are there really four causes?" but we are sure that Aristotle had advanced beyond, produced a better theory of causation than, his predecessors.

Similarly, while we often think that Galileo was a great scientist, and *therefore* has an important place in the history of science, MacIntyre wants to argue that Galileo was an important scientist precisely *because* he had an important place in the history of science. He was great because "he, for the first time, enables the work of all his predecessors to be evaluated by a common set of standards," because with his work, and only then, "the history of late medieval science can finally be cast into a coherent narrative."[23] "How true are Galileo's theories?" asked in isolation, becomes a very puzzling question. But if the question is, "Do Galileo's theories represent an advance on those of his predecessors?" one can answer "Yes" with some confidence—because they help us see the pattern of the earlier theories, and we can tell a persuasive story of how they lead forward. But that kind of argument is even possible only in the context of the earlier tradition.[24]

At the end of chapter 4, I noted that very different cultures can and do interact without having to find universally acceptable starting points. Two persons find what *they* happen to share; they ask questions that arise out of their own particular histories and now the interaction of those histories. In this chapter, I am really only broadening the scope of those conclusions. They do not apply only to the dialogue between two cultures an anthropologist might study. The same kinds of moves get made in debates in the history of science or political arguments—or, as we will see in more detail, in religious discussions. This is, in fact, how people starting from very different assumptions characteristically argue—without either appealing to standards of universal rationality or finding themselves unable to communicate at all.

The most sensitive and developed account that I know concerning argument from within tradition, the kind of middle ground I have been trying to describe in this chapter, is Hans-Georg Gadamer's hermeneutics. In thinking about how we interpret texts, Gadamer has produced a nuanced model for serious conversation, a model that takes tradition seriously.[25]

Gadamer often defined his own position by contrasting it with those of his predecessors, and in questions of how to interpret a text he recognized Schleiermacher as his greatest predecessor. Schleiermacher's hermeneutics taught that the purpose of interpreting a text is to recover the intention or meaning of the author. If I am reading Plato's dialogues, according to Schleiermacher, I try to figure out, "What was Plato thinking when he wrote this?" Gadamer disagrees.

The ordinary purpose of reading a text, he says, is to learn about its subject matter. I read Richard Ellmann's biography of James Joyce to learn about Joyce, not about the mental processes of Richard Ellmann. I read Richard Feynman's lectures on physics to learn about physics, not about Feynman's psychology. Sometimes, of course, I may use the text as a historical source about its author (Gibbon's *Decline and Fall* helps us understand the eighteenth century as well as ancient Rome), or, faced with a puzzling passage, I may say, "What can the author have been thinking when she wrote this?" But to mention such examples is to recognize them as exceptions to our usual procedure.[26]

If we read texts for the sake of their subject matter, Gadamer says—drawing on the hermeneutic tradition of Heidegger and earlier philosophers—then we must bring questions and assumptions to our reading. The Enlightenment project was to overcome prejudice. We were taught to put our assumptions and biases aside and look at a question or read a text afresh. Gadamer denies that we can do it, or that we should try; he attacks the Enlightenment "prejudice against prejudices."[27] We always approach a text with assumptions, biases, particular questions. "In fact, the historicity of our existence entails that prejudices, in the literal sense of the word, constitute the initial directedness of our whole ability to experience. . . . They are simply conditions whereby we experience something."[28] Imagine picking up Ellmann's biography of Joyce with no expectation that the book was about a novelist rather than a chemist, no interest in Joyce, no knowledge of modern literature, no confidence that this was written in standard English and not a secret code—leave out *all* the "prejudices" and it becomes impossible to imagine how I could read the book at all, or why I would want to.

We always begin at a point in history, with a set of assumptions, within what Gadamer calls a "horizon." "The horizon is the range of vision that includes everything that can be seen from a particular vantage point. Applying this to the thinking mind, we speak of narrowness of horizon, of the possible expansion of horizon, of the opening up of new horizons, etc."[29] But we always stand somewhere, and where we stand affects what we can see.

Still, horizons are not fixed. I bring my questions to a text, but the text may give rise to new questions. It may surprise me. "Whoever wants to understand a text is rather prepared to let it say something to him. Hence a hermeneutically schooled consciousness must be sensitive to the otherness of the text from the beginning."[30] To be sure, I begin with prejudices, but "this formulation certainly does not say that we are enclosed within a wall of prejudices and only let through the narrow portals those things that can produce a pass saying, 'Nothing new will be said here.' Instead, we welcome just that guest who

promises something new to our curiosity."[31] Why read a text if we are
confident that our thinking will be utterly unchanged when we have
finished?

In serious reading, then, something happens that Gadamer calls a
"fusion of horizons."[32] I do not get out of my own skin and see things
from within someone else's "horizon," but in confronting a text with
a different point of view, I may reflect on my own previous assumptions
and change a bit. At one level, all of this is trivial common sense: we
start somewhere, but serious reading can help us move somewhere
else. But Gadamer argues that it has some perhaps surprising implications.

For one thing, the "meaning" of a text is different for each interpreter. "The actual meaning of a text, as it speaks to the interpreter,
is not dependent on the occasion represented by the author and his
original public . . . for the meaning is also determined by the historical
situation of the interpreter, and thus by the whole of the objective
course of history. . . . The meaning of a text goes beyond its author,
not only occasionally but always."[33] I bring my set of questions and
assumptions to a text, and its otherness challenges me to think again.
Neither my assumptions by themselves nor the text by itself shapes
what ought to happen in a good reading, but rather the interaction of
the two. "The interpreter dealing with a traditional text seeks to apply
it to himself. But this does not mean that the text is given for him as
something universal, that he understands it as such and only after-
wards uses it for particular applications. . . . He must not seek to
disregard himself and his particular hermeneutical situation. He must
relate the text to his situation, if he wants to understand it at all."[34]
And therefore, "every age has to understand a transmitted text in its
own way, for the text is part of the whole of the tradition in which the
age takes an objective interest and in which it seeks to understand
itself."[35]

All of this is to say what I began to say in chapter 4. We cannot find
an Archimedean point, a universal standard of rationality. On the
other hand, we are not utterly imprisoned within our own current
horizons. In a particular conversation, we learn from a particular conversation partner, in a way shaped by our own previous assumptions
as well as by the insights of the person to whom we speak. As Gadamer
put it:

> Discussion bears fruit when a common language is found. Then the
> participants part from one another as changed beings. The individual
> perspectives with which they entered upon the discussion have been
> transformed, and so they are transformed themselves. This, then, is a
> kind of progress—not the progress proper to research in regard to which
> one cannot fall behind but a progress that always must be renewed in the
> effort of our living.[36]

Gadamer thus painted a very optimistic picture of the way conversation with tradition can expand our horizons. Jürgen Habermas challenged him with the reminder that reliance on tradition can also narrow those horizons, and the debate that resulted was one of the significant events in recent German philosophy. As in many debates, each side distorted the other's position from time to time, and the articles and reviews written back and forth raised far more issues than I can even summarize here.[37] To oversimplify, Habermas thought that Gadamer considered only the *positive* role of tradition. Gadamer, after all, repeatedly talks about both the way my prejudices *help* shape my reading of a text and the way in which texts from the past *help* me expand my own horizons. But sometimes, Habermas says, tradition *oppresses:* the tradition of interpretation gets in the way of a fresh reading of the text; the authority of an honored text prevents us from thinking through a problem for ourselves.[38] For example, some medieval scientists had such an admiration for the authority of Aristotle and Galen that they badly distorted and ignored new empirical evidence to avoid conflict with these "authorities." Similarly, some doctrinaire Soviet Marxists go through considerable intellectual contortions to defend Lenin's interpretations as the correct reading of Marx's texts. Such stultification grows out of a mind-set that always wants to respect tradition. Habermas, of course, thinks that his own critical theory encourages a more democratic, open context in which each voice has an equal chance to be heard—the "ideal speech situation"—and that such a context permits the kind of questioning of tradition that moves inquiry forward.

Not surprisingly, Gadamer denied having opposed all questioning of tradition. His respect for authority, he said, certainly did not mean accepting everything that comes to us out of the past.[39] Rather, he wanted to make at least two commonsense points. (1) When we begin any process of learning, we have to place some initial trust in "authorities"—in parents, teachers, or experts.[40] First-year physics students have to assume that their teachers and textbooks know something useful about the subject if they are ever to get to know enough physics to ask really intelligent questions about what they have been taught. (2) Taking a voice out of the past seriously often provides a useful way of challenging the assumptions of the present—of expanding our horizons. If I assume that Plato or Augustine or Lao-tzu can represent only the dead hand of tradition, then I deprive myself of valuable resources for questioning the way I and my contemporaries look at things. As I argued in chapter 5, Habermas and Rawls both close their horizons to some of the voices of tradition and therefore deprive modernity of some perspectives that might help it see itself afresh.

Of course we ought to question the past, Gadamer insisted: his hermeneutical model implied as much from the start. But when initial trust in a tradition helps us learn enough to ask intelligent questions, or when past texts help us ask hard questions about present beliefs, then respect for tradition liberates rather than oppresses—a possibility Gadamer thought Habermas never acknowledged.[41]

No doubt each participant in this debate exaggerated the position of his opponent. As Paul Ricoeur has written, "For Habermas, Gadamer is an old gentleman who must vote on the right, and so hermeneutics represents the conservatism of the past in a kind of museum. Gadamer, on the other hand, sees Habermas as the radical who made concessions to the students and was punished for it."[42] Beyond the polemics, though, important issues are at stake—important, certainly, for the model of pluralistic conversation I have been trying to develop.

To start with, as a supporter of Habermas might point out, *any* account of how we talk with one another has to assume *some* characteristics of viable conversation. If two people are locked in separate rooms with no means of communication between them, they cannot have a conversation. If one person simply yells at another, without allowing any interruptions, that really does not look like a "conversation" either. But then start extending the argument further by small steps: Suppose one person does not force the other into silence by yelling but by threat of force or intimidation. Suppose the intimidation consists merely of the intimidating presence of a "recognized authority." Until what point would we think such factors were still preventing "real conversation"? If we expand and clarify our list of conditions far enough, do we end up with something like Habermas' "ideal speech situation" after all?[43]

One quick answer to that question would distinguish between basic elements that are simply part of what everybody *means* by "conversation" and additional features that might be part of the conversational ideal of one philosopher but not of another. But that will not work. Remember Quine's criticisms of the analytic/synthetic distinction, reviewed in chapter 2: it turned out that it just is not possible to draw a sharp line between analytic properties that are part of a thing's definition and synthetic ones that are discovered empirically.

Still, the absence of sharp lines does not always leave us unable to make any distinctions at all. One cannot draw a precise line in the dirt where the Rocky Mountains begin, but the topography of Colorado is nevertheless different from that of Kansas. Similarly, it may not be possible to define exactly where to draw the line distinguishing features that are a necessary part of what we mean by conversation, but we can recognize that at one end of a continuum are such things as the physical possibility of communication, while such things as following Robert's Rules of Order lie at the other end. Without characteristics at the first end, we cannot imagine how a conversation would be possible at all, while characteristics at the other end strike us as some-body's idea of a feature it would be nice for conversations to have—but no more than that. When Habermas views all roles for authority or tradition with suspicion, I think he has moved toward the second end of that continuum. He is not defining the necessary features of conver-sation; he is trying to impose one particular ideal of conversation on the rest of us.

Still, might it not be a worthy ideal? After all, the use of force and intimidation does often inhibit serious conversation. We have all seen professors, distinguished lecturers, or elders of the tribe curtly dismiss some nervous youth who, on reflection, had a very good point to make. Should we not therefore attack authority and tradition and encourage equality for the sake of the best conversation?

But at what price? In chapter 5, I tried to make the case that ideals like those of Habermas can do more than inhibit conversation: they can rule some parties—those whose worldviews are strongly shaped by the traditions and authorities of their own communities—out of the con-versation before it even begins, "effectively precluding," as Alasdair MacIntyre puts it, "the voices of tradition outside liberalism from being heard."[44] The goal is pluralism, the most open conversation possible. Repressive tradition can inhibit it—but so can the suspicion of tradition. As Max Horkheimer and Theodor Adorno insisted, En-lightenment can become totalitarian too.

So in the end I return to what, at the beginning of this chapter, was called "good-natured and liberal muddling through." We should be suspicious of authority, but we should also be suspicious of the systemat-ic suspicion of authority. "The time is past," Jeffrey Stout has writ-ten, "when theology can reign as queen of the sciences, putting each other voice in the conversation in its place and articulating, with a conviction approaching certainty, the presuppositions all share." Christianity "must take its place among the other voices, as often to be corrected as to correct."[45] That is the warning Habermas sounds to Christianity or any other tradition. My conviction (and I think Stout would agree with it) is that Enlightenment modernity *also* can no longer reign as queen of the sciences and *also* must take its place as one voice among others. *That* is the point on which Gadamer seems clearer than Habermas. We have to find ways to avoid the stultifying force of tradition without refusing to listen to the voices of tradition altogether. We have to find a middle ground. What all this means in practice can be sorted out only case by case, and in subsequent chap-ters I will try to say more about some of the cases that face contempo-rary Christian theology.

In the meantime, it could be argued that I have thus far avoided the most basic question of all. It is all very well to worry about the rules and conditions of good conversation—but why have conversation at

* But he has depicted the Enlightenment as total; human to make this judgment. ∴ it should be, " as so far as it is totalitarian . . . . "

all? In particular, why should adherents of one tradition feel any need to talk with those who do not stand within their community?

This is itself an ethical question, and like other ethical questions— given everything said so far—it can be answered only in the context of particular traditions. There is no universal rule of rationality which specifies why everyone should talk with everyone else. Christians certainly have reasons internal to our own tradition for seeking out members of other religious communities—or of none—for serious dialogue. Scripture teaches that all human beings are made in the image and likeness of God (Gen. 1:26). A prophet taught ancient Israel that the same God who brought Israel out of Egypt also brought the Philistines from Caphtor and the Arameans from Kir (Amos 9:7), and Acts reports that Paul told the Athenians that the God they worshiped at the altar bearing the inscription "To an unknown god" was the God Christians proclaim (Acts 17:23). Repeatedly, the Bible cites righteous folk from other traditions as examples from whom we can learn: Job, the centurion of Capernaum (Matt. 8:10), that other centurion at the crucifixion (Mark 15:39).

Reflecting on such passages, and on the logic of their faith and the shape of Christian life as they have experienced it, Christian communities have recognized the importance of conversation with "outsiders" for their own life, health, and faithfulness. Vatican II, for instance, called Roman Catholics to "sincere and prudent dialogue" with unbelievers on the grounds that the church "can provide no more eloquent proof of its solidarity with the entire human family with which it is bound up, as well as its respect and love for that family, than by engaging with it in conversation."[46] The Presbyterian Church's Confession of 1967 noted, "Repeatedly God has used the insight of non-Christians to challenge the church to renewal."[47] Other Christian texts include similar passages.

Indeed, the history of the Christian tradition provides evidence of the value of such conversations precisely for Christianity's own faithful development: from patristic lessons learned from Plato to Aquinas' dependence on the Islamic interpreters of Aristotle to the ways Marxists have helped Christians rediscover their call to social witness to the lessons Martin Buber taught a whole generation of Christian theologians. David Tracy offers a helpful list of some possibilities for wider interreligious dialogue: Christians can learn from Buddhists to rediscover the power of Paul's talk of "self-emptying"; Christian ideas of grace can help Pure Land Buddhists clarify their differences with other schools of Buddhism; Buddhists can learn from Christian emphases on social justice to rethink their understanding of what "compassion" means; adherents of many other traditions can learn from a neo-Confucian like Wang Yang-ming strategies for combining political and

mystical elements of faith.[48] Sometimes of course Christians—like anyone else—need to know when to disagree with their conversation
partners, but in these cases and many more Christian theologians
would have been less good at their own tasks had they listened less
attentively and thoughtfully to non-Christian voices. No need to find
universally justifiable reasons to commend such conversations to
Christians: the logic of our own tradition and our own historical experience provide reason enough.

Other traditions will have their own sets of reasons for engaging in
such conversations, and genuine pluralism ought to allow for conversations between people who enter the conversation for quite different
reasons. No doubt some folk's resort to force will constitute such a
danger to life or liberty that we will want to restrain them before we
even begin to converse. No doubt some folk will not want to join the
conversation—not some particular conversation, or perhaps not *any*
conversation with those outside their own tradition. There is no way
of forcing them to do so. Those who believe in founding conversations
on universally defensible ethical principles may claim that they at any
rate can say, "But at least we know they *ought* to join our conversation.
Since they are not part of your tradition, and you justify joining conversations on reasons internal to that tradition, you cannot make such a
claim."

Christians believe, however, that all people, whether they know it or
not, are made in the image of God and that the gospel message comes
to the whole world. They therefore think that everyone ought to join
in conversation with them. People from other traditions will have their
own reasons for believing in the universal value of conversation. Admittedly, in every case, the reasons will be internal to some tradition—
just as the reasons Habermas would give are internal to the tradition
of Enlightenment modernity. There are no reasons not internal to
some tradition.

No one can guarantee success in persuading everyone. If anything,
those who do not demand acceptance of their assumptions right at the
start as the definition of "sanity" or the price of not being dismissed
as "backward" may have better luck at convincing the initially suspicious to join the conversation. They will at any rate manifest greater
sympathy for genuine pluralism.

Those who admit they argue out of a tradition—as I have been
claiming Christians should—can nevertheless believe in the truth of
their claims: truth not just for them but for everyone. They too can
believe that everyone really *should* join the conversation. When Christians say that everyone is made in God's image, for instance, and talk
about the manifestation of that image in human rationality, they really
mean to set out a ground for conversation that applies to all people.

In the context of the kind of pluralism I have been describing, how can one make that kind of claim to truth? That needs to be the topic of a new chapter.

NOTES

1. Stanley Rosen, *Hermeneutics as Politics* (Oxford: Oxford University Press, 1987), p. 138.

2. Aristotle, *The Rhetoric* 3.17, 1418a, trans. W. Rhys Roberts (New York: Modern Library, 1984), p. 212.

3. See William Werpehowski, "*Ad Hoc* Apologetics," *Journal of Religion* 66 (1986), pp. 282–301. Jeffrey Stout makes the point well: "If there is no reservoir of reasons that does not belong to a particular social and historical setting, and the available reasons tend to vary somewhat from setting to setting, it would be naive to expect a single argument to be equally compelling to everybody" (Jeffrey Stout, "The Voice of Theology in Contemporary Culture," in Mary Douglas and Steven M. Tipton, eds., *Religion and America: Spirituality in a Secular Age*, p. 252; Boston: Beacon Press, 1983).

4. "To say to oneself or to someone else 'Doubt all your beliefs here and now' . . . is an invitation not to philosophy but to mental breakdown, or rather to philosophy as a means of mental breakdown" (Alasdair MacIntyre, "Epistemological Crises, Dramatic Narrative, and the Philosophy of Science," *The Monist* 60 [1977], p. 462). The same point gets made in Wittgenstein's *On Certainty* and the anti-Cartesianism of C. S. Peirce.

5. Alvin Plantinga has defined the task of natural theology as showing "that some of the central beliefs of theism follow deductively or inductively from propositions that are obviously true or accepted by nearly every sane man . . . together with propositions that are self-evident or necessarily true" (Alvin Plantinga, *God and Other Minds*, p. 4; Ithaca, N.Y.: Cornell University Press, 1967). George Mavrodes notes, "It is perhaps significant . . . that the author gives no reason whatever as to *why* the natural theologian should construe his task in terms of these limitations." So many of the beliefs we hold with greatest confidence and find most widely shared, Mavrodes points out, are not really necessary truths or "accepted by nearly every sane man." Why should one accept such "a limit upon his own intellectual life"? (George I. Mavrodes, *Belief in God*, pp. 46–47; New York: Random House, 1970).

6. Aristotle, *The Rhetoric* 1.2, 1355b, p. 24. A number of philosophers have recently rediscovered Aristotle's *Rhetoric* with great enthusiasm as the classic text for the kind of argument I am making. I am a bit more cautious. Aristotle indeed defends the methods of rhetoric, but he also sometimes says that rhetoric is distinctly second-best, the kind of argument suitable to the uneducated who cannot follow more rigorous analysis. See *Rhetoric* 1.2, 356b–357a, p. 26, and 2.22, 1395b–1396a, p. 140.

7. Wayne Booth, *Modern Dogma and the Rhetoric of Assent* (Notre Dame, Ind.: University of Notre Dame Press, 1974), p. xiv. For a defense of the rhetorical tradition in contrast to philosophy, see Hans Blumenberg, "An Anthropological Approach to the Contemporary Significance of Rhetoric," in Kenneth

Baynes, James Bohman, and Thomas McCarthy, eds., *After Philosophy: End or Transformation?* (Cambridge, Mass.: MIT Press, 1987), p. 436.

8. "Democratic politics is an encounter among people with differing interests, perspectives, and opinions—an encounter in which they reconsider and mutually revise opinions and interests, both individual and common. It happens always in a context of conflict, imperfect knowledge, and uncertainty, but where community action is necessary. The resolutions achieved are always more or less temporary, subject to reconsideration, and rarely unanimous. What matters is not unanimity but discourse" (Hanna Fenichel Pitkin and Sara M. Shumer, "On Participation," *Democracy* 2 [1982], pp. 47–48; quoted in Richard J. Bernstein, *Beyond Objectivism and Relativism*, p. 223; Philadelphia: University of Pennsylvania Press, 1983). See also Edward H. Levi, *Introduction to Legal Reasoning* (Chicago: University of Chicago Press, 1949), esp. pp. 1–2.

9. Alasdair MacIntyre, "Moral Rationality, Tradition, and Aristotle," *Inquiry* 26 (1983), p. 451.

10. Michael Walzer, *Spheres of Justice: A Defense of Pluralism and Equality* (New York: Basic Books, 1983), pp. 4–5.

11. Ibid., p. 8.

12. Ibid., p. 67. Walzer rarely makes mistakes, but I think it was perhaps Rome rather than Athens that provided free public baths. But the illustration makes his point, in any event.

13. Ibid., pp. 78–79.

14. Ibid., p. xv.

15. Graham Greene's novel *The Power and the Glory* draws its background from such a policy under a Marxist government in one state in Mexico.

16. Alasdair MacIntyre, *After Virtue: A Study in Moral Theory* (Notre Dame, Ind.: University of Notre Dame Press, 1980), p. 207.

17. Jeffrey Stout, *Ethics After Babel* (Boston: Beacon Press, 1988), p. 27.

18. See MacIntyre, "Moral Rationality, Tradition, and Aristotle," p. 451; and Alasdair MacIntyre, "Relativism, Power and Philosophy," *Proceedings and Addresses of the American Philosophical Association* 59 (1985), p. 19.

19. "Only since the year 1900—particularly since 1905—has it become finally evident that intellectual judgments and concepts are exposed to an historico-cultural variety, or relativity, comparable to that of legal practices, moral beliefs, and social institutions. As we now realize, the numbering-procedures, color-nomenclatures, cosmogonies, and technologies of different societies rest on principles that differ as radically as those underlying different moral attitudes and social organizations. Meanwhile, within the citadel of physical science itself, the classical system of Euclid-cum-Newton no longer claims the unique intellectual authority it preserved for much of the nineteenth century. So the chief barrier to extending the relativist argument from practical conduct to intellectual concepts has been removed" (Stephen E. Toulmin, *Human Understanding*, p. 49; Princeton, N.J.: Princeton University Press, 1972).

20. MacIntyre, "Epistemological Crises, Dramatic Narrative, and the Philosophy of Science," p. 467. I suspect it is because they make an effort to fit religion into a narrative that explains why people came to believe it that the critiques of religion from Marxists or Freudians often have more power than more carefully argued ones from some analytic philosophers.

21. Ibid., pp. 455, 460.

22. Alasdair MacIntyre, *Whose Justice? Which Rationality?* (Notre Dame, Ind.: University of Notre Dame Press, 1988), p. 143. See Aristotle, *Metaphysics*, trans. Richard Hope (Ann Arbor, Mich.: University of Michigan Paperbacks, 1960), Book Alpha, esp. secs. 3–7.

23. MacIntyre, "Epistemological Crises, Dramatic Narrative, and the Philosophy of Science," p. 460.

24. "Progress in rationality is achieved only from a point of view. And it is achieved when the adherents of that point of view succeed to some significant degree in elaborating ever more comprehensive and adequate statements of their positions through the dialectical procedure of advancing objections which identify incoherences, omissions, explanatory failures, and other types of flaw and limitation in earlier statements of them, of finding the strongest arguments available for supporting those objections, and then of attempting to restate the position so that it is no longer vulnerable to those specific objections and arguments" (MacIntyre, *Whose Justice? Which Rationality?* p. 144).

Stephen Toulmin's analysis of scientific traditions makes a similar point. Scientists within a particular discipline, he says, set goals, rules, and ideals that define what counts as "good physics" or "good biology." Conflicts within this disciplinary matrix generate a scientific crisis—as, for instance, when the elegance, simplicity, and explanatory power of some theories of quantum mechanics conflicted with the traditional scientific ideal of causal determinism. At such moments, Toulmin says, scientific debate becomes like a debate over constitutional interpretation before the Supreme Court, as each side appeals to precedents, consequences, and public policy. Their place within a tradition is what makes such arguments possible. (Toulmin, *Human Understanding*, pp. 317, 238–241.)

25. In his earlier work, Gadamer sought to defend the independence of the "human sciences" by arguing that his insights showed their legitimate differences in method from the natural sciences; that argument presupposed something like a positivistic account of natural science. Later on, however, Gadamer acknowledged the point I have often noted here: that contemporary philosophy of science helps us see the same issues arising in natural science. See Hans-Georg Gadamer, *Reason in the Age of Science,* trans. Frederick G. Lawrence (Cambridge, Mass.: MIT Press, 1981), pp. 164–166; and the "Nachwort" to the 3rd ed. of *Wahrheit und Methode* (Tübingen: J. C. B. Mohr [Paul Siebeck], 1972), pp. 521–523.

26. Hans-Georg Gadamer, *Truth and Method*, trans. Garrett Barden and John Cumming (New York: Seabury Press, 1975), pp. 148–153, 263–264.

27. Ibid., p. 240. See also Hans-Georg Gadamer, *Philosophical Hermeneutics*, trans. David E. Linge (Berkeley and Los Angeles: University of California Press, 1976), p. 51.

28. Gadamer, *Philosophical Hermeneutics*, p. 9.

29. Gadamer, *Truth and Method*, p. 269.

30. Ibid., p. 238.

31. Gadamer, *Philosophical Hermeneutics*, p. 9.

32. Gadamer, *Truth and Method*, p. 273.

33. Ibid., pp. 263–264.

34. Ibid., p. 289.

35. Ibid., p. 263.

36. Gadamer, *Reason in the Age of Science*, pp. 110–111. "Even if you augment your own culture's collective wisdom about morality by comparative study of distant cultures, so that you have been persuaded to abandon some propositions long held true in your culture and to embrace wisdom from abroad, it will now be a new and (we may hope) improved version of your own culture's collective wisdom you'll need to take into account as you reason about which moral propositions to hold true or justified. You can't somehow leap out of culture and history altogether and gaze directly into the Moral Law, using it as a standard for judging the justification or truth of moral propositions, any more than you can gaze directly into the mind of God. You can, if you possess the requisite virtues, search your available resources for all relevant considerations and deliberate wisely. You can even expand your own culture's horizons in a way that brings new or long-neglected considerations into view. What you can't do, if you are human, is have your judgment determined solely by the matter under consideration without relying on beliefs, habits of description, and patterns of reasoning that belong to a cultural inheritance" (Stout, *Ethics After Babel*, p. 23).

37. For one quite good recent review of the debate, see Georgia Warnke, *Gadamer* (Stanford, Calif.: Stanford University Press, 1987), pp. 107–138.

38. See, among many other passages, Jürgen Habermas, "Review of Gadamer's *Truth and Method*," in Fred R. Dallmayr and Thomas A. McCarthy, eds., *Understanding and Social Inquiry* (Notre Dame, Inc.: University of Notre Dame Press, 1977), pp. 357–358; and Jürgen Habermas, *The Theory of Communicative Action*, vol. 1, trans. Thomas McCarthy (Boston: Beacon Press, 1979), p. 134.

39. "That tradition as such should be and remain the only ground of validity of pre-judgments—a view Habermas attributes to me—flies directly in the face of my thesis that authority rests on knowledge. Having attained maturity, one can—but need not!—accept from insight what he adhered to out of obedience" (Gadamer, *Philosophical Hermeneutics*, p. 34).

40. See Dieter Misgeld, "Critical Theory and Hermeneutics: The Debate Between Habermas and Gadamer," in John O'Neill, *On Critical Theory* (New York: Seabury Press, 1976), p. 179.

41. Gadamer, *Philosophical Hermeneutics*, pp. 32–34.

42. Paul Ricoeur, *Lectures on Ideology and Utopia* (New York: Columbia University Press, 1986), p. 236.

43. For Gadamer's acknowledgment of the need for *some* criteria of appropriate conversation, see Gadamer, *Reason in the Age of Science*, p. 69, and Hans-Georg Gadamer, "Und dennoch: Macht des guten Willens," in Philipp Forget, *Text und Interpretation* (Munich: Emil Fink Verlag, 1984), pp. 59–60. The issue gets stated well in Stephen K. White, *The Recent Work of Jürgen Habermas* (Cambridge: Cambridge University Press, 1988), p. 2.

44. MacIntyre, *Whose Justice? Which Rationality?* p. 399.

45. Stout, *Ethics After Babel*, p. 164.

46. "Gaudium et spes," in Walter M. Abbott, *Documents of Vatican II* (Chicago: Follett Publishing, 1966), pp. 219–220, 201. I am indebted to some as

yet unpublished work by James J. Buckley for my understanding of how Vatican II provides distinctively Christian grounds for such conversations.

47. *The Constitution of the Presbyterian Church (U.S.A.)*, Part I: *The Book of Confessions* 9.42.

48. David Tracy, *Plurality and Ambiguity* (San Francisco: Harper & Row, 1987), pp. 94, 102.

8

TRUTH

The patterns of biblical narrative

Jeffrey Stout has remarked that some positions—and I think both his and mine are among them—can seem moderately relativistic for long stretches and then puzzlingly shift to nonrelativistic claims about "the truth." In earlier chapters, for instance, I have repeatedly emphasized that all argument operates within some particular tradition, that there is no universal standard of rationality. But, as the conclusion of the preceding chapter made clear, as a Christian I believe that the central claims of Christian faith are true—not merely "true for Christians" or "true within the context of the Christian tradition" but in a strong sense just plain true. This chapter will try to clarify that sense of "truth."

As Stout says, a big part of the solution to the puzzle lies in distinguishing between claims about *truth* and claims about *justification.* To use his example: he believes that slavery is wrong—not just in some times and places but everywhere and always. Maybe he is wrong to make that claim across all cultures, but that really is what he believes. On the other hand, he does not know of any way to *argue* for that belief except in the context of some particular tradition. The way we can go about justifying a belief is always context dependent, but the truth claimed for that belief is not.[1]

Similarly, I do not know how to defend Christian faith—or any other belief system—in terms that all rational human beings would have to accept. We argue within the context of some tradition, and we begin with the rules and assumptions a particular conversation partner happens to share. But I also believe that the God in whom Christians believe exists and loves regardless of whether any human tradition acknowledges that God. The preceding chapter emphasized pluralism in argument and justification; this chapter needs to set some limits on pluralism in regard to truth.

In thinking about the kind of truth claims involved in Christian faith, we may find it helpful to begin with the sort of argument we make in many contexts concerning patterns. There is a little drawing in Wittgenstein's *Philosophical Investigations,* borrowed from the work of the psychologist Robert Jastrow:[2]

Some people look at the drawing and "see" it as a duck; others "see" it as a rabbit. Sometimes in initial arguments they grow annoyed and disbelieving. "What do you mean, it looks like a rabbit? Any fool can see it looks like a duck." Communication, however, is not utterly impossible. One can help another see the drawing in a new way: "See, there are the ears, and there's the rabbit's mouth, and its eye." "Oh, of course, I see it now!" We cannot, though, force another into a different way of seeing: "Damn it, man, don't be stubborn; just look at the thing—it's a drawing of a rabbit." "I'm sorry; I'm really trying, but it still looks like a duck to me."

In a pair of eloquently suggestive and "characteristically elusive" articles, Wittgenstein's student John Wisdom applied to religious belief the notion of "seeing a pattern."[3] A Christian sees the universe as the creation of a loving God. A Buddhist sees a pattern of striving and suffering, to be escaped only by Enlightenment. An atheist, perhaps, sees a different pattern—Freud concluded at one point that "obscure, unfeeling, and unloving powers determine men's fate"[4]—or denies seeing any meaningful pattern at all. For most observers, some features come to the foreground, and the whole patterns itself around them.

Many classic religious texts call attention to patterns. King David already knew, we may assume, every detail of his dalliance with Bathsheba, and Nathan did not even remind him of relevant passages from the Torah. He told the story of the rich man who stole his poor neighbor's one little ewe lamb and gave David a pattern for understanding the evil of his deeds. Jesus' parables often function in the same way. "Who is my neighbor?" "A Samaritan, as .he journeyed, came to where he was; and when he saw him, he had compassion."

Of course such forms of argument occur in many fields, not just religion. Basil Mitchell offers a good account of how literary critics argue about the meaning of a text:

> Scholar A takes a certain passage to be the clue to the author's overall meaning. The sense of this passage seems to him quite obvious and also its importance in the work as a whole. However, he recognizes that some other passages are on first reading difficult to reconcile with this one, as he has chosen to interpret it. So he has to bring these apparently recalcitrant passages into line by finding an interpretation of them which will fit; or, failing that, by conceding that they are discrepant, but dismissing the discrepancy as comparatively unimportant. If he can explain why these passages should be in this way discrepant (why Plato nodded *here*) so much the better. In extreme cases he may declare these passages spurious or emend the text; in that case he would benefit from some independent evidence on the point.[5]

One tries to show how the different elements fit into the pattern one perceives; argument takes the form of description, describing the whole as seen in that pattern as persuasively as possible. The argument's persuasive force emerges, in Cardinal Newman's words, from "the culmination of probabilities, independent of each other . . . too fine to avail separately, too subtle and circuitous to be convertible into syllogisms, too numerous and various for such conversion, even were they convertible."[6] "It follows," Newman adds, "that what to one intellect is a proof is not so to another."[7] Some will just not see the pattern. Yet those who do see it will not feel that they are making a tentative and complex inference. "All you have to do is look at the thing!—It's a drawing of a rabbit."[8]

Similar kinds of arguments take place between the proponents of different scientific "paradigms" or in political debates. For instance: Does the lack of causal determinism implied by contemporary quantum theory represent such a radical change in the nature of science that we should reject the theory, or do the other advantages of this theory mean that physicists should be willing to accept a causality that is observed in only a statistical sense? Which are the dominant features that shape the pattern: the Sandinistas' limitations on a free press and Daniel Ortega's visits to Moscow, or the increase in literacy and economic justice in the Nicaraguan countryside? We can in a sense agree about "the facts" and still argue about the shape of the pattern they form.

If we agree about "the facts," however, then are we still debating questions of "truth" at all when we argue about a pattern? Our opinion about that may vary from case to case.[9] Consider, for instance:

The duck-rabbit drawing.

A picture (reproduced in N. R. Hanson's *Patterns of Discovery*)[10] that looks at first like an abstract inkblot. After a while, though, one can see some of the shapes forming a picture of Christ. Might one want to say that that picture is "really there" in a way that the duck—or the rabbit—is not?

A reproduction of a black-and-white photograph of a familiar object, mixed with random inkblots that partially disguise it. Has the person who recognizes the drawing seen something "true" in a stronger sense than in the preceding example?

A photograph of thick grass with a well-camouflaged snake crawling amid the grass.

An actual grassland with a well-camouflaged snake crawling amid the grass.

In the last case, surely, the person who says, "I see a snake" has hold of a truth denied the person looking at the same scene but unable to see that pattern. We might disagree on where to draw the line, or whether to draw one, among the other cases.

Rather than trying to resolve all possible examples, I want to consider the model that seems to fit Christian faith best: claims about an *emerging* pattern. We both look at more or less the same data, but we disagree about the shape it takes and the future it portends. I look at a gifted but troubled adolescent and predict, "This will be a fine novelist someday." You say, "The drinking and the drugs will get him, and he'll end up in jail or an asylum or dead before his time." I point to the candidate's victories in early primaries; you note the shallowness of her support and the growing strength of her opponents. One of us turns out to be right. The loser might say—and might in some cases be justified in saying—"Well, the evidence back then was ambiguous, and you turned out lucky." But in other cases, it might seem more reasonable to admit, "Looking back, I see you were right. I see now what I should have seen then: what seemed to me random and trivial matters were the beginnings of what came to be the dominant pattern." We were certainly arguing about the truth—we both agree that one of us turned out to be wrong—and the truth in dispute concerned not only future predictions but claims about the past and the present.

Christian theology, I propose, makes a claim about an emerging pattern. Christians will admit that the current evidence is ambiguous. They see a pattern in their own lives and the world around them, but they can understand that others do not. They believe, however, that at some future time this now ambiguous pattern will become clear. What we now see in a mirror dimly, we will then see face-to-face. Thus Christians make claims about the future, but also about past events and present realities, about how that which all will someday see clearly will be recognizably the fulfillment—though richer and more developed than anyone can now imagine—of the pattern which some glimpse, in hints and guesses, even now.[11]

Christians see a master pattern in things, however, in at least two quite different ways. These roughly correspond to the traditional theological ideas of typology and the history of salvation.

First, Christian readers of the Bible find in the pattern of Jesus' life a pattern that recurs again and again elsewhere in the Bible, in extrabiblical history, and in their own lives. In Christian exegesis, such reading came to be known as "typological interpretation." In Joseph, who in obedience to his father went off to seek his brothers, was nearly killed by them, but in the end saved them from death in time of famine; in Ruth, who traveled, afraid but trusting, into a foreign land, claimed it as her own, and came to be ancestress of its greatest king; in the Hebrew people, fallen into slavery, into exile, but with its relation to God never sundered, always called again to the Promised Land, to be a light to the nations—one sees a familiar pattern, the pattern of Christ, as if Christ provided the key to all of scripture. As Ronald Hepburn puts it:

> To make one's home in such a structure is like exploring a beautifully designed house. However far you may go from the central hall and staircase, no corridor is without its vista of these, no walk but which finally and graciously returns you to them. The sense quickly and reassuringly arrives—"I know my way about."[12]

For Christians, moreover, this pattern does not apply only to the world of the scriptures. As George Lindbeck puts it, "A scriptural world is . . . able to absorb the universe. It supplies the interpretive *"uniform"?* framework within which believers seek to live their lives and understand reality."[13] In my own life too, if I am a Christian, I find that love and faithfulness never come easily but somehow seem to bring their rewards in time. My best deeds feel like a response to a love that loved me first and my failures not just like mistakes on my part but like betrayals of another's trust in me. The story of Christ, which furnished a key to other stories in scripture, seems to make sense of my story too.

> We thinke that *Paradise* and *Calvarie*,
>   Christs Crosse, and *Adams* tree, stood in one place;
> Looke, Lord, and finde both *Adams* met in me;
>   As the first *Adams* sweat surrounds my face,
>   May the last *Adams* blood my soule embrace.[14]

"What does it mean to become a Christian?" David Tracy asks. "It means at least this: to trust that, empowered, enabled, gifted and commanded by the Christ event of God, I can because I must attempt to risk a life like that disclosed in these gospel narratives."[15]

Christians do not, however, simply understand our own lives after the pattern of Christ's life. Rather, we find the stories of our individual lives making sense only because they are part of a larger story, which has Christ's story at its center—a story of God's initiative which calls for my gratitude and response, a story some theologians have called "the history of salvation." Similarly, on a Christian interpretation, it is not just that the stories of the Old Testament resemble Christ's stories but that the whole sweep of Old Testament narrative seems to point forward to a hope destined to fulfillment.[16] Christ's story provides Christians with a pattern they see again and again but also with the center of a larger pattern that is for them the shape of all things.

Christian theologians need to talk about both sorts of patterns. An exclusive emphasis on the one overarching pattern of the history of salvation can make the lives of individuals seem purely a means to some larger purpose. It loses the sense of the astonishing importance of each individual life in faith. On the other hand, exclusive emphasis on the repetition of patterns in typology can forget that the transformation of our own lives is possible only because of God's prior initiative—that we are part of an epic in which the crucial battle has already been fought. When the Christian story is told most persuasively, then the sweep of that epic gives our own part in it far greater meaning, not less, in a way that becomes most clear not through some argumentative analysis but precisely in the power of a narrative in which the general movement and the character of individual episodes illuminate each other.

In both cases—in salvation history and in typology—Christian faith sorts out the world by seeing a pattern in things. One does not "prove" such a way of looking at the world, if "proof" means a series of syllogisms from universally acceptable premises. Yet Christians want to claim that these really *are* the patterns of reality. The Christian says, "This is what I believe to be true about how the world is. Just as with seeing the pattern of a picture, I find it hard to remember or describe just how the pieces first fell into place for me. I'm not even sure the final trigger of that process should be given too much importance; it may have been something rather trivial which suddenly made things click. What's important is the way I see the whole pattern now. I admit that, just as with such pictures, sometimes I glance back and think, in a moment of panic, that I've lost it, because I can't see the pattern any more. But still: if you ask me how I can think about the world in the way that Christians do, one side of me wants to say, 'But just look!' "[17]

Another side, however, can seek out the kind of conversation described in the preceding chapter. There are ways, after all, of trying to evoke the seeing of a pattern: "There are the ears, and, see, there's the rabbit's mouth." Christians can undertake similar descriptive exercises, tracing biblical themes through exegesis, casting issues in the contemporary world according to biblical patterns, pointing up analogies.[18] The ways in which our own lives, however imperfectly, manifest the pattern we have discerned in things may even exercise its own kind of persuasive power. "The proof of a map," Charles Taylor says, "is how well you can get around using it,"[19] and non-Christians, admiring the way Christians move through the world, may wish they could share their map. But nothing guarantees that another will see the same pattern I do—even if that other person eagerly seeks my way of seeing.[20] Christians will not find this surprising; Ian Ramsey made the point well:

> We can develop what seem to us the best stories, but we can never guarantee that for a particular person the light will dawn at a particular point, or for that matter at any point in any story. Need this trouble us? Is not this only what has been meant by religious people when they have claimed that the "initiative" in any "disclosure" or "revelation" must come from God?[21]

Even for the believer, moreover, seeing the pattern is not incompatible with recognizing that some things do not fit it very well. A scientist, persuaded by a theory's explanatory power, may admit that one aspect of it does not yet work, or put aside some data as admittedly puzzling but the sort of thing that may be resolved by further refinements—or may turn out to be erroneous data. An honest literary critic can concede, "I think my interpretation works, but I admit that's the passage that gives me most trouble." So Christians, confronted with the suffering of children and all the world's other evils, can admit that these things have us mystified and constitute a problem for our vision of things. When we talk about such matters with non-Christians, we will not say, "I don't understand why you think the existence of evil would be a problem for me." It *is* a problem; we understand all too well.[22]

Still, at least for the time being, the way the overall pattern guides our lives and makes sense of things for us leaves us seeing the world that way and holding in abeyance the elements that admittedly seem not to fit. As is often the case with claims about emerging patterns, one cannot specify in advance just what would lead me to change my mind. Suppose I think I recognize a shape emerging in a half-completed jigsaw puzzle. But as I fit more pieces in, perhaps I will come to realize, "No, I was wrong—it isn't an elephant, it's a rhinoceros." Or, "Well, now I don't know what it is, but still, I was wrong; it certainly isn't an elephant." But, looking at the picture now, I find it impossible to specify the list of things that would lead me to reject my elephant hypothesis. And this, of course, is an easy case, compared with a scientific theory or a literary interpretation, much less a religious faith.[23] The believer does say, however, "I'm not claiming this is just my way of looking at things. I really think this is the right way, the way that makes most sense. Oh, of course I'm sure I have a lot of the details wrong, and on some matters those who see things very differently may be closer to the truth than I am—but I think I've got hold of something fundamentally right about the overall picture. By saying that, I mean that I believe that nothing will ever come along that renders this way of looking at things impossible, and that, indeed, someday, as the picture of things emerges more completely, the pattern I see, which I concede is at the moment tricky to catch a glimpse of, will emerge so clearly that anyone who looks will basically see things this way."[24]

In that sense, Christians think that what we believe is true—not just one perspective among others but the right perspective. But what we believe is all tied up with a series of stories, and the way in which those stories are true is a more complicated question. After all, we can use many different stories to make sense of our lives and use them in different ways. Suppose, for instance, someone grew up reading Horatio Alger and finds in those stories of virtuous, hardworking poor boys who reap the rewards of material success after struggle and hardship the key to what life is really about. Such a person would presumably not think of the stories as historically true—one would recognize that they are novels. The truth claims made by an Algerist would concern the general shape of the American economy and American society, beliefs about how much a poor boy (or girl?—Perhaps not) can accomplish.

On the other hand, imagine a young black American who finds a central inspiration in the life of Martin Luther King, Jr. The story of Dr. King's commitment to nonviolent resistance and its success in inspiring black struggle and winning white support seems to offer insights about human nature and the model for one's own life. But in this case, I suspect, some historical claims *would* matter. If it turned out, for instance, that the threat of violence by more militant blacks in historical fact played a key role in Dr. King's greatest triumphs, then perhaps he does not offer such a good model for social struggle after all.

The point is that one cannot say, generally and in advance, "If you use a story to make sense of the world, you are committed to this kind of truth claim concerning the story." As Hans Frei puts it, "Every narrative of the sort in which story and meaning are closely related may have its own special hermeneutics."[25] The kind of claims you make depends on the particular story you use and the way you use it.

Though different people might use the same story in different ways, the story tends to set some limits on plausible ways of using it. Given the interchangeability of Horatio Alger's heroes, for instance, it is hard to think that any one of them matters very much, except as an instance of a general pattern. Even assuming that we did not have independent evidence that Alger was a novelist, therefore, the character of the stories themselves makes it hard to imagine caring about their historical truth. On the other hand, Dr. King seems to emerge from his story as a very particular, noninterchangeable figure.

If we cannot generalize about the truth claims to be made about narratives when they function to shape people's lives, then deciding the truth claims that Christians have to make about the biblical narratives cannot appeal to some universal rule. It will have to involve (1) looking at how those narratives function in the life of the Christian community and (2) carefully reading the texts to see whether something about their own shape implies anything about their proper use. The second criterion will be important in part because the first criterion will no doubt disclose that Christians use them in many different ways. When "use" varies so much, we cannot simply appeal to it to settle the issue.

Some fundamentalist Christians, for instance, will insist that the historical truth of every detail of the story matters to Christian faith. But a careful reading of the Gospels shows that the different Gospels apparently contradict each other as to detail and in other ways sit rather lightly on some questions of historical fact. These texts, then, do not seem very well suited to a use that involves that kind of historical claim about every episode.

At the other extreme, some Christians might say that they use Jesus as an inspiring moral example, and *any* historical question—even of whether there was such a person—does not matter to them. But Jesus' ethic seems tied, in the story, to his person, and to a claim about his relation with God, so that someone who merely draws out moral lessons from his teaching is not being faithful to the character of this story.

The work that Hans Frei and others have begun concerning biblical narratives seems to offer a useful middle ground between these extremes. On this view, the biblical narratives (1) lay out the shape of the world in which, they claim, we live and (2) depict the character of a God to whom they call us to respond.[26] On both counts, they make some general claims about the truth of the story they tell, and those claims are important to the meaning of the narrative. But in neither case is accurately detailed history the point of the text.

Let me consider each of these functions of the Bible in turn. First, the scriptures tell a story about how the whole world has God as its creator, about how all of this world—matter as well as spirit—is intrinsically good, about how, for as long as there have been human beings, we have distorted our relation with our Creator and the world in which we live. In spite of all our sin, the story goes on, God did not give up on us but continued to watch over humankind, and in time established a special relation with the people of Israel, calling them to be a "light to the nations," a visible sign of God's love of this world. Then God's

Word became incarnate in a human being, who died on a cross for our sins and was raised from the dead. In response to Christ's life, ministry, and resurrection, the church came into existence as a witness through which the story could continue.

Any such quick summary becomes obviously superficial. But even the briefest of summaries suggests how the reality of certain events and particular patterns naturally emerges as central to the story's meaning, while many of the details—creation in seven days, which Gospel accurately reports the chronology of Jesus' life, and so on—are peripheral not only to the concerns of modern historical critics but also to the story's own meaning.

Similarly, in reading the Old Testament accounts of God's actions, or the Gospel stories of Jesus, we find ourselves encountering a personality whose characteristics we begin to identify. The story itself captures those characteristics, in the way that a vivid anecdote can convey someone's character; any attempt to discard the story and lay out the personality in analytic description falls flat. It seems abstract and one-dimensional compared with a story's vividness. Yet just as we can often say, "That anecdote sure catches just what my friend Sam is like, better than I would have known how to say it," and then admit, "But I wouldn't swear that the details of the anecdote are true," so with the biblical narratives letting these stories convey to us who God is in a way that only a story could does not commit us to the truth of each episode.

A particularly exciting thing about thinking of the biblical narratives in this way is that it keeps forcing us back to considering our own relation to these stories. If we take the Bible as an accurate history book, then we never have to think about its impact on our own lives when we reflect about its truth. If we take it as illustrating moral lessons, then we never have to worry about its narrative truth at all. But if we pursue this middle route, we face again and again the question of what parts of this story really matter to our lives as Christians. As Charles Wood has written:

> The readers are brought into the narrative; it becomes a context for reflection and action. . . . What is achieved is not simply read off the text and accepted but is rather created through the engagement of the readers—who have their distinctive backgrounds and locations—with the text. . . . Thus, although the text is normative, in that it is by the text that the appropriateness of Christian belief and conduct is to be judged, its normativeness does not stifle diversity and creativity. Indeed, it positively mandates them.[27]

Only in reflecting both on the world described in the story and on the character of a life lived in that world, both on the God depicted in the story and on the nature of a life lived in response to that God, can we begin to sort out what kind of truth claims the story calls us to make.

Speaking of these texts as stories in which we learn the kind of person God is raises another difficult question, for we learn those lessons through seeing how God "acts" in the story. Alasdair MacIntyre states the problem well:

> In the Bible men go on journeys, suffer greatly, marry, have children, die, and so on. So far no difficulty. But they go on their journeys because God calls them, suffer in spite of God's care, receive their brides and their children at the hand of God, and at death pass in a special sense into God's realm. . . . This reference to God introduces all the difficulty. What is said of God is again familiar enough. God calls, God hears, God provides. But these verbs appear to lack the application which is their justification in non-religious contexts. . . . The name "God" is not used to refer to someone who can be seen or heard, as the name "Abraham" is, and when descriptive verbs are used to state that God's call is heard, it is not ordinary hearing that is meant. Hence all the puzzles. If talk about God is not to be construed at its face value, how is it to be construed?[28]

In the first place, God functions as a character in these stories—however oddly, however mysteriously. And sometimes we can identify some of the personal qualities of a character in a story even though the mode of that character's action remains mysterious to us. In reading a science fiction novel, for instance, I can be puzzled about how the creatures of the planet Astrogar talk without sound, act without bodies, and move from one place to another faster than the speed of light. Yet in the context of the story I recognize that Idmar of Astrogar is kind and absentminded, while Sensor of Astrogar is evil and cunning. I may even grow quite fond of old Idmar.

Of course the stories of Astrogar are fiction, and Christians believe that the biblical narratives are not. But in either case, judgments about the personality of a character in the story can be explained and debated even if one cannot currently understand *how* that character could behave in the way one is discussing.

Thus, even as we puzzle over how God acts and speaks, we can nevertheless identify some characteristics of the God who appears in the biblical stories: human beings are unreliable in their allegiances, but God remains faithful; God seeks out those who do justice, love kindness, and walk humbly; and so on. Our puzzles about how God acts make a problem for faith and raise legitimate questions about why we believe these things, but they do not render our talk about God's characteristics meaningless.

As I read the biblical stories and as I use them to try to understand my own life, I also come to realize that in these stories God's initiative has a kind of priority. Abraham does not think he has just taken a notion to travel; he thinks he is responding to God's call. Samuel does not just choose David; he anoints David as God's choice. Jeremiah calls the people back to faithfulness to a God who has never abandoned them. I find myself wanting to say similar things about my own life as a Christian: my acts of love seem a response, however inadequate, to a love that loved me first; my projects, when they are for good, make sense to me as parts of a much larger plan.

Of course I may be wrong, and Jeremiah may have been wrong too. In another story, Vladimir and Estragon act in response to a hope that Godot will arrive, but it does not follow that Godot exists. My claim is only that, to the extent that I take the pattern of these stories to be the pattern for my life and of the world, I am committed to believing that the God they describe is not the projection or useful construct of the people in the story. The logic of the stories is that God's action comes first and generates human responses. *If* I buy into the stories, then I have to buy into that logic.[29] To the extent that the pattern these stories provide me becomes compelling in the way that a pattern can, then I will acknowledge their claims about God, however still mysterious, to be a necessary part of that pattern. As Thomas Tracy puts it:

> Whatever the particular content of our claims about God's acts, our reference to them will involve "telling a story" that ties events together in a meaningful pattern and relates this pattern to the purposive activity of God. . . . Identification of God as a unique subject of speech involves a whole network of claims about the nature of God, the openness of human history and nature to God's influence, God's dealings with us in the past and his purposes for our future, and so on. The effect of this theistic story is to superimpose a pattern of divine intention on the events of human history. It weaves these events together into a meaningful sequence, the central theme of which is the working out of God's purposes in relation to humankind. In doing so, the story suggests that we acknowledge a level of significance in events that would not otherwise enter our description of them.[30]

The persuasiveness of such a pattern depends on the kind of considerations I have described in this chapter, and the persuasiveness of the pattern as a whole counts in favor of the existence of the admittedly mysterious agent who plays such a compelling role within it.

One analogy to this case might be the argument between materialists or behaviorists and those who hold that the interiority of human experience requires reference to another kind of reality—call it mind or consciousness or soul. References to "mind" are for some a crucial element in the way they organize their understanding of human behavior, such that they cannot leave "mind" out of the story, even if they have no clear account of the nature of the mental realm or of how the mental and the physical interact. This analogy does not augur well for clearly settling the question, but it does remind us that, even in complicated cases incapable of clear resolution, evidence and argument of some kinds can still play a role, though the skeptic may have seen the "evidence" all along, and the only "argument" may take the form of description of the world as seen according to a particular pattern.

In explaining the "prolixity" of Karl Barth's *Church Dogmatics,* Hans Frei has noted that besides the fact that Barth was just "naturally talkative," he *had* to write at length because he was trying to re-create "a universe of discourse, and he had to put the reader in the middle of that world, instructing him in the use of that language by showing him how—extensively, and not only by stating the rules or principles of the discourse."[31] If my arguments have been correct, then Christian theology needs to take the form that Frei sees in Barth: a description of the world as seen from a Christian perspective that draws what persuasive power it has from the coherence and richness of the whole. It follows that a small dose of this kind of theology, offered by way of example, will in all likelihood not be very impressive. I am aware that this chapter has therefore remained at a level of abstraction. I have discussed what kind of claims Christians ought to make and how they could argue for them, but I have not made the arguments. I know of no quick way to do that. I hope that even what I have said, however, clarifies the ways Christian theology can claim truth even in the context of a pluralistic conversation. Together with the defense of such conversation offered in previous chapters, that puts us in a place to sort out the questions with which this book began.

NOTES

1. See Jeffrey Stout, *Ethics After Babel* (Boston: Beacon Press, 1988), pp. 24–28 and elsewhere.

2. Ludwig Wittgenstein, *Philosophical Investigations,* trans. G. E. M. Anscombe (Oxford: Basil Blackwell 1968), p. 194.

3. John Wisdom, "Gods," in John Wisdom, *Philosophy and Psycho-analysis* (Berkeley and Los Angeles: University of California Press, 1969), pp. 149–168; and idem, "The Logic of God," in idem, *Paradox and Discovery* (Berkeley and Los Angeles: University of California Press, 1970), pp. 1–22. See also John Hick, "Religious Faith as Experiencing-As," in G. N. A. Vesey, *Talk of God* (New York: St. Martin's Press, 1969), pp. 20–35; Basil Mitchell, *The Justification of Religious Belief* (New York: Oxford University Press, 1980); and Ian T. Ramsey, *Religious Language* (London: SCM Press, 1957). The phrase "characteristically elusive" comes from Mitchell, *The Justification of Religious Belief,* p. 56.

4. Sigmund Freud, *New Introductory Lectures on Psychoanalysis,* trans. James Strachey (New York: W. W. Norton & Co., 1965), p. 147.

5. Mitchell, *The Justification of Religious Belief,* p. 46.

6. John Henry Newman, *An Essay in Aid of a Grammar of Assent,* ed. I. T. Ker (Oxford: Clarendon Press, 1985), p. 187.

7. Ibid., p. 190.

8. See John Henry Newman, *Apologia Pro Vita Sua* (London: Longmans, Green, 1890), p. 19, for Newman's insistence that faith cannot be just a sum of probabilities.

9. For a detailed account of ways in which the duck-rabbit is different from other cases, see Stanley Cavell, *The Claim of Reason* (Oxford: Oxford University Press, 1979), p. 354.

10. N. R. Hanson, *Patterns of Discovery: Inquiry Into the Conceptual Foundations of Science* (Cambridge: Cambridge University Press, 1958), p. 14.

11. John Hick's discussions of eschatological verification sometimes seem to make Christianity purely a matter of claims about the future—indeed, the future after death. In Hick's parable, two men are traveling along a road, and one thinks the road leads to the Celestial City, while the other does not believe it leads anywhere. "They do not," Hick says, "entertain different expectations about the coming details of the road, but only about its ultimate destination" (John Hick, "Theology and Verification," in Basil Mitchell, ed., *The Philosophy of Religion*, p. 60; Oxford: Oxford University Press, 1971). I would argue that a Christian not only expects a different destination but also claims to see a different pattern in the road itself.

12. Ronald W. Hepburn, "Poetry and Religious Belief," in Stephen E. Toulmin and others, *Metaphysical Beliefs* (London: SCM Press, 1957), p. 141.

13. George A. Lindbeck, *The Nature of Doctrine: Religion and Theology in a Postliberal Age* (Philadelphia: Westminster Press, 1984), p. 117.

14. John Donne, "Hymne to God my God, in my sicknesse," *The Poems of John Donne* (London: Oxford University Press, 1912), p. 368.

15. David Tracy, *The Analogical Imagination* (New York: Crossroad Publishing Co., 1986), p. 326.

16. "The Old Testament can only be read as a book of ever increasing anticipation" (Gerhard von Rad, *Old Testament Theology*, trans. D. M. G. Stalker, p. 319; New York: Harper & Row, 1965). I am not claiming that that is the only way to read the Hebrew Bible: to call these texts "the Old Testament" obviously already makes some assumptions. Discussions between Christians and Jews might sometimes resemble discussions between literary critics about the overall pattern of texts. See, e.g., Michael Goldberg, "God, Action, and Narrative: *Which* Narrative? *Which* Action? *Which* God?" *Journal of Religion* 68 (1988), pp. 39–56.

George Lindbeck has pointed the way, I think, toward an appropriate response to the questions Goldberg raises. See George A. Lindbeck, "Critical Exegesis and Theological Interpretation," in Garrett Green, ed., *Scriptural Authority and Narrative Interpretation* (Philadelphia: Fortress Press, 1987), pp. 165–176.

17. I am saying of Christian faith what David Kelsey says of a particular theological position: "it is not itself *taken as a whole* ordered as an argument; rather theological positions taken as wholes might be looked at in a quasi-aesthetic way as a solicitation of mind and imagination to look . . . in a certain way" (David H. Kelsey, *The Uses of Scripture in Recent Theology*, pp. 136–137; Philadelphia: Fortress Press, 1975).

18. I hope I am following Hans Frei's account of Karl Barth's theological method. See Hans W. Frei, "Eberhard Busch's Biography of Karl Barth," in

H.-Martin Rumscheidt, ed., *Karl Barth in Re-View* (Pittsburgh: Pickwick Press, 1981), esp. pp. 110 and 114.

19. Charles Taylor, *Philosophical Papers*, vol. 2 (Cambridge: Cambridge University Press, 1985), p. 111.

20. "There is no single road to Christianity, either as a matter of universal principle or in practice. I am convinced that the passionate and systematic preoccupation with the apologetic task of showing how faith is meaningful and/or possible is largely out of place and self-defeating—except as an *ad hoc* and highly various exercise. In this arena an ounce of living is usually worth a pound of talk, and especially of writing" (Hans W. Frei, *The Identity of Jesus Christ*, p. xii; Philadelphia: Fortress Press, 1975).

21. Ramsey, *Religious Language*, p. 79.

22. In terms of the famous debate on "Theology and Falsification," I am thus in agreement with Basil Mitchell and not with R. M. Hare. Mitchell's believer admits "that many things can and do count against his belief" (Basil Mitchell, "Theology and Falsification," in Mitchell, *The Philosophy of Religion*, p. 20).

23. See Mitchell, *The Justification of Religious Belief*, p. 55. I will return to this question in the next chapter.

24. For now, "we must rather be content to remain in history, to hear the voice of the gospel in proclamation and the biblical narrative, and to struggle to discern his word for the church. . . . The theologian has no privileged access to the gospel's essence but must hear it as all Christians do through written, spoken, and sung words. Informed by Christian practice, yet critically reflecting upon it, the theologian seeks to articulate the gospel so that through it God might mold our Christian identity" (Ronald F. Thiemann, "Piety, Narrative, and Christian Identity," *Word and World* 3 [1983], pp. 156–157).

25. Hans W. Frei, *The Eclipse of Biblical Narrative* (New Haven: Yale University Press, 1974), p. 273.

26. For a good summary, see Charles Wood, "Hermeneutics and the Authority of Scripture," in Green, *Scriptural Authority and Narrative Interpretation*, p. 13.

27. Ibid., pp. 13–14. "Narrative" in the first sentence actually reads "narratives." Given the pronoun that follows, I assume that is a misprint and have corrected it.

28. Alasdair MacIntyre, "The Logical Status of Religious Belief," in Toulmin and others, *Metaphysical Beliefs*, pp. 178–179. See also Langdon Gilkey, "Cosmology, Ontology, and the Travail of Biblical Language," *Journal of Religion* 41 (1961), pp. 194–205. In sorting out these issues, I have found two books particularly helpful: Thomas F. Tracy, *God, Action, and Embodiment* (Grand Rapids: Wm. B. Eerdmans Publishing Co., 1984); and Victor Preller, *Divine Science and the Science of God* (Princeton, N.J.: Princeton University Press, 1967).

29. See Ronald F. Thiemann, *Revelation and Theology: The Gospel as Narrated Promise* (Notre Dame, Ind.: University of Notre Dame Press, 1985), pp. 92–111.

30. Thomas F. Tracy, *God, Action, and Embodiment*, pp. 78–79.

31. Frei, "Eberhard Busch's Biography of Karl Barth," in Rumscheidt, *Karl Barth in Re-View*, p. 111.

9

DIALOGUES

Science and religion; discussions among religions

So far I have set out a model of pluralistic conversation and indicated how Christians might participate in such conversation while preserving their commitment to the truth of their faith. In chapter 1, I suggested that such a model helps in thinking about specific problems like the relation of science and religion, interreligious dialogue, and theological method. It is now time to return to those issues. Chapter 10 will discuss implications for theological method; this present chapter will say something about dialogue between science and religion and among different religious traditions.

Two of the biggest obstacles to serious conversation between science and religion grow out of issues already discussed in this book. If science is a uniquely rational and objective activity, then there is no clear reason why it should engage in dialogue with such a comparatively confused subject as religion at all. On the other hand, if certain kinds of "fideism" are right and the discourse of science and religion is just utterly incommensurable, then dialogue between them seems impossible.

In chapters 2 and 3, I argued that attempts to establish the unique rationality and objectivity of science have broken down. Even scientists cannot appeal to uninterpreted data to settle arguments between important theories by definitive proofs. Scientific arguments, like theological ones, take place within the context of a tradition, and at crucial points in the history of science, one can hope to persuade, but one cannot prove. This does not mean that "science is irrational"; it simply means that "rationality" needs to be defined rather broadly, and science does not have some unique rationality denied to any other kind of inquiry.

One clear-cut difference between science and religion might seem to remain. In the preceding chapter, I suggested how cautious theologians need to be in making claims about the nature of God. Christians tell stories in which God figures as a character, and the God who figures in those stories has some recognizable personal characteristics. Christians insist that this God cannot be just a name for human beliefs or practices, since within the way we see the world the relevant human actions make sense only as responses to prior divine initiatives. Yet none of this introduces much by way of ontological description of God's nature. Therefore, if natural science provides any kind of descriptions of the real nature of the objects of its inquiry, that might make for a big difference between science and religion. Whether science really does provide such descriptions remains a matter of keen debate, and I would not presume to settle it here.[1] Let me just offer two reasons for thinking the question is still open.

First, we often talk of physicists as trying to describe the ultimate forces and particles that make up the objective physical world. The dominant—though not universally held—contemporary interpretation of quantum mechanics raises real questions about such an account. According to quantum mechanics, one can in principle measure either the precise position of a particle like an electron or its precise velocity—but not both. Some physicists believe that the source of this indeterminism lies in an inherent clumsiness of the measuring procedure. They think that the electron itself does have at any moment a precise position and velocity, but because of the limits of or the interference involved in the act of measurement, we can obtain only part of the information on the state of the particle.

Other physicists, however, hold that the significance of the observed indeterminism goes deeper. They believe that precise position does not *exist* with precise velocity; one of these measurements does not *have* any precise value. They therefore infer that it does not make sense to think of the electron as existing on its own with either precise position or precise velocity when it is not being observed at all. While these debates continue, this second interpretation received strong confirmation from experiments by Alain Aspect reported in 1982 following up the theoretical work of J. S. Bell in the 1960s.[2] The interpretation of the experiments remains controversial, but there is at least no consensus among physicists as to the possibility of *any* "realistic" interpretation of quantum theory.[3] Physicists turn out to be storytellers too, and questions about the reference of their stories are in their own way as puzzling as analogous questions in theology.

Arguments from the history of science also raise questions about the "realism" of science. As I argued in chapter 7 with reference to Alasdair MacIntyre, it makes sense to talk of scientific "progress" in the sense of solving the problems generated in the course of a scientific tradition. But it is very difficult to claim that that "progress" consists in getting closer to describing the way the world actually is. Such a judgment would imply, for instance, that, whatever happens in the future of physics, it will at least remain clear forever that "the ultimate constituents of nature are more like fields than like matter and force," a judgment no cautious physicist would make. Historical precedents certainly advise caution: in some ways Einstein's theory of general relativity describes a world ontologically closer to Aristotle's than to Newton's.[4] Pasteur made a great medical breakthrough by rejecting spontaneous generation and insisting on the radical separation of organic and inorganic materials; we have now "advanced" farther by making very nearly the opposite point.[5]

Each step forward in science solves one set of problems and offers a more sophisticated model capable of accounting for a wider range of phenomena or predicting to a greater level of precision—in such senses, science really does "make progress"—but one cannot trace a straight line or a smooth curve showing how science moves steadily in one direction in its "descriptions of reality." It seems significant that working scientists rarely actually talk about "truth." They are using models to solve problems, to help understand. At minimum, the jury is still out on the question of whether science engages in objective descriptions of an objective world.[6] Theologians still debate the same question about religious claims. At this point, then, that issue does not provide the grounds for distinguishing the two fields, and I have already argued that efforts like Karl Popper's to establish science's unique rationality and objectivity do not hold.

This is not to say that natural science and religious discourse use the same methods or work the same way. For instance:

1. Thomas Kuhn and other philosophers of science talk about "conversions" from one scientific paradigm to another, but—to use rather sloppy language—most religious conversions seem "bigger" in scale than scientific ones. Most beliefs about most topics remain in place even in the midst of a scientific "paradigm shift." A religious conversion, on the other hand, may affect every aspect of the way one sees the world. Argument about such matters, therefore, is bound to be more complex and more tentative; fewer constants remain in place to which one can appeal as starting points.[7]

2. In particular, religious beliefs ordinarily have more impact on ethical decisions, on the way we live our lives. In part for this reason, decisions about them are harder to avoid—they represent what William James called a "forced option."[8] If I am convinced that Newtonianism has collapsed but quantum physics strikes me as quite implausible, for instance, I can just stop doing physics. I do not take a stand one way or the other; I simply stop thinking about those issues and devote my time to politics or stamp collecting or something else.

If I am unpersuaded by various religious views, however, I seem to fall into a kind of position—call it agnosticism—whether I want to or not.

3. Christianity and many other religions believe that faith involves a personal relationship with God, and in such relationships other persons can often choose how much of themselves they want to reveal to us. The sky may sometimes be cloudy, the rats sometimes restless, but neither the stars nor even the rats decide whether or not they want to open themselves up to the investigations of the astronomer or the psychologist. But if I want to understand you as a friend, that depends on your cooperation as well as my determination.

If you obtained a particular result in the chemistry lab, I should be able to duplicate your results. If Mary "opened her heart" to you, she may not want to do so with me. It is not clear how I could "repeat your experiment"; I may have to trust your account. If our knowledge of God is at least analogous to our knowledge of other human beings, we would therefore expect to be dependent on divine initiatives and thus sometimes more dependent on the reports of those to whom such initiatives have come.[9]

4. To the adherents of many religious traditions, faith involves not only a way of looking at the world but also a personal trust in God. Therefore, doubts about one's faith seem, from the standpoint of faith, to involve a kind of personal betrayal. Belief in God is, in this respect too, more like trust in a friend or a spouse than like belief in a scientific theory. This alters how we feel about when and how it is appropriate to question or test our belief.[10]

Religion, in short, is not just like natural science—nor is literary criticism just like natural science, nor physics just like geology. They have in common that they are inquiries undertaken by finite, historically embedded human persons who therefore never have unambiguous data or definitively prove their conclusions, and who can never find the supermethod by which all particular methods can be judged. Properly understanding rules like those I have just mentioned shows that they are different kinds of activity and therefore will have different rules—appropriate in each case to the kind of activity involved, no one necessarily less rational than another.

Yet precisely because such rules of inquiry follow from the kind of considerations I have been mentioning, we can argue for or against them. Even these various "language games" themselves thus remain open to critique: a particular religious tradition or a particular kind of scientific inquiry might appropriately have a unique set of rules because of the kind of enterprise it is, but we can ask whether its rules really do follow from the reasons claimed. Sometimes a theologian can legitimately plead, "This is how I have to work, given the nature of my enterprise," but sometimes such pleas represent illegitimate attempts to justify sloppiness or shortcuts. There is relevant evidence to be cited, one way or the other. In such ways, good conversations begin; the fideist claim that such matters cannot be open for discussion does not hold.

Different modes of inquiry, moreover, do not exist in separate boxes and never interact. When psychologists and historians, for instance, both try to understand the life of Martin Luther, they find they are bringing different assumptions and methods to bear on the same patch of territory.[11] They have to ask difficult questions about what each method contributes to illuminating the particular issues at hand, and there is no neutral place to stand while asking those questions—they must take shape in the kind of conversation I tried to describe in chapter 7—but such conversations can take place.

Similar conversations can occur between science and religious faith. Many of the "conflicts" between science and religion result from theologians trying to be scientists or scientists engaging in speculative philosophy, and it is important to get clear on the appropriate range of each field. The defenders of creation science, and Carl Sagan in his speculations about the meaning of it all, seem to me equally guilty, from opposite sides, of confusion in such matters. Both are claiming professional authority to speak of matters beyond their professional competence. Still, here too it seems too simple to say that religious faith and science address totally different questions and therefore *can* never be in conflict and *need* never be in dialogue.

In his day, for instance, Aquinas offered brilliant examples of how dialogue between science and theology can be fruitful. For example: The Aristotelian science of his day argued that the world was eternal. Precisely because Aquinas believed in creation *ex nihilo* on *theological* grounds, he started asking some hard questions and made a good case that, *even in scientific terms,* whether or not the world had a beginning in time was an open question. On the other side of things, much Christian theology had fallen into a Platonically influenced view that we ought to strive to free the soul from the body. Aristotle's psychology, on the other hand, the newly prominent *scientific* view in Aquinas' time, insisted on an ultimate unity between body and soul. Aquinas' reflections on these issues helped him rediscover the importance of the resurrection of the body as the ultimate Christian hope. Serious conversation with science led to a *theological* insight.

Analogous conversations today seem likely to bear fruit too. For theologians who have assumed that we have to think of the world around us primarily in terms of material objects, the conclusions of contemporary physics about the role of the observer in defining what is can come as a bracing shock. My own instinct is that those who hope somehow to rescue free will by way of quantum mechanics are confusing quite different issues, but quantum theory might well imply that the problem of freedom and determinism needs to be restated in new terms. Theology has been worrying about determinism for a long time now, and it may even have some useful lessons—if only about strategies that have been tried and failed—for other disciplines suddenly forced to rethink old problems. On a host of issues, in fact, a time like our own when both physicists and theologians are rethinking basic questions about metaphysics and the way language works has good potential for fruitful conversations between science and religion.

Christians will find, as Aquinas often noted, an explanation for the fruitfulness of such dialogues in the unity of all truth in God. Even those without such faith may acknowledge that sometimes the outsider to a particular field can ask the hard, unexpected question that proves most helpful. Such conversations will probably work best when neither side presupposes some overarching rule of "rationality" that has to be imposed on all forms of inquiry. The good news is that the most methodologically sophisticated contemporary scientists have become aware enough about intellectual pluralism that they may welcome such dialogues, if honest initiatives come from the theological side.

A similarly genuine pluralism provides the best context for dialogue among the different religions. As I suggested in chapter 1, the study of various religions renders it highly implausible that they are all "trying to say the same thing." They make quite different claims about the ultimate nature of things, the destiny of human beings, and the kind of life we ought to try to lead. To be sure, much if not all religious language is symbolic, and no religion can or does claim to grasp ultimate mystery clear and whole. Still, however tentatively religions point the way, it seems clear that they sometimes point in different directions.

For instance, it is not reasonable, Ninian Smart writes, "to think that there is sufficient conceptual resemblance between God and nirvana (as conceived in Theravada Buddhism) to aver that the Theravadin and the Christian are worshiping the same God (for one thing, the Theravadin is not *worshiping*)."[12] Similarly, the great scholar of Buddhism Edward Conze recalled, "I once read through a collection of the lives of Roman Catholic saints, and there was not one of whom a Buddhist could fully approve. . . . They were bad Buddhists though good Christians."[13] Christianity and Buddhism, in other words, give us different instructions about how to live our lives as well as different pictures of the nature of things. As David Tracy puts it, "There are family resemblances among the religions. But as far as I can see, there is no single essence, no one content of enlightenment or revelation, no one way of emancipation or liberation, to be found in all that plurality."[14]

These differences, however, need not lead adherents of one religion to hold adherents of another in contempt.[15] As William Christian has

said, "Understanding each other does not always lead to agreement
and . . . respect for one another does not depend on agreement."[16]
Indeed, the most interesting conversations—about religion or anything else—take place among people who disagree and, while trying
to understand their disagreements and learn from one another, are
willing to defend their own points of view. On the other hand, few
conversational ploys are more infuriating than the claim, "You really
agree with me; you just don't realize it."[17]

Nevertheless, as I said in chapter 1, many contemporary theologians
and philosophers of religion seem extraordinarily uncomfortable with
genuine religious pluralism. They cannot accept the possibility that
there may be just different, even conflicting, religions and no point
from which to evaluate them except from within some one tradition or
another. (I am assuming that the "scientific study of religion" is also
a tradition, or a part of a particular tradition of modernity.) To oversimplify, this discomfort leads to two strategies: either one baptizes the
other religions and claims that they are implicit versions of one's own,
or one develops a philosophical standpoint from which one claims to
be able to evaluate all the religions. The scholarly literature on these
matters is vast and diverse, but looking at Karl Rahner and John Hick
as examples of these two approaches may at least define some crucial
issues.

"Christianity," Rahner once wrote, "encounters the man of the
extra-Christian religion not merely as a non-Christian pure and simple, but as one who, in one respect or another, can and must be
considered already an anonymous Christian."[18] "There are," in other
words, "men who merely think that they are not Christians, but who
are in the grace of God," and we Christians can understand their state
"better than it does itself."[19] Not everyone is an anonymous Christian,
according to Rahner.[20] But the religious views or ethical practices of
some people implicitly contain the essence of Christianity. For example: "Savior figures in the history of religions can certainly also be
viewed as signs that—since man is always and everywhere moved by
the spirit—he gazes in anticipation towards that even in which his
absolute hope becomes historically irreversible and is manifested as
such" (in other words, to Christ). A non-Christian religion can therefore be "a positive means of gaining the right relationship to God and
thus for the attaining of salvation."[21] Indeed, the Christian church
hopes to offer "the historically and socially constituted explicit expression of what the Christian hopes is present as a hidden reality even
outside the visible Church."[22]

In one sense, the devout adherents of any faith indeed believe that
they understand the adherents of other traditions better than those
folk understand themselves. Christians believe that Buddhists are crea-

tures of a loving God but sinners whether they know it or not; Buddhists believe that Christians are caught on the wheel of samsara whether they know it or not; and so on. Furthermore, adherents of one tradition *may* think that another tradition provides real help in moving toward the true goal of human life. A Buddhist might think that, at least up to a point, Christian piety helps to free Christians from striving and desire. A Christian might believe that God was somehow at work in ancient India in the life of the Buddha.

It goes a step farther, however—and a step Rahner sometimes took—if I as a Christian say that I understand the real aims of the faith and practice of Buddhism better than the Buddhists themselves do. If Christians are more nearly right, then maybe the God revealed in Jesus Christ is nevertheless at work when Buddhists seek nirvana—but the Buddhists are not trying to achieve salvation in Jesus Christ in a rather confused way; they are *trying* to achieve nirvana. If the Buddhists are ultimately right, then maybe Christians' prayers nevertheless help us move toward nirvana. But we are not seeking nirvana; we are seeking salvation in Jesus Christ. In both cases, it seems ethnocentric and finally a bit insulting to use the categories of one tradition to explain the underlying intent of the beliefs and practices of another.[23]

John Hick recognizes the dangers of that kind of ethnocentrism, but he solves them, I think, by developing his own syncretistic beliefs and presenting them as the essence of all religions. Hick insists that a Christian should acknowledge "that the Real, which he or she has encountered as the divine Thou, is known by Buddhists as the ineffable 'further shore' or *nirvana*. "[24] Indeed, he claims that in general "different forms of religious awareness are not necessarily competitive, in the sense that the validity of one entails the spuriousness of the others, but are better understood as different phenomenal experiences of the one divine noumenon; or in another language different experiential transformations of the same transcendent informational input."[25] What happens with Hick is what tends to happen with theories of the common ground of all religions, namely, that a particular philosophical-religious theory—in Hick's case a kind of late nineteenth-century British idealism with some Hinduism thrown in—gets elevated to the status of the core of all religion, the criterion according to which other religious points of view can then be judged.[26]

Hick rejects the traditional Christian interpretation of the incarnation,[27] for instance. He also argues that after death each of us goes through a kind of dream period "of self-revelation and self-judgment, a kind of psychoanalytic experience" before being reembodied in some other physical universe, so that in a series of lives we can "gradually progress towards the completion of the divine purpose" for each of us.[28] Whether he is right or not—I happen to disagree with him on both counts—in both cases, he is one participant in the conversation, advocating one point of view. When he claims instead to be the neutral moderator of the whole discussion, the representative of "religion in general," who is bringing the rest of us together and therefore occupies a privileged position, he is cheating at the rules of genuine conversation.[29]

It is arguably true, for instance, that giving up belief in the uniqueness of God's incarnation in Christ would bring a Christian closer to the beliefs of Hindus and Jews. Similarly, acknowledging that no one can achieve the true goal of human life without the help of a kind of divine grace would bring a Theravada Buddhist closer to Christianity and Islam. But the Trinitarian Christian might reply that she did not want to become a Unitarian, and the Theravadin respond that he did not want to be a Mahayana Buddhist. The leader of an interreligious dialogue does not have the right to dictate the position that each participant should take within his or her own tradition. The fact that moving from A to B brings one closer to C does not in itself prove that B is better than A—unless one has a map of all positions already in the back of one's mind, with the location of the truth already marked, presumably somewhere near the middle.

Hick's approach to interreligious dialogue has interesting parallels to Jürgen Habermas' theory of communication—and some similar consequences. In chapter 5, I discussed how Habermas and Kohlberg argue for openness, equality, and tolerance. The form of their argument, I proposed, leads to a kind of *intolerance,* for anyone who defends the authority of tradition or questions the central values of the Enlightenment gets dismissed as primitive or backward or, in any event, not a legitimate candidate to join in authentic conversation. Analogously, Hick and many other contemporary philosophers of religion claim to want to foster a universal religious dialogue, but it turns out that evangelical Christians, Hasidic Jews, traditional Muslims, and so on are not really eligible to join that dialogue, because they will be unwilling to accept the proposed rules of the game, rules that seem to emerge from a modern, Western, academic tradition.

Perhaps a real commitment to religious pluralism could lead, in George Lindbeck's words, to letting the different religions "regard themselves as simply different and . . . proceed to explore their agreements and disagreements without necessarily engaging in the invidious comparisons that the assumption of a common experiential core makes so tempting."[30] Once we recognize that we are not all trying to say the same thing, then we can recognize that *some* of the things that other people are saying seem to be genuine insights which we can appropriate for ourselves and that different points of view can often pose hard questions for our own position and lead us to new insights.

Perhaps we can serve others in similar ways. In such conversations, it may turn out that those who are most committed to their own traditions, least sympathetic with syncretistic efforts toward a "world theology," sometimes have the most to contribute. In any event, there will be no reason to keep them out of the discussion.

To summarize, I propose the following rules for Christians eager to engage in interreligious dialogue that accepts the kind of authentic pluralism I have been trying to describe:

1. Remain aware that you speak from a Christian point of view. Suggest, if you like, rules for the conversation or common themes, but do not presume the right to declare the rules all participants *must* accept or the "real" agenda all share whether they realize it or not. Do not, in short, pretend that you can stop being a Christian and become the neutral and therefore authoritative moderator of the whole discussion. Do not let a representative of "modernity" or anyone else assume that role either.

2. The most interesting conversation partners may well be those persons who have entered most deeply into the particularities of their own traditions.[31] Therefore, view with grave suspicion any proposed rules for interreligious dialogue that rule the Hasidic Jew, the conservative Roman Catholic, the Tibetan Buddhist, or the Sufi mystic out of the conversation in advance and admit only those whose worldviews have been in particular ways shaped by the assumptions of Western modernity.

3. In the normal course of things, dialogue with other religious traditions will take the form of dialogue with *particular* traditions. Christians will talk to Jews or to Muslims or to Buddhists, and so on, and they will find different common ground, and different topics for fruitful conversation, with each. It may sometimes be interesting to explore what several different traditions *all* share—I do not want to rule out such inquiries on principle—but we should always remember that we are not talking to adherents of some sort of generic "non-Christian religion." Our conversations do not reach one anothers' traditions only by way of some construct called "religion in general."

At the end of chapter 7, I discussed some of the reasons for engaging in such conversations, the ways in which adherents of one religious tradition can learn from those of another. Sometimes what one learns leads to a deepening and enriching of one's own faith; conversion is not the only significant result of conversation. But another reason for pursuing serious discussion on any topic is the possibility that I might be wrong, and the discussion might help me recognize my error. Indeed, if before we begin I absolutely rule out the possibility that you might be right and I might be wrong, then our exchange becomes in some degree superficial.

On matters as central to our lives as faith, however, an emphasis on openness to the other's point of view can lead to a different kind of superficiality. Consider the following passage from John Cobb:

> In faithfulness to Christ I must be open to others. When I recognize in those others something of worth and importance that I have not derived from my own tradition, I must be ready to learn even if that threatens my present beliefs. . . . I cannot predetermine how radical the effects of that learning will be. . . . I cannot even know that, when I have learned what I have to learn here and been transformed by it, I will still see faithfulness to Christ as my calling. I cannot predetermine that I will be a Christian at all. That is what I mean by full openness. In faithfulness to Christ I must be prepared to give up even faithfulness to Christ. If that is where I am led, to remain a Christian would be to become an idolater in the name of Christ. That would be blasphemy.[32]

Cobb raises important issues in a characteristically sensitive way, but his remarks seem not wrong, exactly, but rhetorically misleading. In contrasting religion and science earlier in this chapter, I suggested that religious faith involves a sense of a trusting relationship, more like trust in a person than belief in an idea, and that this means that doubt in such matters carries overtones of betrayal.

That changes our attitude to the possibility of doubt. If I say, "Can you imagine what would lead you to abandon belief in such and such a theory in physics?" you might comfortably reply, "Yes, such and such evidence, combined with a new theory that had such and such characteristics."[33] If I ask, "Can you imagine evidence that would lead you to conclude that your husband had been unfaithful to you?" you might reply, "Yes, I suppose if he moved out of the house, I found him in bed with another woman, and he laughed in my face." In both cases, belief is not independent of relevant evidence.

Yet if I then say, "Ah ha! You admit that you can imagine what would persuade you of your husband's unfaithfulness! What kind of trust is this?" you respond, "No, that's unfair. I can describe a situation that would lead me to judge him unfaithful, but I am confident that that situation will never arise. I suppose, come to think of it, that that's one way my situation is different from that of most scientists, who *expect* that the further progress of science will refute current theories."

Similarly, in the case of religious faith, I would not be a serious conversation partner if I said (and meant), "Nothing anyone could say or show me could conceivably alter my Christian faith." Yet it does not follow that I *expect* that my faith will be undercut; such an expectation, in fact, seems contrary to the nature of faith. Cobb's remarks unnerve me a bit, because they seem to lose sight of the shocking unexpectedness with which the loss of a faith always comes.

More generally (and at this point I no longer have Cobb in mind), openness should not invite us to become what Paul Ricoeur contemp-

tuously calls "Don Juans of the myth," who court every religious tradition in turn.[34] A lifetime often seems too short a time to complete the
journey into the depths of one faith. Dabbling in various traditions
seems accordingly superficial.[35] As a Christian, I talk with a Buddhist,
in part because I hope to learn how to be a better Christian from the
Buddhist's insights. If the conversation is to be serious, then, yes, I
acknowledge the possibility of my own conversion to Buddhism. But
if, in the name of openness, someone says, "Why don't you try out
Buddhism for a while?" then that sounds not only like an invitation to
betray my Christian faith but also like a rather superficial picture of
what it would mean to "become a Buddhist." Faith embodies a powerful vision of the world, and such visions are neither abandoned nor
entered into lightly. *Serious* dialogue indeed requires openness to
change, but it also demands a sense of how significant changing one's
faith would be. No doubt Christians have often lacked the first of these
virtues, but many recent writers on these topics lack the second. Genuine pluralists will try to remember both. Openness really is important,
but arguments for openness can encourage an ideal of occupying many
different positions which then becomes a surrogate for the old dream
of occupying no particular position at all. If we are honest, we will
admit that we stand somewhere. If we are serious, we will feel serious
commitments to the place we stand. Those whose ideal of interreligious dialogue calls us to abandon such commitments as a precondi-
tion of conversation invite us either not to be honest or not to be
serious.

NOTES

1. For a balanced recent discussion of the issues, see Nicholas Jardine, *The Fortunes of Inquiry* (Oxford: Clarendon Press, 1986).

2. For an introduction, see Bernard d'Espagnat, "The Quantum Theory and Reality," *Scientific American* 241, no. 5 (1979), pp. 158–181. The classic articles are J. S. Bell, "On the Einstein Podolsky Rosen Paradox," *Physics* 1 (1965), pp. 195–200; and Alain Aspect and others, "Experimental Realization of Einstein-Podolsky-Rosen-Bohm *Gedankenexperiment:* A New Violation of Bell's Inequalities," *Physical Review Letters* 49 (1982), pp. 91–94.

3. Hilary Putnam, *Realism and Reason* (Cambridge: Cambridge University Press, 1983), p. 228. See also Bas van Fraassen, "The Charybdis of Realism: Epistemological Implications of Bell's Inequality," *Synthese* 52 (1982), pp. 25–38.

4. Thomas S. Kuhn, "Reflections on My Critics," in Imre Lakatos and Alan Musgrave, eds., *Criticism and the Growth of Knowledge* (Cambridge: Cambridge University Press, 1970), p. 265.

5. Mary Hesse, *Revolutions and Reconstructions in the Philosophy of Science* (Brighton, Eng.: Harvester Press, 1980), p. 35.

6. See Earl MacCormac, *Metaphor and Myth in Science and Religion* (Durham, N.C.: Duke University Press, 1976), pp. 100–101. Quine states an extreme thesis: "Physical objects are conceptually imported into the situation as convenient intermediaries . . . as irreducible posits comparable, epistemologically, to the gods of Homer" (Willard Van Orman Quine, *From a Logical Point of View*, p. 44, 2nd rev. ed.; New York: Harper & Row, Harper Torchbooks, 1963).

7. This may still be a matter of degree. The change in physics during one lifetime from, say, 1900 to 1950, for instance, might be more fundamental and wide-reaching in terms of a whole set of beliefs than Newman's conversion from Anglicanism to Roman Catholicism. But it is probably significant that the former took place in a series of stages and that I did not choose the example of a conversion to Buddhism.

8. William James, *The Will to Believe and Other Essays in Popular Philosophy* (New York: Longmans, Green, 1897), pp. 3–4.

9. See George I. Mavrodes, *Belief in God* (New York: Random House, 1970), p. 53.

10. Basil Mitchell, *The Justification of Religious Belief* (New York: Oxford University Press, 1980), p. 139.

11. See, e.g., Roger A. Johnson, *Psychohistory and Religion: The Case of Young Man Luther* (Philadelphia: Fortress Press, 1977).

12. Ninian Smart, "Truth and Religions," in John Hick, ed., *Truth and Dialogue in World Religions: Conflicting Truth-Claims* (Philadelphia: Westminster Press, 1974), p. 55.

13. Edward Conze, "Buddhist Saviors," in S. G. F. Brandon, ed., *The Saviour God: Comparative Studies in the Concept of Salvation* (Manchester: Manchester University Press, 1963), p. 82; quoted in Joseph A. DiNoia, "The Universality of Salvation and the Diversity of Religious Aims," *Worldmission* 32 (1981–82), p. 11. "If certain theories about human life held in India are true, for example, the theories of Karma and reincarnation, then morality in the sense in which Western culture understands it is false. The understanding of the meaning and causes of human actions that are supported not only by metaphysical beliefs in Hinduism but also in its religious myths and rituals and its social practices simply do not sustain the views of human accountability, rational autonomy and respect for individuals qua persons that ground Western conceptions of morality" (James M. Gustafson, *Ethics from a Theocentric Perspective*, vol. 1, p. 123; Chicago: University of Chicago Press, 1981).

14. David Tracy, *Plurality and Ambiguity* (San Francisco: Harper & Row, 1987), p. 90. To quote the thirteenth-century Zen Buddhist, Dogen, "Those who are lax in their thinking are saying that the essence of Taoism, Confucianism and Buddhism is identical, that the difference is only that of the entrance into the Way. . . . If people say such things, Buddhism has already gone from them" (*The 'Shobogenzo' of Dogen, the Book of Buddhist Sutras*, in Phra Khantipalo, *Tolerance: A Study from Buddhist Sources*, p. 154; London: Rider, 1964; quoted in William A. Christian, *Oppositions of Religious Doctrines*, pp. 115–116; New York: Macmillan Co., 1972).

15. Or to consign them to hell—a point I discussed in chapter 1.

16. Christian, *Oppositions of Religious Doctrines*, p. 5. "It is both logically and practically possible for us, as Christians, to respect and revere worthy representatives of other traditions while still believing—on rational grounds—that

some aspects of their world-view are simply mistaken" (Paul Griffiths and Delmas Lewis, "On Grading Religions, Seeking Truth, and Being Nice to People—A Reply to Professor Hick," *Religious Studies* 19 [1983], p. 78).

17. For such a view: "Even before dialogue actually takes place, the assumption is that all are alike. One anticipates what the eventual conclusion must be, and that kills any real discussion" (Arnulf Camps, *Partners in Dialogue*, p. 30; Maryknoll, N.Y.: Orbis Books, 1983). "Dialogue, as I understand it, means a sustained conversation between parties who are not saying the same thing and who recognize and respect the differences, the contradictions, and the mutual exclusions, between their various ways of thinking" (John V. Taylor, "The Theological Basis of Interfaith Dialogue," in John Hick and Brian Hebblethwaite, eds., *Christianity and Other Religions: Selected Readings*, p. 212; Philadelphia: Fortress Press, 1981).

18. Karl Rahner, "Christianity and Non-Christian Religions," in Hugo Rahner and others, *The Church: Readings in Theology* (New York: P. J. Kenedy & Sons, 1963), p. 131.

19. Karl Rahner, *Theological Investigations*, vol. 4, trans. Kevin Smyth (Baltimore: Helicon Press, 1966), p. 366.

20. See, e.g., Karl Rahner, *Theological Investigations*, vol. 6, trans. Karl-H. and Boniface Kruger (Baltimore: Helicon Press, 1969), p. 394.

21. Karl Rahner, *Theological Investigations*, vol. 5, trans. Karl-H. Kruger (Baltimore: Helicon Press, 1966), p. 125.

22. Ibid., p. 133. For good recent discussions of Rahner on anonymous Christianity, see Maurice Bouten, "Anonymous Christianity: A Paradigm for Interreligious Encounter?" *Journal of Ecumenical Studies* 20 (1983), pp. 602–629; and Gavin d'Costa, "Karl Rahner's Anonymous Christian—A Reappraisal," *Modern Theology* 1 (1985), pp. 131–148.

23. Rahner himself recalled the awkward moment when the great Zen teacher Nishitani asked him if he would mind being called an anonymous Buddhist. That particular encounter ended graciously on both sides, but it does point up the problem. See Karl Rahner, *Theological Investigations*, vol. 16, trans. David Morland (New York: Crossroad Publishing Co., 1983), p. 219.

24. John Hick, *Problems of Religious Pluralism* (New York: St. Martin's Press, 1985), p. 94.

25. John Hick, "Towards a Philosophy of Religious Pluralism," *Neue Zeitschrift für systematische Theologie* 22 (1980), p. 135. Elsewhere Hick refers to a transcendental reality *an sich:* "the Eternal One—a term which draws ambivalently upon two different sets of associations: on the one hand the mystical One of Plotinus and the One without a second of the Upanishads, and on the other hand the One who is the divine Thou of the biblical narratives" (John Hick, *God Has Many Names*, p. 83; Philadelphia: Westminster Press, 1982).

26. He explicitly thinks he can judge the superiority of some religious points of view to others. See John Hick, "On Grading Religions," *Religious Studies* 17 (1981), p. 451.

27. John Hick, "Whatever Path Men Choose Is Mine," in Hick and Hebblethwaite, *Christianity and Other Religions*, p. 186.

28. Hick, *Problems of Religious Pluralism*, pp. 141–143. Hick is a particularly clear case, but I would make similar points in connection with Paul F. Knitter's *No Other Name? A Critical Survey of Christian Attitudes Toward the World Religions*

(Maryknoll, N.Y.: Orbis Books, 1985) and Wilfred Cantwell Smith's *Towards a World Theology* (Philadelphia: Westminster Press, 1981).

29. "Some suggest that we should attempt to overcome our traditional parochialism by moving to what they claim is a 'universally human' position, one that penetrates beneath all the 'accidental' and 'historical' differences among humans and their religions to some supposed 'essential oneness' we all share. Then, on the basis of this deep unity underlying everything human, we can understand and negotiate the differences with which the several great religious traditions confront us. But there really is not such a universally human position available to us; every religious (or secular) understanding and way of life we might uncover is a *particular* one, that has grown up in a particular history, makes particular claims, is accompanied by particular practices and injunctions, and hence is to be distinguished from all other particular religious and secular orientations" (Gordon D. Kaufman, "Religious Diversity, Historical Consciousness and Christian Theology," in John Hick and Paul F. Knitter, eds., *The Myth of Christian Uniqueness*, p. 5; Maryknoll, N.Y.: Orbis Books, 1987).

30. George A. Lindbeck, *The Nature of Doctrine: Religion and Theology in a Postliberal Age* (Philadelphia: Westminster Press, 1984), p. 55.

Paul Knitter writes that serious dialogue "requires that the theology of all the partners take as a *hypothesis* that there is a common ground and goal for all religions. . . . Without this deeper sharing in something beyond them all, the religions do not have a basis on which to speak to each other and work together" (Knitter, *No Other Name?* p. 209). For reasons I will shortly explain further, this just seems false to me. Indeed, I sympathize with Lindbeck's view that such an assumption can precisely become the *enemy* of serious dialogue.

More recently, Knitter has proposed that a common *goal* of religion should become the starting point for interreligious dialogue. All the religions may not share any symbol, he admits, and even talk of "belief in God" may impose our categories on some other traditions, but all religions pursue the mystery of salvation. This does not seem to me to escape the problem. He quotes Aloysius Pieris' remark that religions share the pursuit of *"liberation* (vimukti, mokṣa, nirvana)." That seems to me to equate a number of radically *different* goals. When Knitter concludes that "the absolute, that which all else must serve and clarify, is not the church or Christ or even God—but rather, the kingdom and its justice," that looks to me like the imposition of Christian categories. See Paul F. Knitter, "Toward a Liberation Theology of Religions," in Hick and Knitter, *The Myth of Christian Uniqueness*, pp. 187, 190. In this article, Knitter also acknowledges (pp. 183–185) the existence of contemporary trends in philosophy such as those I have been discussing, and their potential challenge to his point of view. But one senses that he does not take them very seriously. At any rate, it is unnerving that he consistently refers to the philosopher Richard Bernstein, on whose work he depends heavily at this point, as "Jeremy Bernstein," mixing him up with the *New Yorker*'s fine science writer.

31. See David Tracy, "Defending the Public Character of Theology," *The Christian Century* 98 (1981), p. 353.

32. John B. Cobb, Jr., "The Meaning of Pluralism for Christian Self-Understanding," in Leroy S. Rouner, ed., *Religious Pluralism* (Notre Dame, Ind.: University of Notre Dame Press, 1984), pp. 174–175.

33. Though a physicist might not always be able to specify such conditions.

34. Paul Ricoeur, *The Symbolism of Evil,* trans. Emerson Buchanan (Boston: Beacon Press, 1967), p. 306.

35. I therefore mistrust Paul Knitter's claim (in Knitter, *No Other Name?* p. 211) that the deepest kind of interreligious dialogue requires at least "some attempt at" being able to "belong to, share in, more than one religion."

10

THEOLOGY

Revisionist and postliberal theologies revisited

Given the conclusions developed in previous chapters, how should Christian theologians go about their business? I hope that the ideal of pluralistic conversation I have explained helps sort out a number of contemporary debates about theological method. At the end of chapter 1, I described two widely discussed recent models for theology. To oversimplify, the concern of the *revisionist* theology which dominates most academic circles in the United States is to preserve the *public* character of theology, that is, to find ways in which Christians can explain what they believe and argue for its truth in ways that non-Christians can understand. For the recently emerged *postliberal* theology, the theologian's task is more nearly simply to describe the Christian view of things. Postliberal theologians note ad hoc conjunctions and analogies with the questions and beliefs of non-Christians, but their primary concern is to preserve the Christian vision free of distortion, and they mistrust systematic efforts to correlate Christian beliefs with more general claims about human experience, which seem to them always to risk constraining and distorting the Christian "answers" to fit the "questions" posed by some aspect of contemporary culture.

Given what I have said about conversation and pluralism, I recognize the importance of both of these concerns. Christians need to find means of serious conversation with non-Christians. They also need to resist overarching theories that see Christianity as one local instance of some universal essence of religion or set out some general theory of what it means to be "rational" which Christians and everyone else must accept before real conversation can begin. In pursuing these issues, both revisionist and postliberal theologians have, in my view, sometimes fallen into errors. I hope that my conclusions provide a context for preserving the best insights of both. In that sense, I am trying to find a compromise.

At the same time, I have warned against self-proclaimed mediators who claim to stand in neutral territory, so I should say that I end up with more sympathy for the postliberal side. In large part, I simply think that academic theologians in the United States just now are more in danger of losing authentic pluralism by trying to find a common essence of religion or requiring that everyone accept certain Enlightenment assumptions as presuppositions for any conversation than by denying any value in religions other than Christianity. I do not know people in academic circles who dismiss all religions except Christianity as intellectually trivial or morally dangerous. I encounter quite a few people who think that those who do not share the presuppositions of a certain kind of Enlightenment modernity are intellectually trivial and morally dangerous. Genuine pluralism opposes both of these theses; at the moment, the second seems more widely accepted, and so the corrective provided by postliberal theology seems the more necessary one.

Another conclusion I want to draw, however, is that the dividing of theology into these two (warring?) camps is itself a distortion. There is a considerable range of opinion within each position, and it is possible to have more in common with some on the "other side" than with some on "one's own side." However briefly, any serious discussion of these matters therefore needs to stop generalizing and start looking at individual theologians.

Any discussion of the revisionist side appropriately begins with David Tracy, who introduced the term "revisionist theology" and strikes me as its greatest current exponent. But interpreting Tracy's work poses some problems. A scholar of astonishing erudition and great generosity, he seems to have read everything and to have found something of value in everything he has read. Amid all this appropriation, sometimes of writers who strongly disagree with each other, it is often hard to get clear on just what Tracy *rejects.* He is generous even to himself: to most readers it seems that his more recent work has moved away from some of the views he stated earlier, but Tracy is reluctant to admit this and tends to claim that he is merely approaching the same questions from a different angle.

In his first book of constructive theology, *Blessed Rage for Order* (published in 1975), Tracy wrote that from his revisionist perspective, "contemporary Christian theology is best understood as philosophical reflection upon the meanings present in common human existence and the meanings present in the Christian tradition."[1] If the theologian is engaged in *philosophical reflection* and considers *common human experience,* he went on to argue, then "the fundamental loyalty of the theologian *qua* theologian is to that morality of scientific knowledge which he shares with his colleagues, the philosophers, historians, and social scientists. No more than they, can he allow his own—or his tradition's—beliefs to serve as warrants for his arguments."[2] Therefore, Christians cannot appeal simply to the Bible or distinctively Christian experience or the Christian tradition; they have to show that what they say at least addresses questions and makes some kind of sense in terms of experience all human beings share, and they have to be willing to submit the "cognitive claims" they make to investigation by the methods of philosophy: "metaphysical or transcendental reflection."[3]

In the contemporary university, Tracy feels, appeals to tradition and authority carry little weight and get one quickly dismissed as an obscurantist. He wants the intellectual community to take Christian theology seriously, and that means explaining and arguing for it in terms that community will accept. Beyond the academic community, moreover, there is a pluralistic society debating important moral issues—from feeding the hungry to abortion to nuclear disarmament. Tracy wants the Christian voice to be heard in those debates, but he thinks that will not happen unless Christians are willing to play by the rules of contemporary society—which means, among other things, not appealing to our own tradition or scripture as if such appeals settled the issue at hand.

Such concerns lead Tracy to advocate a "public theology." Christianity, he says, must not become "no more than a set of personal preferences and beliefs making no more claim to either publicness or universality than the Elks Club."[4] But what does it mean for theology to be "public"?[5] In this book, I have been questioning the possibility of a fully "public" standpoint, if "public" means "universal," arguing that *any* argument always takes place within some particular community and tradition. Tracy has always acknowledged this, but the issue seems to have come more to the fore in his recent works.

"The absolute standpoint," he writes, "is no more";[6] "the surest mark of contemporary theology is precisely a profound acceptance of finitude and historicity. The Enlightenment 'prejudice against prejudice' is discountenanced by systematic theologians not because it is inconvenient but because it is implausible."[7] Christians stand within the Christian tradition; their "trust in and loyalty to the reality of the God disclosed in Jesus Christ finally determine and judge all other loyalties."[8]

> Each of us contributes more to the common good when we dare to undertake a journey into our own particularity . . . than when we attempt to homogenize all differences in favor of some lowest common denominator. Like the ancient Romans who made a desert and called it peace, we are tempted to root out all particularity and call it publicness.[9]

It is a temptation Tracy clearly wants to resist. But how does he fit that awareness that we always stand within a particular tradition with a commitment to "public" theology? Tracy has two answers: a distinction between fundamental theology and systematic theology, and the concept of the "classic."

His definitions of fundamental and systematic theology come from his teacher Bernard Lonergan, who defined these as two of the "functional specialties" of theology.[10] Tracy explains that they have different purposes:

> *Fundamental* theologies will be concerned principally to provide arguments that all reasonable persons, whether "religiously involved" or not, can recognize as reasonable. . . . *Systematic* theologies will ordinarily show less concern with such obviously public modes of argument. They will have as their major concern the re-presentation, the reinterpretation of what is assumed to be the ever-present disclosive and transformative power of the particular religious tradition to which the theologian belongs.[11]

If *The Analogical Imagination* (published in 1981) seems more conscious of its place within a particular tradition than *Blessed Rage for Order* was, Tracy claims, it is thus not because he has changed his mind but because he is now engaged in a different "functional specialty"— *subdiscipline* systematic theology rather than fundamental theology.

But even systematic theology, he says, has its own kind of "publicness." Systematic theology involves the interpretation of a religious "classic"—in the case of Christian theology, the Bible—and "any classic . . . is always public, never private."[12] Any text comes out of a particular tradition, but a *classic* text addresses great human questions in such a profound way that it speaks to an audience far beyond the particular community that produced it. I do not have to be a medieval Catholic to learn from thinking about Aquinas, or a Russian to learn from thinking about Dostoevsky—and I do not have to be a Christian to learn from thinking about the Bible. Since systematic theology starts with scripture and seeks to work out its implications, it might at first seem to presuppose the authority of scripture in a way that would make it pointless for non-Christians, who do not share that assumption. But since the Bible is one of the classics of our culture, its interpretation *will* be of wider interest, since non-Christians can learn from reflection on this classic text.[13] "The notion of the religious classic as a cultural classic can assure the entry of all theological classics into the public realm of culture." This argument, for Tracy, is crucial: if one could not appeal to the status of the classic in this way, "then systematic theology would be eliminated."[14]

In seeking to defend the public character of theology, then, Tracy has used two different strategies. In *Blessed Rage for Order,* he empha-

sized universal human experience; in his more recent work, he appeals
more to the role the Christian classic can play in the conversation of
our culture—though one can find *both* themes in *all* his work.[15]

In earlier chapters, I have tried to show flaws behind both such
strategies. As Tracy himself admits, there is no absolute standpoint, no
place to stand outside any tradition, no universal criterion for judging
truth and rationality. The language we use and the tradition in which
we have lived shape the way we experience things and indeed the kind
of experience we can have. Sometimes, indeed, they yield a rather
harshly negative judgment against the way we experienced the world
before we encountered this tradition and its language. There is no
such thing as raw data of experience. Tracy's appeals, particularly in
Blessed Rage for Order, to the religious dimension of human experience,
tend, in Francis Fiorenza's words, "to view the Christian tradition
primarily as a specification of what is universally experienced as religious. The historical particularity of the tradition as well as the force
of its conflict with experience tends to be minimized in such a
model."[16] The world's religions are *not* different attempts to do the
same thing, to be judged by how well they measure up to a universal
standard of religious adequacy. Tracy never believed that; indeed, I
have been able to cite him at many points in this book in support of
my critique of such views. But the effort to find a universally "public"
theology sometimes has driven him to make statements that *sound* like
a move in this direction.

As his work has reflected more awareness of the dangers of such
moves, Tracy has turned increasingly to his second strategy. Granted
there are no universal criteria of publicness, still the study of Christian
classics stands as a legitimately public activity *in our culture.* This seems
to give our culture (whose boundaries never get clearly defined) a
puzzlingly privileged status. For the sake of particular conversations,
I can see why Western Christians would want to appeal to the ground
they share with others in the broad Western tradition—just as, for the
sake of other particular conversations, they would want to appeal to
the ground they share with Buddhists or the ground they share with
Marxists but not with Western liberals, and so on. But Tracy seems to
claim that we live in *one* culture and that its place in that culture
provides *the* justification of Christian theology's public character. Advocates of the cultural importance of Africa and Asia, feminists, and
many others have been attacking such notions of "culture" recently.
Just as Richard Rorty is not a neoconservative but can sometimes
sound like one, so David Tracy is certainly not Allan Bloom but can
sometimes sound like him in his confident references to cultural classics. I have tried to argue that no single "conversation" determines our
culture but that we live in a number of interrelated "cultures" whose
pluralism manifests itself in a plurality of conversations—overlapping

and interrelated to be sure, but not subsumable as elements of a single superconversation. Christians will find particular occasions for joining many of those conversations, but there is no single set of rules to which they must conform or single set of classics they must acknowledge in order to join *"the* conversation of our culture."

Both of Tracy's strategies for "public theology" therefore seem to involve more systematic criteria for the "publicly" acceptable than I think can be justified. Yet these strategies both appear often in contemporary theology—often in versions less nuanced than Tracy's. To take two examples, Schubert Ogden exemplifies the appeal to universal human experience, and Gordon Kaufman the reference to the context of our culture.

Theology, Ogden says, has fallen under suspicion because people believe that it "involves an appeal to special criteria of truth to establish some or all of its statements" and "that the theologian must be a believer, already committed to the Christian understanding of reality." Not so, Ogden insists: the claims of theology "are true (insofar as they are so) only because they meet the requirements of completely general criteria," and "the personal faith of the theologian" is not necessary for "his or her theological understanding."[17] Theology, therefore, does not presuppose faith in any way; it has to be argued on the same sort of criteria, available to everyone, that one would use in an argument in philosophy or the social sciences.[18] Indeed, "Christian theology is necessarily dependent not simply on some philosophy or other, but on an integral theistic metaphysics. For how can the venture of faith be reflectively confirmed, or theology's assertions rationally justified, except on the basis of just such a metaphysics?"[19]

In short, Ogden thinks that theology has to defend its claims according to universal criteria of truth and to subsume itself under the categories of a rationally established metaphysics, if it is to be intellectually viable. I have tried to show in earlier chapters, however, that most sophisticated philosophers and social scientists thinking about methodology these days do not believe in universal criteria of truth or rationally establishable metaphysics. Ogden seems to be trying to adjust to a set of rules that have already become obsolete.

Gordon Kaufman, on the other hand, has pursued Tracy's other strategy; indeed, he more explicitly defends theology's public character by locating it within Western culture. "Theology," he writes, ". . . has public, not private or parochial, foundations. It is not restricted either to the language and traditions of a particular esoteric community (the church) or to the peculiar experience of unusual individuals."[20] The view that "the task of theology . . . is to work out of tradition and to hand on tradition," he says, is "authoritarian. . . . I do not think it is justifiable any longer to do Christian theology in this way."[21]

What is the alternative? As Tracy appeals to the cultural role of the religious classic, so Kaufman appeals to the public role of the concept of God in our culture:

> The roots of theology are not restricted to the life of the church or to special dogmas or documents venerated in the church, nor are they to be found in something as inchoate as "raw experience." They are to be found, rather, in the ordinary language(s) of Western culture at large, i.e., in the living speech of people for whom the word "God" has peculiar weight and significance.

And therefore, "whether the church as an institution lives or dies, theology has an important cultural role to play—so long as people continue to use and understand the word 'God.' "[22] Kaufman, moreover, is confident that talk about God will *not* disappear from our culture, since "reflection on the ultimate point of reference for all life and thought and reality must surely go on in some form so long as human life persists."[23] That cultural concept of God, he says, provides the appropriate starting point for the imaginative work of the Christian theologian.[24]

Kaufman's appeal to the standards of "Western culture" is even more explicit than Tracy's, so the question of why that particular ongoing conversation should have a uniquely privileged status arises even more forcefully. After all, Christianity these days is growing most rapidly in Latin America, Asia, and, above all, Africa, places where it is involved in many different conversations, to some of which "Western culture" may seem a bit peripheral. Moreover, as Alfred North Whitehead argued, the dominant picture of God in Western culture has often come to be centered on power and arbitrary will in a way that "gave unto God the attributes which belonged exclusively to Caesar."[25] Ideologies of power and supremacy have contributed to creating our nuclear mess. If Kaufman wants to write, as he says, a "theology for a nuclear age," surely he should start with the gospel's vision of a God whose greatness lies in humility and suffering love, and radically *challenge* our culture's dominant picture of God.

My point is really a simple one. Revisionist theologians are trying to get Christian theology involved in the public conversations of our culture. It is a laudable aim. Their strategies for accomplishing that end, however, risk cutting and trimming the gospel to fit it to the categories and assumptions of a particular philosophical or cultural position. Moreover, they risk appealing to assumptions about universal criteria of rationality or the superiority of one particular cultural conversation which I have argued do not stand up on *philosophical* grounds.[26]

Postliberal theologians' concern for preserving Christian distinctiveness provides a useful corrective to such mistakes, but, as I have admitted, postliberals can fall victim to their own set of excesses. The problem of what it means to call theological claims "true" has led to particular confusion. Before we tackle those issues, however, a bit of review seems in order.

"Postliberal theology" really began with Hans Frei's reflections on biblical hermeneutics. Much of the Bible, Frei pointed out, consists of stories, realistic narratives. What is the meaning of such stories? Frei wants to say that they mean what they say, in the way that the sentences of a realistic novel do. If I take a typical sentence from a realistic novel—say, for instance, "Mr. Tench went out to look for his ether cylinder"—the *meaning* of this sentence does not involve reference to historical characters or events, but neither can it be reduced to some moral lesson or general claim about human nature. I understand what the sentence means when, in a rather simpleminded way, I understand what each of the words means and how they fit together.

This seems obvious to the point of triviality, but Frei persuasively argues that most biblical hermeneutics for the last two hundred years has denied it—and for significant reasons. If I begin with the world of my experience as a "modern" person, with all its assumptions, and ask, "Are the biblical stories true?" then the answer can be "Yes" only if either (1) they report accurate history or (2) they reveal or illustrate general lessons about human existence. Biblical scholars recognized that many biblical narratives do not accurately report history—so, if they were to be true, their meaning could not be reference to historical events. Scholars then assumed that the only other kind of meaning a story *could* have was to illustrate some general lesson about human existence, so that was what the biblical narratives *must* mean.[27] Any careful reader of a good story, however, knows that you lose something if you try to translate it into such a nonnarrative form. In a story, we hear something about particular characters and events; the moral of a story is not the whole meaning of the story. But biblical interpreters have ignored the possibility that much of the Bible might "mean" in the way that a realistic narrative does, and therefore they have distorted the text by trying to find a nonnarrative meaning for it.

Frei proposes a radical solution. Suppose we do not start with the modern world. Suppose we start with the biblical world, and let those narratives define what is real, so that *our* lives have meaning to the extent that we fit them into *that* framework. That is, after all, the way a great many Christians—Augustine, Aquinas, Luther, Calvin—read the Bible for a long time. If we do that, then the truth of the biblical narratives does not depend on connecting them to some other *real* world. *They* describe the real world. A theology based on that way of reading scripture would operate in the way I tried to describe in chapter 8, narratively describing how the world looks from a Christian perspective, making connections with other perspectives only unsystematically.[28] Frei's fascinating argument is that any other way of doing it, any attempt to begin theology with a systematic apologetics, inevitably leads to a hermeneutics that distorts the meaning of the biblical texts by ignoring their special narrative character.

While Frei was thinking about such matters, his colleague George Lindbeck was reading sociologists, anthropologists, and philosophers of science, and he concluded that what Frei was saying made far more sense than most contemporary discussions of theological method. Most theories of religion, Lindbeck said, take either a *propositionalist* form, which "emphasizes the cognitive aspects of religion and stresses the ways in which church doctrines function as informative propositions or truth claims about objective realities," or an *experiential-expressivist* form, which "interprets doctrines as noninformative and nondiscursive symbols of inner feelings, attitudes, or existential orientations."[29] A propositionalist will judge religions in terms of how many accurate truth claims they make, and how few false ones. An experiential-expressivist will judge them in terms of how effectively they "articulate or represent and communicate that inner experience of the divine . . . which is held to be common to them all."[30]

Lindbeck's book devotes little—perhaps too little—attention to the propositionalists. There are obvious reasons for dismissing them. With our modern awareness of history, we are conscious that the same doctrinal formulation can have different meanings in different historical periods. Even something as apparently simple as "Christ is Lord" has meant something different to a Jew, a Hellenistic Greek, a medieval peasant, or a modern American.[31] But if a doctrinal statement functions as an objective description of some reality, then it seems its meaning should not so change from one age to another. At least since Kant, moreover, theologians have been nervous about thinking of religious language as very straightforwardly "describing objective realities" anyway. Talk of God seems to use the categories of human experience to talk about matters that lie beyond the realm of that experience, and that makes us very conscious of its problematic character.

In any event, Lindbeck dismisses the propositionalists quickly and clearly thinks that experiential-expressivism is the dominant current view; he tends, perhaps unfairly, to see revisionist theology generally falling into this camp. In the preceding chapter, I repeated one of the arguments that Lindbeck makes against this position: there is no "common core" which all religions are trying to express and against which they could be measured.[32]

Moreover, Lindbeck thinks this approach gets the relation of experience and language backward. We do not first have "religious experience"—or any very complex human experience—and then look around for the language to express it. Rather, it is only language that makes any kind of sophisticated human experience possible—and language inevitably shapes the experience's character.[33] Therefore, prelinguistic experience can hardly provide the criterion for judging linguistic formulations. We cannot argue for Christianity by saying that it best captures the essence of universal religiousness, since there is no coherent "religiousness" prior to a particular tradition's language.

Lindbeck, therefore, proposes a *cultural-linguistic* model for understanding religion. On this model, religious doctrines function primarily "as communally authoritative rules of discourse, attitude, and action."[34] "The proper way to determine what 'God' signifies, for example, is by examining how the word operates within a religion and thereby shapes reality and experience rather than by first establishing its propositional or experiential meaning and reinterpreting or reformulating its uses accordingly."[35]

On the cultural-linguistic model, then, "religions are seen as comprehensive interpretive schemes, usually embodied in myths or narratives and heavily ritualized, which structure human experience and understanding of self and world. . . . Stated more technically, a religion can be viewed as a kind of cultural and/or linguistic framework or medium that shapes the entirety of life and thought."[36] A good Lindbeckian, postliberal theologian will therefore operate less like a philosophically oriented apologist and more like a sensitive anthropologist, who tries to describe the language and practice of a tribe in terms of how they function in the life of that community and how they shape the way that community sees the world, rather than trying to defend these people's way of talking by the standards of some universal human rationality or experience.

This way of thinking about theology raises two related questions: In respect to *truth*, does it imply radical relativism?[37] In respect to *ethics*, does it imply radical sectarianism?

Questions about truth and relativism arise naturally enough for postliberal theology. After all, Lindbeck says that Christian doctrines describe the rules of the Christian community—suggesting that other communities might have other sets of rules—and contrasts his position with "propositionalist" views in which religious doctrines make truth claims. Frei insists that the biblical narratives do not "mean" by referring—either to historical facts or to ontological entities—and thereby sometimes leaves what he wants to say about their truth a bit unclear.

Other writers associated with the postliberals have gone at least a step farther. David Kelsey, for instance, in his discussion of the uses of scripture in recent theology, has concluded, "To call a set of texts 'scripture' is, in part, to say that they ought so to be used in the common life of the church as to nurture and preserve her self-identity."[38] Indeed, to say that "Scripture is authoritative for theology" is not to identify some property that these books have but to describe *"how they are used* in the Christian community."[39]

Why do scriptures have authority? Because the community treats them as authoritative! It is a good answer for a descriptive sociologist to give, but as a piece of Christian theology it seems distressingly circular. The community uses these texts in a particular way, surely, because of beliefs it has about the texts—about how God inspired them, or they speak with unusual power, or whatever—and not just about the community's own practices. We think of ourselves as *acknowledging* an authority the texts somehow possess, not as *granting* them such authority.

I am not sure of the force of Kelsey's claims here; Stanley Hauerwas pushes similar points farther—in what seems to me the wrong direction. Hauerwas approvingly cites Kelsey for believing that "claims about the authority of scripture are . . . claims about the function of scripture in the common life of the church" so that "scripture's authority for that life consists in its being used so that it helps to nurture and reform the community's self-identity as well as the personal character of its members."[40] He has praised Lindbeck for believing that "religion is not primarily a set of propositions to be believed or disbelieved, but a set of skills that one employs in living."[41] Further, he believes "it is impossible to distinguish . . . questions regarding the truth of the narrative from its normative status. At least part [but not all? what else?] of what it means to call a significant narrative true is how that narrative claims and shapes our lives."[42] "Just as scientific theories are partially judged by the fruitfulness of the activities they generate, so narratives can and should be judged by the richness of moral character and activity they generate."[43] And therefore, "the truthfulness of Jesus creates and is known by the kind of community his story should form."[44]

If I understand such remarks correctly, they do seem mistaken. After all, many different communities with quite different stories produce ethically admirable people. Only on a quite extreme pragmatic theory of truth—more extreme than Hauerwas appears to lay claim to—could one say that the virtues of the people *make* their stories true, or even very directly count as evidence that they *are* true. The Black Muslim teaching of Elijah Mohammed, for instance, narrated how all black people are descended from the original man, by way of the tribe of Shabazz, which settled in the Middle East sixty-six trillion years ago, while white people came into being only around six thousand years ago, as a result of an experiment by the evil scientist Yakub.[45] Black Muslims have certainly had success in reforming drug addicts and instilling pride and self-discipline in members of the ghetto underclass no one else seems able to reach. We would, however, not ordinarily think of the moral transformation of their converts as counting in favor of the truth of the story they tell. But if Black Muslim effectiveness does not count in favor of claims about Yakub and the tribe of Shabazz, why should the virtues of the Christian community count in favor of claims about Jesus? Lindbeck at one point notes that the behavior of a speaker can count *against* the truth of his or her utterance: when a crusader proclaims, *"Christus est Dominus"* as he bashes the head of an infidel, then we want to say there is something false about that statement, made in that context.[46] But the converse does not follow: the virtue of the speaker may make beliefs admirable, but it does not make them true. Even assuming that one could argue back from the virtue of the tellers to the truth of their tale, any such argument on behalf of Christian narratives either would fall victim to a strong form of relativism, in which different stories are "true" for different groups, or else would have to claim that the Christian community makes people demonstrably more virtuous than other communities do—I claim I would not want to try to defend on empirical grounds.[47]

"If Christ was not raised," Paul says, "then our gospel is null and void, and so is your faith; and we turn out to be lying witnesses for God" (1 Cor. 15:14–15, NEB). No matter our virtue, no matter the cohesiveness of our community: the story might still be false.[48] Ronald Thiemann's work has emphasized the crucial point here: Christian theology claims that Christian efforts in faith come as a response to God's gracious initiative. We do something because God did something first. Therefore, it cannot be the virtue of our people or the practices of our community that make true the story we tell about what God did.[49]

Postliberal theologians generally do not want to say that it is. Hauerwas himself writes that "the only reason for being a Christian . . . is because Christian convictions are true."[50] Frei acknowledges that, "About certain events in the Gospels we are almost bound to ask, Did they actually take place?"[51] In particular he admits that, however impossible it may be to "describe what happened" at the historical moment of Jesus' resurrection, still, "the New Testament authors were right in insisting that it is more nearly correct to think of Jesus as factually raised, bodily if you will, than not to think of him in this manner."[52] Lindbeck notes a variety of ways in which, while doctrines function primarily as rules for proper communal usage, they can also make truth claims.[53]

Christian theologians ought to avoid letting philosophers or anyone else set their agendas or the rules for their activity. The best philosophers these days do not want to do that anyway. And postliberal theologians have brought this point into clear theological focus. Sometimes, however, that emphasis risks sounding like radical relativism— like the claim that Christian doctrines express merely the rules for talking within the Christian community. Other communities, other rules—and no ontological claims, one way or the other.

Going that far is a mistake. The internal logic of Christian faith itself requires stating stronger claims than that. In chapter 8, I tried to specify a minimal account of what a Christian theologian needs to say. To summarize: (1) Christians believe that no subsequent experience will refute the essential pattern we as Christians now see in things. (2) We believe that the pattern of which Christians now catch a glimpse will ultimately be perspicuous to all. (3) Mysterious as all talk of God is, we believe that our actions in faith respond to prior acts of God, and therefore talk of God cannot be interpreted without remainder as a way of talking about human thoughts or practices.

Christians mean at least that much, I suggest, when they say, "This is what we believe." Christians who hold particular philosophical beliefs about the nature of truth may want or need to mean more than that; the conjunction of their philosophical views with these minimal claims may entail further assertions. Exploring such questions would entail another book than this one. Even the minimal claims just made, however, which would hold in the context of a very wide range of philosophical assumptions, suffice to distinguish Christian faith from extreme forms of subjectivism and relativism and are therefore all I need to say here.[54]

Postliberal theologians, however, have not been attacked only regarding questions of truth. They are also criticized on ethical grounds for retreating from public debate into a theological ghetto.[55] After all, the argument goes, we live in a pluralistic society with non-Christian neighbors, and therefore we cannot hope to have real influence in political debate if we appeal to warrants that only Christians would accept. Suppose, for instance, I think that the federal government ought to do more to house the homeless. Someone says, "Why should we bother? Why shouldn't they fend for themselves?" In response, I simply quote some biblical passages about seeking justice and caring for the poor. My questioner replies, "Maybe that's a good reason for the *church* to do something, but this isn't a Christian nation, and the fact that the Bible prescribes some policy doesn't provide a reason for our *society as a whole* to follow it."

At that point, it might seem, either (1) I offer some general reasons, not applicable only for Christians, why we ought to adopt this policy, or (2) I undertake some general defense of the Christian point of view, to indicate why non-Christians ought to listen to it, or (3) I admit that Christian faith guides Christians in how to lead their private lives and the life of Christian communities but does not have implications for matters of public policy. Postliberal theology's critics argue that its reluctance to do (1) or (2), at least in any systematic way, drives it to (3). But the conclusion that Christian faith has nothing much to say about the shape of society as a whole seems inconsistent with much of scripture and the Christian tradition.

I certainly concede the importance of this question. Let me make three points in response.

1. Christians acting in the way I have advocated will at least offer a model of a community that knows what it believes, that interprets the widest range of issues in terms of its beliefs, and that puts its beliefs into action. As Hauerwas has argued often and eloquently, the existence of such a community has its own kind of persuasive power in the wider society.[56] It is striking that early Quaker abolitionists and Christian pacifists in different ages had a public impact precisely by witness rather than by argument according to "publicly acceptable" criteria. Reinhold Niebuhr and Martin Luther King, Jr., have probably been the recent American theologians of greatest public impact, and both of them spoke with fascinating combinations of explicitly and unapologetically Christian language and ad hoc connections with all sorts of other contexts. Even today, as James Gustafson has acknowledged, the Roman Catholic bishops writing their pastoral letter on the nuclear issue "did not need to forge a hermeneutical theory, or a theory about 'public theology,' or a moral theory on which all rational persons could agree (when the moral philosophers quit arguing with each other because they have reached consensus I will be more persuaded that such is possible) in order to write a document that has been taken very seriously by some important persons in public life."[57]

2. As I have argued throughout this book, Christians can and should seek common ground with particular non-Christians on particular issues. We can work together with Jews and Marxists, for instance, to help the homeless, and even recognize that we have common reasons for doing so. We can work together for common goals even with people who have reasons for pursuing those goals very different from our own. Our social concerns and cooperation will therefore reach well beyond the boundaries of the Christian community.

The intellectual background for such efforts can be subsumed under the slogan "ad hoc apologetics," which Hans Frei introduced and William Werpehowski has developed.[58] But like all slogans, this one can hide some disagreements. By "ad hoc apologetics," Werpehowski and Frei both mean that we should let the common ground we share with a given conversation partner set the starting point for that particular conversation, not looking for any *universal* rules or assumptions for human conversation generally. Werpehowski, however, thinks of that kind of activity as a necessary and important part of Christian life. Frei seems to use the phrase "ad hoc" in a stronger sense: if such conversations arise, this is how to pursue them; but, if not, not. For reasons indicated earlier in this book, I would agree with Werpehowski. The logic of Christian faith drives us to conversation beyond the borders

of Christian faith; it is only the rules for those conversations that
emerge ad hoc.

3. Still, the critic will say, such ad hoc alliances do not yet develop
moral standards which we can prove that any reasonable, responsible
person ought to follow—and only that kind of standard provides a
legitimate foundation for public policy in a pluralistic society.

I have been maintaining, however, that that kind of standard simply
does not exist. All that we ever have is the common ground that
happens to exist among different particular traditions. If I am right,
then *pretending* that some such contingent common ground is in fact
a provable universal standard of human morality is a dangerous business: socially dangerous because it dismisses all those who do not
share one set of cultural norms as primitives to be forcibly educated
or lunatics to be locked up, and theologically dangerous because it
turns into a form of idolatry in which these cultural standards become
the norm according to which we judge our faith. We have to think
about how to set public policy in the midst of *genuine* pluralism, and
that means evolving the rules of temporary alliances and the limits of
pressing one's own case which I have described as characteristic of
genuine conversation.

Such genuine conversation, with a commitment to genuine pluralism, can serve the concerns of both revisionist and postliberal theology. It seeks out serious interaction with non-Christians in a variety of
contexts, but it preserves a distinctive Christian voice in the conversation. It avoids the errors of philosophical foundationalism on one side
and radical relativism on the other. It really accepts contemporary
pluralism, and therefore it knows that we cannot ignore non-Christian
voices but also that we can no longer assume that the assumptions of
the Enlightenment set the rules for all rationality.

As I said at the beginning of this chapter, while I recognize the
concerns expressed on both sides of this debate, it seems to me that
the postliberal voice needs particularly to be heard just now—and that
for two reasons, one related to our intellectual context, one to our
political situation.

I realize that Southern Baptist and even some Roman Catholic institutions face significant challenges to intellectual freedom from church
authorities. We should not treat those challenges lightly. Nevertheless,
the dominant context of the American academy just does not seem to
me to be one where we need to worry about the Christian voice drown-
ing out all others. Indeed, just to state such a concern in the midst of
a typical contemporary American college or university is to recognize
that it misses the mark. Those of us who do theology in such contexts
cannot help being aware of our pluralistic context.

On the other hand, the danger that an imperialistic Enlightenment
rationalism and liberalism will silence other voices in the academy, in

spite of all the philosophical arguments against it noted earlier in this
book, seems a real one—even if it adopts a new and somewhat different
neoconservative rhetoric of preserving "Western culture." Religion
departments are particularly vulnerable to the assumption that the
methods of the social sciences or of a generalized phenomenology of
religion provide the only appropriate styles of academic study of religion. As Langdon Gilkey, no postliberal, has remarked:

> To the academy . . . there appears the illusion of a new universality, the
> universality of the culture as a whole as opposed to the partiality of the
> church within the culture. But . . . modern Western philosophy is as
> particular, as located in space and time, as are the Christian or the Bud-
> dhist traditions.[59]

Discussions of interreligious dialogue seem above all vulnerable to the
imposition of assumptions about the "common core of all religions"
and opposition to the honest expression of religious disagreement. In
that context, the postliberal determination to preserve a distinctively
Christian voice in the conversation seems particularly important.

Beyond the academic context, there are other concerns. Peter
Berger once remarked, "In a world full of Nazis one can be forgiven
for being a Barthian."[60] By that, I take it, he meant that in a culture
like Germany in the 1930s, with the values that had somehow come to
dominate it, Christian theology should follow Barth's course and emphasize the gospel's judgment of contemporary culture rather than
trying to reinterpret Christian faith in the terms of that society.

But what about our society? In every major city, the homeless sit
hungry at the doorsteps of greatest wealth. Many of the children of
privilege find their existence so unbearable that they seek self-destructive escape through drugs. We finance the maiming of children by
various semisecret operatives in far-off countries in pursuit of goals no
one can quite explain. Other societies in the modern world, to be sure,
are just as bad, and some are a great deal worse—we should never lose
sight of that. Still, measured by the standard of the gospel, we fall
desperately short.

Of course Christians need to face the challenge of other points of
view to help them grow. Of course we need to follow the gospel
injunctions to reach out to all the world. Of course, in pursuit of all
sorts of practical goals, we need to make all sorts of alliances with
non-Christians. But we also need to make vivid the judgment the
gospel casts against our culture. Perhaps, in service of such a witness,
even a modest dose of sectarianism is not such a terrible thing. Perhaps
those whose particular calling is the strange task of theology can even
be forgiven for being postliberal theologians. Theology by itself will
not solve the social problems that face us. If Christianity has a contribution to make, it will require churches and Christian people with

greater moral commitment and intellectual self-confidence. Maybe, though, even a book like this one can in a very modest way help some Christians think about how to face the problems and move toward such commitment and self-confidence.

NOTES

1. David Tracy, *Blessed Rage for Order: The New Pluralism in Theology* (New York: Seabury Press, 1975), p. 34.

2. Ibid., p. 7.

3. Ibid., p. 56. Gordon Kaufman says that Tracy claimed that "theology should turn to metaphysics for its final legitimation" (Gordon D. Kaufman, *The Theological Imagination*, p. 241; Philadelphia: Westminster Press, 1981). That states it a little more strongly than I would.

4. David Tracy, *The Analogical Imagination* (New York: Crossroad Publishing Co., 1986), p. 132.

5. I have discussed this question at greater length in William C. Placher, "Revisionist and Postliberal Theologies and the Public Character of Theology," *The Thomist* 49 (1985), pp. 392–416.

6. Tracy, *The Analogical Imagination*, p. 48.

7. Ibid., p. 100.

8. Ibid., p. 48.

9. David Tracy, "Defending the Public Character of Theology," *The Christian Century* 98 (1981), p. 353.

10. Bernard Lonergan, *Method in Theology* (New York: Herder & Herder, 1972), pp. 127–133.

11. Tracy, *The Analogical Imagination*, p. 57.

12. Ibid., p. 14.

13. Ibid., p. 132.

14. Ibid., pp. 68–69.

15. There is an intriguing parallel with the intellectual odyssey of John Rawls. This account really does oversimplify, but I find it hard to sort out Tracy's position. Tracy admits that theological arguments can achieve only "relative adequacy," only a persuasive truth (David Tracy, *Plurality and Ambiguity*, pp. 22–23; San Francisco: Harper & Row, 1987; and idem, *The Analogical Imagination*, p. 86 n. 34). But he continues to believe that *all* forms of theology need to be "public" and that "to speak in a public fashion means to speak in a manner that can be disclosive and transformative for any intelligent, reasonable, responsible human being" (Tracy, "Defending the Public Character of Theology," p. 351).

16. Francis Schüssler Fiorenza, *Foundational Theology: Jesus and the Church* (New York: Crossroad Publishing Co., 1984), p. 283.

17. Schubert M. Ogden, *On Theology* (San Francisco: Harper & Row, 1986), pp. 19–20.

18. Ibid., pp. 10–11.

19. Ibid., p. 90. In some of his earlier work, like *Theology and the Philosophy of Science,* Wolfhart Pannenberg seemed to be developing a much more quali-

fied position that had learned lessons from Kuhn and others. But in more recent books, he advocates universal criteria of rationality as flatly as Ogden: "Without a sound claim to universal validity Christians cannot maintain a conviction of the truth of their faith and message. . . . In the modern age they must conduct this defense on the terrain of the interpretation of human existence and in a debate over whether religion is an indispensable component of humanness. . . . For these reasons, Christian theology in the modern age must provide itself with a foundation [!] in general anthropological studies" (Wolfhart Pannenberg, *Anthropology in Theological Perspective*, trans. Matthew J. O'Connell, p. 15; Philadelphia: Westminster Press, 1985).

20. Gordon D. Kaufman, *An Essay on Theological Method* (Missoula, Mont.: Scholars Press, 1975), p. 8.

21. Gordon D. Kaufman, *Theology for a Nuclear Age* (Philadelphia: Westminster Press, 1985), pp. 17–18.

22. Kaufman, *An Essay on Theological Method*, pp. 15–17.

23. Ibid., p. 17.

24. Kaufman, *Theology for a Nuclear Age*, pp. 22–23.

25. Alfred North Whitehead, *Process and Reality: An Essay in Cosmology* (New York: Free Press, 1969), p. 404.

26. My own feeling is that David Tracy falls victim to those risks less often than most other revisionists—in part because his philosophical allegiances have grown to lie more with Paul Ricoeur, as opposed to, for instance, Ogden's dependence on Heidegger and Whitehead and Kaufman's on Kant. As effectively as any contemporary philosopher, Ricoeur reminds us that we always stand within a tradition and that there can be no universal hermeneutical theory that sets out the rules for all processes of interpretation. See, e.g., Paul Ricoeur, *The Conflict of Interpretations*, trans. Willis Domingo (Evanston, Ill.: Northwestern University Press, 1974), p. 19; and Paul Ricoeur, "Naming God," *Union Seminary Quarterly Review* 34 (1979), p. 215. See also William C. Placher, "Paul Ricoeur and Postliberal Theology," *Modern Theology* 4 (1987), pp. 35–52. Still, I have tried to argue that Tracy's concern for public theology sometimes leads him away from genuine pluralism.

27. Hans W. Frei, *The Eclipse of Biblical Narrative* (New Haven: Yale University Press, 1974), p. 11; and idem, *The Identity of Jesus Christ* (Philadelphia: Fortress Press, 1975), p. xiv.

28. Frei's best brief account of such a method comes when he describes how Barth did it. See Hans W. Frei, "Eberhard Busch's Biography of Karl Barth," in H.-Martin Rumscheidt, ed., *Karl Barth in Re-View* (Pittsburgh: Pickwick Press, 1981), pp. 103–104, 110–111.

29. George A. Lindbeck, *The Nature of Doctrine: Religion and Theology in a Postliberal Age* (Philadelphia: Westminster Press, 1984), pp. 16–17.

30. Ibid., p. 47.

31. For a parallel point, see ibid., p. 83.

32. "There can be no experiential core because . . . the experiences that religions evoke and mold are as varied as the interpretive schemes they embody. Adherents of different religions do not diversely thematize the same experience; rather they have different experiences" (ibid., p. 40).

33. This goes back to the attacks on the Myth of the Given discussed in chapter 2.

34. Lindbeck, *The Nature of Doctrine*, p. 18.

35. Ibid., p. 114.

36. Ibid., pp. 32–33.

37. For an introduction to the issues, see Michael Root, "Truth, Relativism, and Postliberal Theology," *dialog* 25 (1986), pp. 175–191.

38. David H. Kelsey, *The Uses of Scripture in Recent Theology* (Philadelphia: Fortress Press, 1975), p. 150.

39. Ibid., p. 89, emphasis added; see also pp. 97–98.

40. Stanley Hauerwas, *A Community of Character: Toward a Constructive Christian Social Ethic* (Notre Dame, Ind.: University of Notre Dame Press, 1981), p. 55.

41. Stanley Hauerwas and William Willimon, "Embarrassed by God's Presence," *The Christian Century* 102 (January 30, 1985), p. 98. I am not sure Lindbeck would be comfortable with this praise.

42. Hauerwas, *A Community of Character*, p. 97.

43. Ibid., p. 95.

44. Ibid., p. 37. "A truthful telling of the story cannot be guaranteed by historical investigation . . . but by being the kind of people who can bear the burden of that story with joy" (ibid., p. 52). If this passage means only that there is something hypocritical and therefore false when someone who has not incorporated something of the story of Jesus into his or her own life tells the story, then I agree. But "truthful telling" is ambiguous, and I worry that for Hauerwas a people's willingness to bear the burden of the story with joy somehow makes the story itself true, as well as making this particular telling of the story morally appropriate. That seems to me to confuse two completely different issues.

45. See C. Eric Lincoln, *The Black Muslims in America* (Boston: Beacon Press, 1961), pp. 77–79. I am referring to beliefs Elijah Mohammed held at one time. The development of his views, much less those of various Black Muslim groups since his death, is much too complex a story to tell here.

46. Lindbeck, *The Nature of Doctrine*, p. 64.

47. Paul Nelson and Thomas W. Ogletree both worry that Hauerwas' view becomes Pelagian: the emphasis falls on claims about what the Christian community does, not on what the Holy Spirit does or on grace. See Paul Nelson, *Narrative and Morality* (University Park, Pa.: Pennsylvania State University Press, 1987), p. 116; and Thomas W. Ogletree, "Character and Narrative," *Religious Studies Review* 6 (1980), p. 26.

48. "If the ontological truth-claims of the New Testament are false, then the Christian religious life, understood and pursued as the knowledge and service of God in Jesus Christ, is founded on an illusion" (Julian N. Hartt, "Theological Investments in Story: Some Comments on Recent Developments and Some Proposals," *Journal of the American Academy of Religion* 52 [1984], p. 121).

49. See, e.g., Ronald F. Thiemann, *Revelation and Theology: The Gospel as Narrated Promise* (Notre Dame, Ind.: University of Notre Dame Press, 1985), p. 61. Those who read all the way to the end of Kierkegaard's *Concluding Unscientific Postscript* (as many who write about it seem not to do) will find, I think, the same point made: in the end, subjectivity is *untruth*, because sin distorts our subjectivity apart from grace.

50. Hauerwas, *A Community of Character*, p. 1.

51. Frei, *The Identity of Jesus Christ*, p. 132.

52. Ibid., p. 150.

53. Lindbeck's position is very complex, but includes at least three elements:

1. Doctrines qua doctrines may set rules, but they may also function, though nondoctrinally, to make truth claims. For instance, the *doctrine* of the Trinity requires that one follow a certain set of rules (affirm the unity of God, do not think of Father, Son, and Spirit simply as different activities of one personal agent, etc.) and does not necessarily imply anything about God's ontological nature, but a Christian *theologian* could speculate "on the possible correspondence of the Trinitarian pattern of Christian language to the metaphysical structure of the Godhead"—and thereby make ontological truth claims. But someone who follows the rules and remains agnostic about such speculations is still doctrinally orthodox. (Lindbeck, *The Nature of Doctrine*, p. 106.)

2. As Aquinas suggested, in our language about God, the way we signify *(modus significandi)* does not correspond to anything in the divine being, but what is signified *(significatum)* does. A rough analogy: if I as a nonphysicist imagine atoms as made up of little marbles, I am thinking about it all wrong, but if, for instance, I say, "Helium has two electrons," I am saying something right, even though I hardly understand what it means. Our language about God can be like that. (Ibid., p. 66.)

3. "As actually lived, a religion may be pictured as a single gigantic proposition. It is a true proposition to the extent that its objectivities are interiorized and exercised by groups and individuals in such a way as to conform them in some measure in the various dimensions of their experience to the ultimate reality and goodness that lies at the heart of things. It is false to the extent that this does not happen" (ibid., p. 51).

I am not sure how all this fits together.

54. This is one of the places where I feel confident speaking only on behalf of Christians. Obviously, some or all of these rules would apply to other traditions too, but I do not want to generalize. I am not sure, for instance, that Theravada Buddhists would need to make any claim analogous to my third point.

55. See in particular James M. Gustafson, "The Sectarian Temptation: Reflections on Theology, the Church, and the University," *Proceedings of the Catholic Theological Society* 40 (1985), pp. 83–94.

56. See Stanley Hauerwas, *Against the Nations* (Minneapolis: Winston Press, 1985), p. 1. Since I have criticized Hauerwas on the question of truth, it is particularly important to emphasize how much I owe him, and agree with him, on these ethical issues.

57. James M. Gustafson, "The Bishops' Pastoral Letter: A Theological Ethical Analysis," *Criterion* 23 (Spring 1984), p. 10.

58. See Frei, "Eberhard Busch's Biography of Karl Barth," in Rumscheidt, *Karl Barth in Re-View*, p. 114; and William Werpehowski, "*Ad hoc* Apologetics," *Journal of Religion* 66 (1986), pp. 282–301.

59. Langdon Gilkey, "Plurality and Its Theological Implications," in John Hick and Paul F. Knitter, eds., *The Myth of Christian Uniqueness* (Maryknoll, N.Y.: Orbis Books, 1987), p. 42. "The secular academy . . . regards our discovery of religious parity among the world religions as a kind of childlike awakening

from naivety and self-centeredness. And yet the same academy has not yet conceived the shock that is to come to it when the cultural parity of the West, among the world's other cultures, comes to the forefront of consciousness" (ibid., p. 40).

60. Peter L. Berger, *A Rumor of Angels* (New York: Doubleday & Co., Anchor Books, 1970), p. 18.

INDEX OF NAMES